Introduction to
Africana Demography

Studies in Critical Social Sciences Book Series

Haymarket Books is proud to be working with Brill Academic Publishers (www.brill.nl) to republish the *Studies in Critical Social Sciences* book series in paperback editions. This peer-reviewed book series offers insights into our current reality by exploring the content and consequences of power relationships under capitalism, and by considering the spaces of opposition and resistance to these changes that have been defining our new age. Our full catalog of *SCSS* volumes can be viewed at https://www.haymarketbooks.org/series_collections/4-studies-in-critical-social-sciences.

Series Editor
David Fasenfest (Wayne State University)

Editorial Board
Eduardo Bonilla-Silva (Duke University)
Chris Chase-Dunn (University of California–Riverside)
William Carroll (University of Victoria)
Raewyn Connell (University of Sydney)
Kimberlé W. Crenshaw (University of California–LA and Columbia University)
Heidi Gottfried (Wayne State University)
Karin Gottschall (University of Bremen)
Alfredo Saad Filho (King's College London)
Chizuko Ueno (University of Tokyo)
Sylvia Walby (Lancaster University)
Raju Das (York University)

Introduction to Africana Demography

Lessons from Founders E. Franklin Frazier, W.E.B. Du Bois, and the Atlanta School of Sociology

Edited by
Lori Latrice Martin

Haymarket Books
Chicago, IL

First published in 2020 by Brill Academic Publishers, The Netherlands
© 2020 Koninklijke Brill NV, Leiden, The Netherlands

Published in paperback in 2021 by
Haymarket Books
P.O. Box 180165
Chicago, IL 60618
773-583-7884
www.haymarketbooks.org

ISBN: 978-1-64259-611-3

Distributed to the trade in the US through Consortium Book Sales and Distribution (www.cbsd.com) and internationally through Ingram Publisher Services International (www.ingramcontent.com).

This book was published with the generous support of Lannan Foundation and Wallace Action Fund.

Special discounts are available for bulk purchases by organizations and institutions. Please call 773-583-7884 or email info@haymarketbooks.org for more information.

Cover design by Jamie Kerry and Ragina Johnson.

Printed in the United States.

10 9 8 7 6 5 4 3 2 1

Library of Congress Cataloging-in-Publication data is available.

In Loving Memory of Lorri Burgess

Contents

Acknowledgements   IX
List of Figures and Tables   X
Notes on Contributors   XI

Introduction   1
   Lori Latrice Martin

PART 1
Africana Demography and Migration, Fertility, and Mortality

1   Carceral Migration: an Africana Demographic Reframing of Post-release Pathways for Formerly Incarcerated Populations   25
    Brianne Painia

2   Child Support Enforcement as Social Control: Black Fathers and Multi-partner Fertility   47
    Maretta McDonald

PART 2
Africana Demography and Policing

3   Us versus Them: "We Are More Fearful of the Police than the Actual Criminals"   81
    Melinda Jackson-Jefferson

4   Policing the Black Community: History, Reality, and the Rudiments of Change   103
    Edward Muhammad and Jack S. Monell

5   African Americans' Response to Discrimination: Does Region Matter?   121
    Jas M. Sullivan

PART 3
Africana Demography and Bridging Racial Gaps

6 Rethinking Black Families in Poverty: Postcolonial Critiques and Critical Race Possibilities   143
   Deadric Williams

7 Embodying a Hybrid Habitus: Identity Construction and Social Mobility among Working-class Black Women   165
   Tifanie Pulley and Arthur Whaley

8 A Black Theology of Liberation: the Black Church and a Living Wage   187
   Weldon McWilliams

9 Reducing the Achievement Gap of African Americans through a Mental Health Lens   200
   David I. Rudder and Anthony Hill

Index   223

Acknowledgements

I wish to thank the following individuals and organizations for their continued support and encouragement throughout my academic career and the development of *Africana Demography*: Lee and Edith Burns, Derrick Martin, Jr., Ann and John Thornton, Sharon and Marvin Broome, Sarah Becker, Stephen C. Finley, Annie Daniel, Maretta McDonald, Ify Davis, Brianne Painia, Cassandra Chaney, Andre Sigmone, Ewart Forde, Mahilia Howard, Ashley Maryland, Dominique Dillard, Lynette Coto, Alana Peck, John Aggrey, Derrick Lathan, Caleb Young, David and Shannon Rudder, Raymond Jetson, Chris Tyson, Shanille Mosley Thomas, Luke St. John McKnight, Jeremiah-Anthony Righteous-Rogers, Tat Yau, Robyn McGee, T'Asia Holmes, Dorothea Swann, Frances Pratt, McKinley and Sue Johnson, Reggie Sanders, Dione Footman, Wil Glover, Constance Slaughter Harvey, Constance Harvey Burwell, Barbara Ann Johnson, Larry Mathews, Rachel Nichols, Ray Nichols, Bill Batson, Village of Nyack, Antoinette Bennett, Bobbie Commodore, and Emir Sykes.

Figures and Tables

Figures

2.1 Predicted probability of child support enforcement type by multi-partner fertility   69
4.1 Crime rates for the zone containing Westside and the university center   116
6.1 Conceptual model indicating a critical race theory of the overrepresentation of Black families in poverty   151

Tables

2.1 Descriptive statistics of sample   62
2.2 Multinomial regression coefficients predicting child support enforcement sanction type of Black fathers by multi-parent fertility status   65
2.3 Multinomial regression coefficients predicting child support enforcement sanction type of Black fathers by multi-parent fertility status   68
5.1 Demographic characteristics, 2001–2003 National Survey of American Life   127
5.2 Reactions to discrimination, 2001–2003 National Survey of American Life   128
5.3 Odds ratios for reactions to discrimination by region and demographic characteristics, 2001-2003 National Survey of American Life   129
7.1 Sample questions   172
9.1 Student views on persistence and retention   191
9.2 Student views on self-care and developing healthy relationships   212
9.3 Student views on nurturing and self-actualization   214

Notes on Contributors

Anthony Hill
is an associate professor of Social Work in the School of Social Work and Behavioral Sciences at Springfield College. He earned a Doctorate of Education from University of Massachusetts, Amherst. Dr. Hill has extensive experience in both the fields of social work and education and has been employed as a clinician, adjunct faculty member, school social worker, assistant principal, principal, and college administrator.

Melinda Jackson-Jefferson
joined the Sociology Department at Nicholls State University in August of 2017 after receiving her Ph.D. in Sociology from Louisiana State University as an assistant professor. Her primary research interests join the sociological literatures on fear of crime and intersectionality that explores issues of inequality related to underrepresented populations. At present, Dr. Jackson-Jefferson has published research on inequality, race and racism in the criminal justice system, social justice, critical race theory, intersectionality (gender, race and class) and fear of crime. Much of her attention, however, has focused on projects that use qualitative and quantitative methodologies to study crime. Her research has appeared in *Democracy & Education, Crime & Delinquency, Gender and Education, Culture and Education* and *The Journal of Pan African Studies*.

Lori Latrice Martin
is professor in African and African American Studies and the Department of Sociology at Louisiana State University (LSU). Dr. Martin is also LSU Faculty Athletics Representative. Her research areas are race and ethnicity, racial wealth inequality and black asset poverty, and race and sports. Dr. Martin is the author of numerous scholarly works. Martin's most recent publications include *South Baton Rouge* (Arcadia Publishing, 2017), *Black Asset Poverty and the Enduring Racial Divide* (FirstForumPress, 2012), and *Big Box Schools: Race, Education, and the Danger of the Wal-Martization of American Public Schools* (Lexington Books, 2015).

Maretta McDonald
is a doctoral candidate and Louisiana Board of Regions/Southern Regional Education Board doctoral fellow at Louisiana State University (LSU). Her primary research interests are race and ethnicity, crime, family, gender, and public policy. She earned her Master's Degree from Southeastern Louisiana

University in Applied Sociology. McDonald's Master's thesis examined the relationship between race and child support enforcement system outcomes. She is currently researching the impact of race on various topics such as: support for child support enforcement policy, representation in mass media, and social movements.

Weldon McWilliams

graduated from SUNY Stony Brook in 2002 with a B.A. in Africana Studies. He obtained his M.A. in African-American Studies and Ph.D. from Temple University. Dr. McWilliams is an associate professor of History at Dutchess Community College in Poughkeepsie, NY.

Jack S. Monell

is an associate professor and Program Coordinator of Justice Studies at Winston-Salem State University with over twenty years of working in the fields of social work, criminal justice and human services. A scholarly practitioner with a broad range of experiences (both personal and professional), he has worked for nonprofit, local, state and Federal government agencies. He is the author of "A Preliminary Examination of Hegemonic Masculinity: Definitional Transference of Black Masculinity Effective Lethal Tactics against Black Males," in: *The Handbook of Research on Black Males: Quantitative, Qualitative, and Multidisciplinary*, (Michigan State University Press, 2018) which explores the issues faced by African American males and the violent encounters they face due to stereotypical perceptions and biases. Dr. Monell received his Ph.D. from Walden University, M.S.W. from Howard University, B.A. from Towson State University, and a Post Graduate certificate in Sociology, respectively.

Edward Muhammad

is a doctoral student in Qualitative Research & Evaluation Methodology at the University of Georgia. His research focuses on qualitative methodologies and critical qualitative research. Muhammad's current research interests include the phenomenology of the black lived experience, philosophical hermeneutics, and qualitative investigations of the Nation of Islam. He holds a Bachelor's and a Master's degree in Psychology from Southern University and the University of Baltimore, respectively.

Brianne Painia

is an instructor of Interdisciplinary Studies at Louisiana State University (LSU). Her research interests include: black femininities and masculinities; the intersection of race, gender, and religion in black religious spaces; and black feminist sociology. Dr. Painia received her Ph.D. in Sociology from LSU in May 2018.

She received a Master of Arts in Sociology from The George Washington University in 2014 and her Bachelor of Science in Business Administration from The University of Southern Mississippi in 2012.

Tifanie Pulley

is currently an adjunct faculty at Tidewater Community College. She holds a Ph.D. in Sociology and Women's and Gender Studies from Louisiana State University (LSU). As a sociologist with an interdisciplinary focus, the role of economic marginalization and related decision making-processes in education, health, work, and crime across categories of race, gender and class, undergird her research interests. Dr. Pulley's greatest hope is to use scholarship as a tool for creating a more just and equitable tomorrow.

David I. Rudder

is Associate Dean at the School of Professional and Continuing Studies at Springfield College. He earned a Bachelor of Arts degree from Canisius College, Masters of Science degree from the University of Buffalo, State University of New York, and Doctorate of Philosophy degree from University of Delaware. Dr. Rudder's research interests include urban policy and economic development.

Jas M. Sullivan

is a professor of Political Science, Psychology, and African and African American Studies at Louisiana State University. Dr. Sullivan studies race, identity and political behavior. His current projects explore the effects of African American racial identity on political attitudes and behavior. Dr. Sullivan has published numerous articles and book chapters. He is also the co-author (with Jonathan Winburn and William E. Cross, Jr.) of *Dimensions of Blackness: Racial Identity and Political Beliefs* (SUNY Press, 2018) and co-editor (with William E. Cross, Jr.) of *Meaning-Making, Internalized Racism, and African American Identity* (SUNY Press, 2016).

Arthur Whaley

is an independent research and evaluation consultant. He has over 30 years of experience in higher education as a faculty, administrator, and researcher. He received his A.B. in Psychology from Princeton University, and a Ph.D. in Clinical Psychology from Rutgers University. He completed a Doctor of Public Health degree in Epidemiology from Columbia University. His main research interests involve understanding the role of cognitive and cultural factors in the etiology, diagnosis, and treatment of mental disorders, and in the prevention of health-damaging behaviors, of underserved ethnic and racial populations with a particular focus on African Americans.

Deadric Williams is an assistant professor of Sociology at the University of Tennessee. Professor Williams' research lies at the intersection of race and racism, families, and health. His emerging research focuses on integrating race and racism theory with research on African American families and health. This line of research seeks to make explicit that (1) race is socially constructed, (2) racial groups are hierarchically organized, and (3) although racial domination changed over time from overt (i.e., slavery, genocide) to covert (e.g., hegemony), dramatic differences in the life chances between African Americans and Whites persist in the United States. Taking this approach to race has important implications to family and health research. Professor Williams' research has appeared in the *Journal of African American Studies, Society and Mental Health, American Journal of Human Biology*, and other scholarly outlets.

Introduction

Lori Latrice Martin

Four hundred years after the first settlement of enslaved people of African ancestry in Jamestown, Virginia, sociologists and demographers, using a host of techniques, are still trying to explain persistent disparities between black and white people in the United States, especially the lack of black progress on a host of social and demographic outcomes.[1] There are many theoretical and methodological challenges associated with understanding such issues as persistent antiblack violence (at the hands of both state agents and vigilantes), racial income and wealth inequality, enduring asset poverty, school and residential segregation, the overrepresentation of black children in under-resourced public schools, the criminalization and incarceration of black bodies, the political disfranchisement of black communities, displacement through gentrification, distressed neighborhoods, and poor health outcomes for black people across the life course, among others. What are some factors that explain the difficulties sociologists and demographers face in adequately studying these important social issues? Why haven't sociologists and demographers been more successful in influencing public policy to address the challenges facing black people in America? In what ways has the inability of sociologists and demographers to positively impact the lived experiences of black people in America eroded public trust in these disciplines, and what can be done to (re)establish public trust in these disciplines? It is my contention that what is needed is a new intervention I call *Africana Demography*, which builds upon the strengths of black sociology and critical demography. The intervention proposed here should have the added benefit of affording recognition for many of the scholars denied their rightful place in the sociological and demographic canons.

1 How Does It Feel to Be a Problem?

Sadly, people of African ancestry in America have most often been viewed as a problem and seldom as a people. This has been true from the day that the first people of African ancestry arrived and were brought and "settled" in Jamestown,

---

1 An earlier version of this chapter was accepted for publication in *Issues in Race and Society* in 2019. At the time of this writing, the article was still in press.

Virginia, in 1619. Members of the dominant group have viewed those identified sociologically and demographically as black as a problem. The problem during much of the seventeenth century was how to exploit the labor of individuals from central and West Africa for the benefit of the developing colonies. How could the dominant group justify the treatment of human beings of darker hues as property and not people? The answers came gradually over the century and with the outpouring of black people's blood, sweat, and tears. Efforts to dehumanize and criminalize individuals with their own history and culture were pursued through private practices and public policies. The sentencing of John Punch to servitude for life in the 1640s was one of the first indications that black people were to be treated differently from white people by the law. White indentured servants would be punished by having years added to their period of servitude, but never for life. Laws determining the status of children born to enslaved women—as always following the condition of the mother regardless of the identity of the father—were another example of the idea that blackness was pathological. The problem of how to maintain the supply of forced and unpaid labor changed course after the U.S. Congress banned the importation of slaves in 1808. Slave owners had to rely more on the natural increase of the slave population through the breeding of slaves like livestock and through other means—including the horrific sexual violence enacted upon black women slaves, oftentimes by the individuals who claimed ownership of them.

How should the enslaved population be counted to prevent the political dominance of one region over another region? In order for the U.S. Constitution to be ratified by southern states, a notorious compromise was reached to count slaves as three-fifths of a person. What should become of the free black people who gained their status through manumission and gradual emancipation was another problem members of the dominant group faced. Colonization societies were organized and many introduced plans to send free black people back to Africa or to places in the Caribbean to prevent them from working with enslaved black people to dismantle slavery in America. What types of policies should be in place to return enslaved people who dared seek freedom in states and territories where slavery did not exist? Fugitive slave laws were passed; the infamous Dred Scott decision of the U.S. Supreme Court upheld the constitutionality of such laws. What would white people do about the black population if the institution ended? Even Abraham Lincoln did not believe whites and blacks could coexist peacefully. Black people were considered a burden that white people had to bear.

After the Civil War ended and the Thirteenth and Fourteenth Amendments to the Constitution, bestowing upon black people citizenship, due process, and the right to vote, were passed, these changes presented a unique set of problems some white people resented being forced to address. The dominant group still viewed black people as a problem where political representation, land ownership, and economic competition were concerned, as evidenced by the sadly short-lived period known as the Reconstruction era. The backlash to this relatively successful period of history included increases in the number of black people who were lynched, the organization of antiblack terrorist organizations like the Ku Klux Klan, land takings, race riots, restrictive codes, convict leasing, and sharecropping, to name a few.

The problem of the New Negro in the early twentieth century meant the dominant racial group had to determine how to respond to a new level of consciousness among former slaves and their descendants who sought to take ownership over their newfound albeit tenuous freed status through accomplishments in sports, the arts, music, and literature, and through demands for the control of their images and resistance to challenges to self-determination.

The movement of millions of black people moving from the South to the North in the Great Migration presented a problem for the dominant group. The limitations on immigration from Southern, Eastern, and Central Europe in 1924, like the bans of Chinese (1882) and Japanese (1908) immigration earlier, led to labor shortages in some industries, which caused many businesses to recruit black laborers from the South. Whites in the South were faced with the dilemma of black laborers seeking greater economic opportunities in the North and leaving the Jim Crow South behind. Northern whites had to address the problem of welcoming black laborers and at the same time not angering white laborers, especially white union laborers, who saw the migrants as unwanted competitors for limited employment positions, and whose presence might depress their wages. Despite the presence of so-called liberal whites in the North, formal and informal practices kept black people residentially segregated and relegated to under-resourced schools far away from their children, families, and friends.

The Great Depression introduced a new set of challenges for the nation as a whole. How to lift Americans—namely white Americans—out of the proverbial economic ditch was a priority. But domestic and agricultural workers—predominantly black—were explicitly excluded from New Deal labor reforms and opportunities.

Black people had the audacity to want to take part in one of the greatest single opportunities for mass wealth accumulation in the nation's history with the establishment of the Home Owner's Loan Corporation (HOLC) in 1933 and the Federal Housing Administration (FHA) in 1934. The problem of how to exclude black people from what is the most recognizable symbol of the American dream, home ownership, was resolved by excluding black people from the first opportunity for average Americans to own their own homes. HOLC and FHA underwrote loans for average Americans, thus fundamentally changing the terms of the home-buying process so that the dream of owning a home was open to (white) people beyond just the truly wealthy, while black people were systematically kept out of the home buying process through such practices as redlining. The mass construction of homes after the Second World War and the mass accumulation of wealth derived from it played important roles in the suburbanization of America and the assimilation of white ethnic groups formerly considered as separate and distinct races. In many ways, suburbanization served as a proxy for whiteness.

Accepting the shedding of black blood in the world wars as enlisted men and women was fine but respecting their service by treating them and other black people as human beings and as full citizens was a problem. The armed forces were not integrated until President Harry Truman's executive order of 1948.

The problem of educating black and white children in separate facilities dominated the first half of the twentieth century. Black children were deemed intellectually inferior relative to white children and there were also concerns that if black and white children attended the same schools they might interact socially, including sexually, which might lead to violations of miscegenation laws and informal norms regarding sexual relations between black and white people. For some members of the dominant group acceptance of interracial relations was tantamount to racial genocide.

The bus boycotts by black people in Baton Rouge, Louisiana, in 1953, and later in Montgomery, Alabama, in 1955, was a problem for many. The refusals to accept segregated buses by black patrons, who made up a substantial majority of the ridership, hurt the local communities economically. The loss to municipal bus services in these two cities were substantial and caused many members of the dominant racial group to ramp up efforts to quell movements to fight ongoing racial discrimination and antiblack sentiments. Black people complaining about the torturing of a fourteen-year old boy in Money, Mississippi, in 1955 was a problem because their demands for justice in the case of Emmett Till brought attention to the ongoing antiblack sentiments that existed in the country.

The presence of new social movements, such as civil rights organizations, Black Power groups, and the Nation of Islam, was so problematic that federal, state, and local agencies infiltrated them and engaged in activities to influence the organizations, including creating dissension between key figures.

Not only were emerging black organizations viewed as a problem, but also black families themselves. Daniel Patrick Moynihan published a report where he identified what he viewed as the pathology of the black family as a national crisis. His misuse of the works of the black sociologist E. Franklin Frazier has not only negatively impacted how some view Frazier's legacy, but it provided great fodder for scholars, public policymakers, and the general public to blame black women, especially black mothers, for the challenges facing black people as a whole. Although Moynihan was engaged in what W.E.B. Du Bois might consider "car window sociology," many other sociologists and demographers have provided some legitimacy for his work by making it among one of the most widely cited reports on the subject of black families.

Increases in the number of distressed neighborhoods, crime, educational disparities, health challenges, and incarceration among the black population were characterized as evidence of the pathology of black families and black culture. The problem, as told by many prominent scholars including sociologists and demographers, was that black people followed a street code. Black people were influenced by a culture of poverty. Black communities suffered from a lack of social organization. Black people who were already in a position to benefit from some of the changes brought about the Civil Rights Movement constituted a new black middle class. This black middle class fled their communities of origin for more affluent areas, thus causing two critical problems. One problem was how to keep these more affluent black people out of the white neighborhoods where they were not wanted but could afford to buy housing without ending up as a litigant in a housing discrimination suit. The other problem was how to police and contain the relatively larger number of unemployed and underemployed black people who were concentrated in communities where many of the residents were both poor and black.

Claims of a post-racial society notwithstanding, "How does it feel to be a problem?" is a question that has plagued black people over the past few decades and continues to linger in their everyday experiences today. The Great Recession is a good example. Although people from Wall Street to Main Street were affected by the economic crisis, black people not only suffered more than other racial and ethnic groups, as evidenced in the amount of loss to their overall net worth, but also were blamed by some for the crisis.

The election of the nation's first black president did not significantly alter the perception that black people were a problem. On the contrary, much of the fear among members of the dominant racial group, especially white men, was that the Obama administration would seek to address some of the problems associated with the black population at white people's expense and to their detriment. This perception of black people as a perpetual problem fuels white fervor and may be responsible, at least in part, for the election of Donald J. Trump and the upsurge in white supremacist ideology, evidenced by such events as the tiki-torch-carrying demonstrators in Charlottesville.

The time has long passed for sociologists and demographers to cease viewing black people as a problem—intentionally or unintentionally—and to consider new ways of thinking about ways to study the black people in which they are not objects and where their experiences, culture, and engagement with multiple sources of oppression are central to scholarly inquiries. Otherwise, the black population is the perpetual square peg, which sociologists and demographers attempt to fit into theoretical and methodological round holes that simply don't fit. What is needed is a new intervention that I call *Africana Demography*, which draws from black sociology and critical demography. While black sociology has much to offer on the study of the black population, it is limited in important ways, to which we turn our attention now.

2 What Is Sociology Missing? More Black Sociology

Efforts to establish black sociology have a long history despite the fact that some contemporary sociologists remain unaware of its existence or the necessity for such an area of study. One need only look back at recent debates on social media regarding whether programs for some learned societies, such as the Eastern Sociological Society, are elitist and/or white-male-dominated for examples.

Although scholars such as W.E.B. Du Bois and E. Franklin Frazier were engaged in research centered on the black population in the late nineteenth century well into the twentieth century, what they were doing was not codified as black sociology. Irving Louis Horowitz sought to establish the principles of black sociology in the early 1970s. He did so by identifying broader problems within the discipline of sociology, particularly when it came to studying race. He described the transformation of studies about race into studies about small groups, which were more reflective of "psychological-introspective evaluation" (Horowitz 1973, 8) than a systematic study of social structures and social systems.

Horowitz made another important observation about problems in sociology as they related to inquiries into the human behavior, social interactions, and social institutions involving black people. For most sociologists, he argued, the so-called Negro problem was essentially a "deviant problem" (Horowitz 1973, 8). This problem led to another problem, namely the ignoring of black culture as a "liberating agency" and an emphasis on how to free black people from a set of social conditions (Horowitz 1973, 8).

The consequences of the problems identified by Horowitz were far-reaching for the sociology of the black experience in America. The limitations were evidenced in the discipline's inability to impact social and public policy and to bring about any meaningful societal change. Indeed, Horowitz when as far as to say that sociology was "proven so impotent in the face of current mass unrest" (Horowitz 1973, 8).

Wilburn Watson (1976) built upon the work of Horowitz to not only provide a definition of black sociology but also to distinguish it from sociological studies about people of African ancestry in the United States. In other words, Watson clarified the various ways in which people have defined or imagined black sociology and then offered a working definition. Watson described one definition of black sociology as any sociological studies conducted by black sociologists. Another definition viewed any research conducted by black sociologists that was specifically on the topic of race relations as black sociology (Watson 1976). Studies that included some theoretical frame or substantive issues that were of concern to black people were also a commonly held definition of black sociology (Watson 1976). Finally, black sociology was best identified "by the ideological commitment of the sociologist to the release of Black people from race-related social oppression" (Watson 1976, 116).

The last definition is in keeping with the kind of work done by scholars like W.E.B. Du Bois, whose work Watson described as "inquiry initiated and implemented by sociologists whose social identity is Black, whose ideological allegiance, as expressed in the formulation of research problems and the interpretation of research results, is for the release of Black people from race-related social oppression, and whose primary research population is constituted by Black people" (Watson 1976, 118).

Du Bois was also likely to have understood that the concerns that some sociologists had about "value intrusion" was in many ways an illusion (Watson 1976, 118). While many white sociologists studying race, presumably like many other white scholars studying race, believed that they could and should check their values at the door as they entered their research space, black sociology recognizes the role of values and seeks to minimize its influence "through careful research design" (Watson 1976, 118).

As Horowitz (1973) believed, for Watson black sociology stands in sharp contrast to other so-called sociologies about black people. Watson described these other forms of *race-related* sociologies. For example, there are undoubtedly black sociologists engaged in research on the white population. But what Watson categorized as mainstream white sociology explores the social behavior of black people within the context of beliefs that black people have very little identity or culture worthy of preserving. Finally, Watson (1976) reviewed a body of literature where white sociologists studying race-related topics primarily studied white people with little concern for social change, which he understood as the antithesis of black sociology.

Black sociologists draw, according to Watson (1976), from a rich "cultural 'data bank,'" including from sources of black thought. Sociologists have long devoted themselves to legitimizing their existence and refuting any arguments or perceptions that sociology and other social sciences were not *real* sciences. Consequently, sociologists have built of thick disciplinary walls and constructed fortified silos that often limit their ability to understand the multilevel and multidimensional nature of a host of social issues, including challenges facing the black population. Another consequence is that sociologists tend to lay patterns created for studying nonblack populations over observations of black populations. When there is an empirical mismatch they declare the black population pathological (Watson 1976). Watson contended that this is most evident in the application of three dominant theories to explaining the social condition of black people: immigration-assimilation, structural functionalism, and culture of poverty. Current studies about the black population in America still have the goal of "fitting the black–white situation into a model rather than letting the situation determine the mode of explanation" (Watson 1976, 389).

Watson concludes black sociologists are in fact humanists and implies that black sociology is generative. The work of black sociology, while intended to address the race-based oppression faced by black people, has implications for other historically marginalized groups in America and beyond. Thus black sociology provides both the theory, methods, and action to aid others in mobilizing to address the tough challenges they face based upon other sources of oppression, such as gender, ethnicity, religion, social class position, etc.

In more recent years, Earl Wright II and Thomas Calhoun (2016) published articles and an edited book on the topic of black sociology, citing the works outlined here and laying out key principles. Wright and Calhoun provide an important genealogy for black sociology. The pair point to the first American school of sociology, not the Chicago School, but the Atlanta Sociological Laboratory. American sociology and black sociology emerged with the work of people like W.E.B. Du Bois and E. Franklin Frazier, whose research interests grew out of their personal commitments to social justice, and also to bias in existing disciplines and a general lack of interest in treating the study of the black population as worthy of scholarly attention and inquiry.

In an attempt to further clarify the essential elements of black sociology, Wright and Calhoun (2016) identified five principles. First, black sociology should be led primarily by black Americans. Previous definitions of black sociology excluded nonblack sociologists altogether. Second, research is centered on black Americans. Third, the research is interdisciplinary. Fourth, whenever possible, black sociological research should be generalizable to other populations experiencing oppression based upon their racial identity, for example. Finally, research findings should have social and public policy implications.

There are a number of reasons that the idea of the existence of black sociology historically and in contemporary times is hard from some white and some black sociologists to accept. Some white and black sociologists believe the United States and the discipline of sociology have entered a new era where race matters but maybe less. They cite the election of President Obama as one example. An increase in the number of black students in sociology courses at both the undergraduate and graduate levels may also provide some evidence for such claims. More sessions at professional meetings on the subject of the black population than in past years might be another measure. Even the election of black people as presidents of American Sociological Association and regional associations might provide merit to the claim that sociology is more unified on the matter of race than ever before or that sociology is certainly more unified on the matter of race than other disciplines.

Many sociologists holding the aforementioned viewpoint are likely to be living in an academic bubble where they fail to realize how the reward system in the discipline is structured in such a way as to penalize black sociologists, and others, who seek to critique or challenge the theories and methods that are deemed central to understanding virtually all sociological phenomenon and peoples. Black sociologists, for example, understand that the very decision to study the black population may limit their ability to become tenured and get promoted. They are also aware that doing what they were trained to do by studying the black population, which necessitates engagement with whiteness and the white populations, also places their very employment and at times their safety at risk. Let's look at the former argument in greater detail.

Frazier and Du Bois knew very early in their careers that the work they devoted themselves was not considered on par with research conducted in other areas and on other populations. One need only look at the ways in which both were either misunderstood or virtually ignored as evidence of the marginalization of scholarship on the black population, especially scholarship that was counter to the dominant narratives about the group. Similarly, black sociologists today find it difficult to have their work appreciated in ways that nonblack sociological studies are conducted. In fact, many black sociologists bypass so-called mainstream journals altogether based on anecdotal impressions or a careful empirical review of what typically is published in these mainstream sociological journals. They make a cost-benefit analysis and reach the conclusion that their work might find greater acceptance and a more informed pool of reviewers in journals with the word "critical" in the title or in Africana studies journals that may or may not be discipline specific. Black sociologists can be penalized during the tenure and promotion process for not reaching what a department or an institution deems the minimum basic standard for productivity, or criticized for publishing in journals outside of the top-tier, in outlets that are not considered competitive by such often-controversial measurable outcomes as the impact factor. Moreover, black sociologists may find it challenging to secure a book contract from a standard-bearer university press, given the nature of their work, or due to the limited number of potential reviewers. Thus they can risk being denied promotion, especially at institutions where a monograph is a prerequisite to tenure and promotion.

Stephen C. Finley, Biko Mandela Gray, and Lori Latrice Martin (2018) wrote about the challenges facing black professors at predominately white institutions (PWIS) in a recent article published in the *Journal of Academic Freedom*. Several of the most high-profile cases where black professors were the subject of attacks by "white virtual mobs" and constructively abandoned by the white administrators who hired them involved black sociologists engaged not solely in studies on the subject of race, but specifically in black sociology. Drs. Zandria Robinson and Dr. Johnny Smith are two such examples. The inability of white sociologists is acknowledge even the existence of black sociology is evidenced in the debates on social media referenced earlier. The need for black sociologists to periodically revisit definitions of black sociology for the sake of clarifying what it is and is not has placed the relevance of sociology more broadly in question and has placed black sociologists at personal and professional risks.

3   What Is Demography Ignoring? More Critical Sociology

Sociology is not alone as the subject of the criticisms that have been raised. The limitations of conventional or mainstream demography were noted in a special issue of *Sociological Forum* at the close of the twentieth century. Hayward Derrick Horton introduced a new paradigm called *critical demography* in 1999. The special issue featured an essay by one of the most prominent conventional demographers then and now, Douglas Massey. The issue also included a host of articles related to race and gender to highlight the potential of critical demography to transform the ways demographers apply their techniques.

Horton (1999) came up with the idea of introducing a critical demography paradigm based upon his observation that demographers were unwilling to even consider using the term "racism" in their work. Power dynamics are central to understanding the social structure and thus central to understanding the many variables and concepts of interest to demographers. Horton proposed that critical demography would be explicit about the characterization of the social structure by dominant and subordinate groups.

Horton made several comparisons between conventional demography and critical demography. Conventional demography could be considered "mainstream" or white, male, heteronormative. For Horton, conventional demography not only ignores power dynamics, including discussions about racism and sexism, but also appears consumed with merely describing trends and reporting estimates, while critical demography is predictive and places the subject of analysis within an appropriate social context. Moreover, Horton observed that conventional demographers contend that data are mute and that theory gives them meaning. Contrariwise, critical demography holds that theory must take "a back seat to the articulation, elaboration, and application of theory" (Horton 1999, 364–65). Conventional demography, Horton contends, operates from a position that demographic inquiries are apolitical and it thus accepts the status quo. He described that acceptance as tacit acceptance, while critical demography explicitly challenges the social order. Finally, another major difference between conventional and critical demography is that the former assumes objectivity and views demographers as independent actors engaged in rigorous scientific inquiry. In other words, conventional demography is assumptive (Horton 1999). Critical demography not only questions the area of study but also questions demographers, hence, Horton made the claim that critical demography is reflective.

In an effort to get ahead of criticisms that it was too narrowly focused, Horton makes it clear that critical demography is best understood as "an umbrella large enough to accommodate a broad range of topics" (1999, 364). This is evidenced in many of the other articles published in the special issue of *Sociological Forum*. For example, there is an article about feminist demography and another about nuptiality and fertility within the context of the collapse of the Soviet Union.

In the same issue, Douglas Massey (1999), a demographer and coauthor of the book *American Apartheid*, described what critical demography meant to him. Massey appeared to equate critical demography with scholar-activism, which is not something that Horton included in his description of the paradigm. Nevertheless, Massey made it clear that writing for and reaching out to audiences beyond demographers was different and distinct from the creation of rigorous scientific research. He thought that this was particularly important for demographers receiving public funding to support their research. Massey described several ways in which he engaged with the public, from responding to media inquiries to writing books and other reports for public consumption.

It is noteworthy that Massey (1999) felt the need to let conventional demographers know that engagement with the public for the purpose of bringing about social change was not outside of the scope of the work of demographers. He did see this work as separate and distinct from works where demographers establish scientific validity. Black sociologists have rarely made such distinctions, as mentioned previously, and often engaged in scholarship on the black population for the primary purpose of challenging the status quo and bringing about the liberation of black people. Engaging in work Massey (1999) described as the signature of a "critical demography" is and was foundational for black sociologists and for other black scholars in other fields of study.

Despite support from critical demography as evidenced in the special issue referenced above, including the essay from Massey, few people have responded to the call to consider critical demography as a paradigm of the future. Much like black sociology, critical demography has much to offer but is limited. What is required is a unifying area of study I call *Africana Demography*.

4 What Is Needed? Africana Demography

Black sociology is an important discipline that has been ignored for many generations despite its impact on American sociology more broadly. The failure to account for the significant role of black sociology and black sociologists means that generations of scholars have not been adequately exposed to the theories and methods of people like W.E.B. Du Bois, despite Du Bois's historical importance, and despite E. Franklin Frazier's having served as the first black president of what is now known as American Sociological Association (ASA) as the first black person ever to become president of a learned society in the nation. Far too many graduate students across America do not read Du Bois in their required theory courses; undergraduate students may read a paragraph or two in introductory textbooks about Du Bois and the existence of racism and sexism in the discipline's past. When asked why Du Bois is not required reading, typical answer is, "Well, we can't read everyone." Du Bois, Frazier, etc., are not just run-of-the-mill sociologists, however; they are giants in the field and deserve to be denied no longer.

Alton Morris' award winning book, *The Scholar Denied,* as well as works by Earl Wright, II, have highlighted the many contributions Du Bois made to sociology in America and many other fields. *The Philadelphia Negro* was one of his most important and impactful works. Du Bois highlighted the importance of studying black people to further science in *The Philadelphia Negro*. Failing to empirically study black people would be a missed opportunity to study the development of a great race, argued Du Bois. Morris (2015) outlined many of Du Bois' innovations and concluded that "Du Bois emerged from *The Philadelphia Negro* as the first number-crunching, surveying, interviewing, participant-observing and field-working sociologist in America, a pioneer in the multi-methods approach" (Morris 2015, 47).

Although many sociologists consider themselves demographers and engage in a range of population studies, all demographers are not sociologists and not all sociologists are demographers. Consequently, one cannot equate black sociology with a particular form of demography. Black sociology can undoubtedly inform ways of thinking about demography, especially in studies concerning people of African ancestry in the United States.

Similarly, while critical demography is useful in critiquing conventional demography, it is also limited in so far as the black population in America is concerned. Critical demography, admittedly, accommodates "a broad range of topics" (Horton 1999:364). It may be used to understand the case of African Americans, as Horton (1999) addressed in a follow-up article to the 1999 article in *Sociological Forum* where he introduced the concept of critical demography, but the African American or black population is not its focus.

Africana Demography must include research that is led primarily by black Americans. Africana Demography involves research that is centered on black Americans. It derives much of its explanatory and predictive power from the cultural data bank of black Americans. Additionally, Africana Demography generates research that is, when possible, generalizable to other populations experiencing similar types of oppression. Research findings must have social and public policy implications and must involve sharing findings with non-academic audiences.

5   Discussion: Mistrust, Policy Monitoring and the Color Wall

The implications and potential for Africana Demography are great. Sociology and demography are both often silent on some of the most important and historical social and demographic events of American history. Failing to account for the impact of the historic baby boom of the 1950s is just one example. Baby boomers have changed virtually every social institution over their life course from the construction of schools to shortfalls in social security. Additionally, absent an understanding of and appreciation for Africana Demography the mass exodus of hundreds of thousands of black people from the South to the North beginning in the early part of the twentieth century is referred to as the Great Migration, while Africana demographers, such as E. Franklin Frazier, contend that a more appropriate label is the Second Emancipation.

Moreover, the social and demographic significance of not only the Civil Rights Movement but also other important social events has been ignored by sociologists and demographers or misunderstood and therefore examined in very limited ways. For example, much attention has focused on the black middle class without a reasonable definition for the group. Attention has also been devoted to the poor or black underclass, with little to no attention devoted to the black working class, which, historically, has been far more numerous than either the black middle class or the black underclass. It is important to note too that there were a number of resistance organizations during the 1960s and 1970s—the Nation of Islam, black nationalist groups, and the Black Power movement—that had an impact on the social and demographic lives of black people in the United States. These seldom figure in interpreting changes over time for the black population, especially in geographical areas where these groups and movements had the most influence. To be clear, their influence reached far beyond arbitrary geographical boundaries and were viewed by government and police agencies as so influential that many were under surveillance or infiltrated.

Sociologists and demographers have been largely silent more recently on the killings of black people by law enforcement officials and vigilantes. Most seem willing to leave the work to criminologists, who often provide the theory and the data to support the actions of those involved with the unnatural deaths of black men and black women across the country. The silence and the failure to engage in debates about a matter that has so gripped the attention of the nation—leading to the #BlackLivesMatter movement and white responses like #BlueLivesMatter—has contributed to the mistrust and indifference some feel toward social sciences such as sociology and demography.

Sociologists and demographers have become in some ways monitors of social and public policies, including those impacting black people, while doing very little to bring about positive changes that would lead to their liberation. Taken together all of these issues have ensured that W.E.B. Du Bois's claim that the color line would be the defining issue of the twentieth century would be true through the foreseeable future. Sociologists and demographers have not succeeded in erasing the color line but have succeeded in fortifying walls of whiteness around the disciplines.

6 Conclusion

Africana Demography is an important intervention with the potential to make sociology and demography as relevant as in the days of W.E.B. Du Bois and E. Franklin Frazier by linking the techniques and rigorous scholarly inquiry of both disciplines to the principles of black sociology and the fundamental tenets of critical demography with blackness, not whiteness, as the center.

Understanding that whiteness is not normative and blackness is not essentially pathological is important.

It is also imperative that sociologists and demographers afford W.E.B. Du Bois and E. Franklin Frazier and others from the Atlanta School of Sociology their rightful place in the annals of history. If colleges and universities, especially PWIs, are serious about recruiting and retaining a diverse student body and they are serious about recruiting and retaining black professors then they must allow undergraduate students and graduate students to see themselves reflected in the curriculum. The days of excluding Du Bois from introductory textbooks or making only a passing reference to him have long passed. Similarly, mentions of Frazier's work only within the context of controversial works by people like Daniel Patrick Moynihan in disingenuous. Both scholars are deserving of far more. Including their work in graduate-level courses may not only help to attract black graduate students but also help to retain them. Showing a respect and appreciation for black sociologists and black demographers may also assist with the recruitment and retention of black professors.

Feeding the pipeline from undergraduate programs to doctoral programs is key to the future of demography and sociology. Regional and national organizations, such as Eastern Sociological Society, Population Association of America, and so forth are also likely to see increases in the membership of black graduate students and black professors and more diversity on the programs and in leadership positions.

Black scholars within sociology and demography have an expectation that their fields would do better because they presumably know better. Sadly, this is not the case. Racial disparities between blacks and whites in America persist and they persist for a multitude of reasons. Mainstream sociologists and conventional demographers can no longer bury their heads in the sand or remain on the sidelines. They must be open and honest about the roles they have played in the maintenance and fortification of the color line over time and embrace Africana Demography as a legitimate field that can be in dialogue with mainstream sociology and conventional demography to bring about the liberation of black people in America—or else both disciplines will continue to celebrate narrow improvements in the racial income gap, while all but ignoring the insurmountable racial wealth gap. They will forever join in the chorus of those blaming the victim, all the while claiming concern for social structures and social systems. Africana Demography is needed now more than ever.

Together, the chapters in this book highlight Africana Demography in action. In Part 1: Africana Demography and Migration, Fertility, and Mortality, Briana Painia examines the mass incarceration of black people as a demographic phenomenon. In Chapter 1, "Carceral Migration," Painia reconsiders prisoner reentry as a carceral migration sharing many characteristics with both domestic and international migration.

Maretta McDonald's chapter, "Child Support Enforcement as Social Control," addresses a common topic of conventional demography, the black family. More specifically, McDonald examines racism as a factor in explaining variation in family structure and outcomes of black families as a unit and their individual members. McDonald also explores how the laws and policies that govern Child Support Enforcement system are used to punish black fathers who do not conform to conventional norms of fertility and family structure. Using Fragile Families and Child Wellbeing study data, McDonald shows how multi-partner fertility is associated with the harshness of the penalties against non-custodial black fathers who are behind in their child support payments.

In Part 2: Africana Demography and Policing, Melinda Jackson-Jefferson's chapter, "Us versus Them," focuses on a "system" that focuses on locking up black and brown bodies in physical and metaphorical prisons. She understands the criminal justice system to be one that serves as an overarching racial caste system and validates discrimination. Jackson-Jefferson's focus on fear of crime reflects Africana Demography in that it brings light to the disparities that exist between black and white people on a subject matter popular in conventional demography by putting black Americans at the forefront and addressing racism.

Edward Muhammad and Jack S. Monell offer a critical analysis of policing by scholars from the black community with recommendations emanating from the inherent resources and cultural sensibilities within the black community. Muhammad and Monell's chapter, "Policing the Black Community" frames their work on policing as a form of population control within the traditions of critical and Africana Demography. Muhammad and Monell also contextualize perceptions of police by discussing attitudes about police and policing. The scholars also address the fatal consequences of black encounters with police, drawing from national data sets.

Jas Sullivan, in "African Americans' Response to Discrimination," observes that prior research on racial discrimination explored its presence, health effects, and coping mechanisms. He argues that much of the work is in the area of presence and health effects. Less is known about the ways one lessens a stressor such as discrimination. The purpose of Sullivan's chapter is to explore reactions to experiences with discrimination. Sullivan's chapter addresses the following research question: Do African Americans in the non-South react to discrimination differently than African Americans in the South? His study uniquely identifies regional differences in the reactions to discrimination.

Part 3 includes chapters that utilize the Africana Demography framework for understanding and addressing persistent racial gaps, especially economic inequality. Deadric Williams presents a theoretical perspective for understanding black families in poverty that centers race and racism in the chapter, "Rethinking Black Families in Poverty." The theoretical perspective offered in this chapter builds on recent debates about racial inequality in poverty. Specifically, Williams explores the early arguments on low-income black families with a specific emphasis on cultural and structural arguments. He provides a summary of scholarship by mostly black scholars who have presented a more dynamic understanding of black family life, but their research has been largely ignored. Williams also critiques conventional family sociology and offers a critical approach to the study of black families in poverty.

Tifanie Pulley and Arthur Whaley contribute to the emerging field of Africana Demography with their chapter called, "Embodying a Hybrid Habitus." Pulley and Whaley observe that not enough is known about black women and upward social mobility. The scholars are particularly interested in understanding how black people behave within their class status. As part of Africana Demography Pulley and Whaley use this study to explore the meaning of social class and upward mobility in the lives of working-class black women. The scholars focus on how these women construct and negotiate their identities. A critical question for Pulley and Whaley is how do black women professors acquire the habitus for their occupational role as academicians, which is usually inconsistent with the experiences of their working-class background?

Drawing on Black Liberation Theology, Weldon McWilliams addresses the relatively poor economic status of many Americans, especially black people in America. McWilliams focuses on the creation of a living wage. In the tradition of Africana Demography, McWilliams draws from historic black intellectual traditions and institutions to re-imagine how the nation can offer more people a living wage and argues that this must involve the Black Church.

Introduction to Africana Demography concludes with a chapter by David Rudder and Anthony Hill. The scholars focus on the racial achievement gap in education and mental health. Rudder and Hill call for re-examination of higher education to aid in the recruitment and retention of students of color, especially black students, with the importance of incorporating self-care strategies and other important skills. Rudder and Hill present a more holistic approach to student success and thus greater academic achievement through an emphasis on the social and mental well being of African American males. The aim of this chapter is to improve the persistence and retention of diverse male students.

The contributors to *Introduction to Africana Demography: Lessons from Founders E. Franklin Frazier, W.E.B. Du Bois, and the Atlanta School of Sociology* speak to innovative ways of addressing pressing issues with the added benefit of affording many of the *scholars denied* their rightful place in the sociological and demographic canons. Specifically, *Introduction to Africana Demography* provides a critique of conventional demographic approaches to understanding race and social institutions, such as the family, religion, and the criminal justice system.

Bibliography

Armstrong, Edward G. 1979. "Black Sociology and Phenomenological Sociology." *Sociological Quarterly* 20 (3): 387–97.

Blackwell, James, and Morris Janowitz. 1974. *Black Sociologists.* Chicago: University of Chicago Press.

Bonilla-Silva, Eduardo. 2018. *Racism without Racists.* Lanham, MD: Rowman & Littlefield.

Collins, Patricia Hill. 1990. *Black Feminist Thought.* New York: Routledge.

De La Cruz-Viesca, Melany, Paul M. Ong, Andre Comandon, William A. Darity Jr., and Darrick Hamilton. 2018. "Fifty Years after the Kerner Commission Report: Place, Housing, and Racial Wealth Inequality in Los Angeles." *RSF: The Russell Sage Foundation Journal of the Social Sciences* 4 (6): 160–84.

Du Bois, W.E.B. 1903. *The Souls of Black Folk.* Chicago: A.G. McClurg.

Du Bois, W.E.B. 1899. *The Philadelphia Negro.* Philadelphia: University of Pennsylvania Press.

Farley, Reynolds. 1988. "After the Staring Line: Blacks and Women in an Uphill Race." *Demography* 25 (4): 477–95.

Finley, Stephen C., and Biko Mandela Gray. 2015. "God Is a White Racist: Immanent Atheism as a Religious Response to Black Lives Matters and State-Sanctioned Anti-Black Violence." *Journal of Africana Religions* 3 (4): 443–53.

Finley, Stephen C., Biko Mandela Gray, and Lori Latrice Martin. 2018. "Affirming Our Values." *Journal of Academic Freedom* 9: 1–20.

Frazier, E. Franklin. 1927. "The Pathology of Racial Prejudice." *The Forum* 70: 856–62.

Frazier, E. Franklin. 1937. "Negro Harlem: An Ecological Study." *American Journal of Sociology* 43 (1): 72–88.

Frazier, E. Franklin. 1939. *The Negro Family in the United States.* Chicago: University of Chicago Press.

Frazier, E. Franklin. 1957. *Black Bourgeoisie.* Glencoe, IL: Free Press.

Frazier, E. Franklin. 1974. *The Negro Church in America.* Sourcebooks in Negro History. New York: Schoken Books.

Guo, Guang, Fu, Yilan, Lee, Hedwig, Cai, Tianji, Li Yi, and Kathleen Mullan Harris. 2014. "Recognizing a Small Amount of Superficial Genetic Differences across African, European, and Asian Americans Helps Understand Social Construction of Race." *Demography* 51 (6): 2337–42.

Hine, Darlene, William Hine, and Stanley Harrold. 2010. *African American Odyssey.* London: Pearson.

Horowitz, Irving Louis. 1973. "Black Sociology." *Transaction* 4 (9): 7–8.

Horton, Hayward Derrick. 1999. "Critical Demography: The Paradigm of the Future?" *Sociological Forum* 14 (3): 363–67.

Killewald, Alexandra. 2013. "Return to 'Being Black, Living in the Red': A Race Gap in Wealth That Goes Beyond Social Origins." *Demography* 50 (4): 1177–95.

Kochhar, Rakesh, and Anthony Cilluffo. 2018. "Key Findings on the Rise in Income Inequality within America's Racial and Ethnic Groups." Washington, DC: Pew Research Center. http://www.pewresearch.org/fact-tank/2018/07/12/key-findings-on-the-rise-in-income-inequality-within-americas-racial-and-ethnic-groups/.

Krein, Shelia, and Andrea Beller. 1988. "Educational Attainment of Children from Single-Parent Families: Differences by Exposure, Gender, and Race." *Demography* 25 (2): 221–34.

Ladner, Joyce. 1973. *The Death of White Sociology.* New York: Random House.

Le Duff, Darryl. 1975. "Perspectives on the Caucus of Black Sociologists and the 1975 Program." *Black Sociologist* 5: 6–7.

Martin, Lori Latrice. 2013. *Black Asset Poverty and the Enduring Racial Divide.* Boulder, CO: First Forum Press.

Martin, Lori Latrice. 2015. *Big Box Schools: Race, Public Schools, and the Danger of the Wal-Martization of Public Schools in America.* Latham, MD: Lexington Books.

Massey, Douglas. 1999. "What Critical Demography Means to Me." *Sociological Forum* 14 (3): 525–28.

Massey, Douglas, and Nancy Denton. 1993. *American Apartheid.* Cambridge, MA: Harvard University Press.

Morris, Aldon. 2015. *The Scholar Denied.* Berkeley: University of California Press.

Pratt-Clarke, Menah A.E. 2014. "Building a Foundation for Africana Sociology: Black Sociology, Afrocentricity, and Transdisciplinary Applied Social Justice." *Critical Sociology* 40 (2): 217–27.

Rosenbaum, Emily. 1992. "Race and Ethnicity in Housing: Turnover in New York City, 1978–1987." *Demography* 29 (3): 467–86.

Saenz, Rogelio, and M. Cristina Morales. "Demography and Race and Ethnicity." In *Handbook of Population*, edited by D.L. Poston and M. Micklin, 169–208. New York: Springer.

Sakamoto, Arthur, Huei-Hsia Wu, and Jessica Tzeng. 2000. "The Declining Significance of Race among American Men during the Latter Half of the Twentieth Century." *Demography* 37 (1): 41–51.

Sharkey, Patrick. 2012. "Temporary Integration, Resilient Inequality: Race and Neighborhood Change in the Transition to Adulthood." *Demography* 49 (3): 889–912.

South, Scott, and Kyle Crowder. 1997. "Residential Mobility between Cities and Suburbs: Race, Suburbanization, and Back-to-the-City Moves." *Demography* 34 (4): 525–38.

St. Drake, John Gibbs. 1945. *Black Metropolis: A Study of Negro Life in a Northern City*. Chicago: University of Chicago Press.

Sullivan, Laura, Tatjana Meschede, Lars Dietrich, and Thomas Shapiro. 2015. "The Racial Wealth Gap: Why Policy Matters." New York: Demos. Retrieved September 27, 2018. Iasp.brandeis.edu/pdfs/2015/RWA.pdf.

Wagmiller, Robert. 2007. "Race and Spatial Segregation of Jobless Men in Urban America." *Demography* 44 (3): 539–62.

Watson, Wilburn. 1976. "The Idea of Black Sociology: Its Cultural and Political Significance." *American Sociologist* 11 (2): 115–23.

Wilson, William Julius. 1979. *Declining Significance of Race*. Chicago: University of Chicago Press.

Wortham, Robert. 2005. "Introduction to the Sociology of W.E.B. Du Bois." *Sociation Today* 3 (1): 1–16. http://www.ncsociology.org.libezp.lib.lsu.edu/sociationtoday/v31/atlanta.htm.

Wright, Earl II. 2002a. "Using the Master's Tools: Atlanta University and American Sociology, 1896–1924." *Sociological Spectrum* 22 (1): 15–39.

Wright, Earl II. 2002b. "Why Black People Tend to Shout!: An Earnest Attempt to Explain the Sociological Negation of the Atlanta Sociological Laboratory Despite Its Possible Unpleasantness." *Sociological Spectrum* 22 (3): 325–61.

Wright, Earl II. 2002c. "The Atlanta Sociological Laboratory, 1896–1924: A Historical Account of the First American School of Sociology." *Western Journal of Black Studies* 26 (3): 165–74.

Wright, Earl II, and Thomas C. Calhoun. 2016. "Jim Crow Sociology: Toward an Understanding of the Origin and Principles of Black Sociology via the Atlanta Sociological Laboratory." *Sociological Focus* 39 (1): 1–18.

Wright, Earl II, and Edward Wallace. 2015. "Black Sociology: Continuing the Agenda." In *The Ashgate Research Companion to Black Sociology*, edited by E Wright, II and E. Wallace, 3–14. Burlington, VT: Ashgate Publishing Company.

Wright, Richard, Holloway, Steven and Mark Ellis. 2013. "Gender and the Neighborhood Location of Mixed-Race Couples." *Demography* 50 (2): 393–420.

Wyse, Jennifer Padilla. 2015. "Black Sociology: The Sociology of Knowledge, Racialized Power Relations of Knowledge, and Humanistic Liberation." In *The Ashgate*

Research Companion to Black Sociology, edited by Earl Wright II and Edward Wallace, 15–32. Burlington, VT: Ashgate Publishing Company.

Zuberi, Tukufu, and Eduardo Bonilla-Silva. 2008. *White Logic, White Methods: Racism and Methodology.* Latham, MD: Rowman & Littlefield.

PART 1

Africana Demography and Migration, Fertility, and Mortality

CHAPTER 1

Carceral Migration: an Africana Demographic Reframing of Post-release Pathways for Formerly Incarcerated Populations

Brianne Painia

1   Introduction

The movement of formerly incarcerated persons has been studied from a multitude of angles across race, class, and gender studies. Both incarceration and reentry have been thoroughly discussed in terms of their impacts on the people, places, and institutions affected by both phenomena. Within the last decade multiple scholarly, political, and activist works and initiatives have focused on the negative financial, social and emotional costs associated with incarceration (van Dooren, Kinner, Forsyth 2013; NeMoyer et al. 2019), particularly in the United States where more people are locked up than anywhere else in the world (Kozlowska 2017). One of those costs is the disenfranchisement of millions of Americans due to carceral association. Researchers have estimated there is may be roughly 3 million African Americans 'missing' from their communities due to murder, premature death, or incarceration. As a result of pushbacks to the mass incarceration phenomenon in this country, many states have committed to reducing both their incarceration and their recidivism rates by revising legislation and shifting state funding into the improvement and maintenance of better reentry systems. This movement by thousands of Americans, many of them Black males, from their home communities to carceral facilities and back to their home communities is a migratory process that can, and should, be studied as demographic in- and out-migration to releasees' pre-incarceration environments.

The field of Africana Demography expands space within demography for a reimagining of the journey of returning citizens to their communities as a carceral migration sharing many characteristics with both domestic and international migration. Africana Demography as an emerging demographic field has the potential to reshape understandings of critical demography due to its emphasis on questioning structures and their impact on Black persons, acknowledging the validity and variety of Black American experience and heritage, and applying scientific analysis to those experiences without pathologizing those behaviors. This chapter discusses relevant aspects of Africana Demography, which differentiate it from prior fields of scientific inquiry, its relation to the phenomenon of carceral migration, and the implications of the study of carceral migration.

2   Africana Demography's Ancestries

Before delving into the tenets of Africana Demography, it is necessary to review the scholarly fields which precede it. Africana Demography represents the intersection of critical demography and Black sociology—a previously undefined marriage of both disciplines—which amounts to an acute goal of improving and bettering the lives and livelihoods of members of the Diaspora through the scientific study of their processes and social realities. This intersection represents a joining of the inquiries of power structures inherent to critical demography and the social investigation of Black Sociology in a way that allows Black demographers and social scientists to appropriately address and progress the issues of Black American population. Yet, both of these fields derive from larger umbrella disciplines which seek to define and explain the social world—social demography and Sociology.

Demography at its base simply concerns itself with the scientific investigation of human population trends, behaviors, and maintenance (Nam 1979; Morgan and Lynch 2001) with an objective lens to influence and address applied or 'real world' implications. Formal demography is understood to encompass much of the statistically and mathematically modeling and analysis common to the field, whereas population studies refers to a broader scope of work which engages demographic data and variables in conjunction with theoretical work from other disciplines (Hirschman and Tolnay 2005). The breadth of scope available in population studies which can be used to describe, explain, and empower the Black American experience as a cultural unit is reflected in Africana Demography's commitment to contemplating new ways of studying Black people and the scopes of marginalization and identity which intersect their lived experience (Martin, in press).

Critical demography's eye on structures and institutions creates an area of overlap between itself and Black sociology via the explicit focus on the relationship between the individual (or groups of individuals) and the structures around them. Institutions comprise systems or structures which act in the interest of the most powerful entities and individuals within the country (Gorga 2017). To study institutions is to study the dynamics of power, domination, and marginalization that guide and influence them and through studying these dynamics a scholar hopes to shed light on the ways to improve or resist these oppressions. Horton and Sykes state that, "wealth, status and power...are the valued resources that dominant groups in any society struggle to maintain for themselves and to exclude from others" (2008, 241). It is the opportunity to acquire wealth, status, and power that is of potential interest to critically demographic scholars who are aware of how those three factors great impact fertility, mortality, and one's ability to migrate themselves and their families. As a people with an extensively long and predominantly negative relationship with the American criminal justice system, Black people represent a research body that is in constant struggle against institution-enforced oppressions and in constant pursuit of an oppression-free humanity.

Sociology recognizes society is guided by a web of invisible forces that are created and maintained by humans who share physical, cultural, or national space and our individual interactions with these forces are guided and refracted by our social identities and locations (Alinia 2015; Collins 2000). Black sociology adds to this scientific investigation of the social world with the specific nod to Black persons' culture, history, and relationship to the collective racial identifier of 'Black'. Africana Demography's Black Sociology ancestry mandates that it calls out any power dynamics (whether within or outside of the community) which work against the interest of Black persons while highlighting and sharing the nuanced stories which comprise the Black cultural tradition. Africana Demography—through the immediate paring of critical demography and black sociology—represents a lineage of scholarly methods, traditions, and disciplines that look to the social world for its analysis of the human experience. Yet, as stated throughout this edited volume, all these parent fields of social science lack a specific focus on the demographic and population-related phenomena unique to Black Americans. It is in this void that Africana Demography as a sub-field finds its niche.

3 Africana Demography

Africana Demography holds the following four major distinctions from its predecessors: A Black American specific focus, acknowledgment of Black American cultural background and context, the assumption of valid black personhood, and commitment to sharing academic knowledge with non-academics.

The first important distinction of Africana Demography is its target of Black American populations. Studies about the experiences of Black South Africans or Black British Women are included in the school of Black sociological thought and research (Mahon 2015). Africana Demography's specific focus on the Black American experience borders Africana Demography's scope to reflect the diverse array of Black nationalities and ethnicities present in the United States. This country's unique history with Black Americans, immigrants, and their descendants via chattel, race-based slavery creates a social backdrop that affects every aspect of American life from educational outcomes to residential choices to spiritual practices (Cross 1991). Africana Demography is rooted in the Black American experience with hopes to be applicable to non-American Black populations as well. Creation of theory and social demographic analysis situated in American Blackness—a melting pot of demographic, social, and cultural legacies—contributes to the international field of Black social population studies. Documenting and expanding the canon of the Black American experience reinforces our space within the global story of the Pan-African experience and the social forces which pertain to our birth, death, health, and migration processes. Africana Demography uses the Black American experience at the center around which our relationships to one another and society as a whole rotate in an effort to tell more about and improve the condition of the Black American population.

Africana Demography acknowledges, includes, and progresses from the sociohistorical cultural base that is unique to Black persons. This 'Africana' base can be contextualized to any combination of national or ethnic backgrounds that a Black American may possess (e.g. first-generation Americans whose parents immigrated from West African and/or West Indian nations) and used to provide the needed context for the authentic and effective study of Black populations. Africana Demography recognizes the multitude of webs and connections that comprise the Africana collective history (slavery, immigration, structural racism, sexism) and empowers Black demographers to use their lived experiences to situate the study of Black peoples. Oris, Brunet and Bideau reinforce the value of culture to the demographic study of minority groups when they describe it as "necessarily cultural and social…its scientific study is also influenced by national cultures and even dependent upon these cultures to a certain extent" (2005, 2). Cultural context is crucial in the effective demographic studies of people of color. Africana Demography acknowledges the multitude of national histories represented within the Black American population (McDonald and Cross-Barnet 2018) and centers that variety in any analysis of those populations.

Another tenet of Africana Demography is the assumption of valid personhood of the black subjects without pathologizing Black ways of being. A black demographic focus should not treat black people as mere voiceless numbers, as some demographic and social studies may frame them, but as persons whose lives and stories are deserving of scholarly recognition because they tell us more about the American experience. Patricia Hill Collins made popular the notion of 'everyday knowledge' to refer to the valuing of subjects' lived experience as valid sources of scientific study and the recognition of subjects of social study as valid scholars of their own experience (Collins 1992). In a similar fashion, Tara J. Yosso argues that communities of color possess a number of social capitals that are integral to its inhabitants' progression and success in their professional and academic life as well as their survival in a world where they are marginalized (2005) despite hegemonic narratives that label those same communities as under-privileged or imply the members of those communities as lacking in moral and/or ethical fiber. A demography of Black American peoples must also look to Black subjects as the authorities of their experience and valid producers of scholarly knowledge. This emphasis on subject experience does not overshadow or repress the presence of rigorous social scientific data collection but enhances its validity and accuracy in accounting the Black experiences which shape our population and its demographic processes.

Black persons have been the objects of many an academic study with a variety of misnaming and pathologizing of behaviors, beliefs, and identities (Frazier 1939). As seen with a slew of public and scholarly publications which ignore the factors bearing upon the black experience (such as racism, classism, or sexism) and replace those factors with racist, patriarchal myths about the population, scholarship has not always been kind or objective to Black populations. Comparison against white, patriarchal ideals about family life, sexuality, and access to upward mobility has many times left black person in the margin of research about their experience—constantly being measured against a standard never meant to represent or reflect their ways of being (Harris-Perry 2013). Africana Demography cannot use white American traditions and cultural norms as the litmus test for black behavior, morality, and scholarship; instead it invites new measures and tools to tell the story of Black American populations. Africana Demography uses its various scholarly ancestors to investigate and report the authentic and unique cultural norms and behaviors specific to black folk.

A final distinction of Africana Demography is its respect for the sharing of academic knowledge with those outside of the academy. Calling back to black feminist works *Black Feminist Thought* (Collins 2000) and *Sister Citizen* (Harris-Perry 2013), much of the lived experience and collective knowledge we as Black scholars draw from come from our familial and social interactions within our social communities and residential neighborhoods. Many of us were empowered to become scholar activists in our barbershops and salons (Doyle et al.

2016), indoctrinated into civic engagement via our community and religious organizations, or introduced to applied feminism via our own gender role non-traditional homes (Lawrence, Webb, Littlefield, Okundaye 2004). In other words, we as Black sociologists and demographers recognize the knowledge and power we received in our communities of origin and realize our responsibility to share the things we've learned about our social world with our initial teachers. Emphasizing the import of creating understanding for those who may have never crossed the seals of institutions of higher learning reinforces the debt that many of our educational institutions owe but never acknowledge to the Black American community. Many universities in our country were built via the funding accrued from the American slave trade (Johnson 2007). Even once slavery was outlawed and segregation became illegal systemic attacks on Black communities and economies barred many African Americans of the middle twentieth century from filling the halls of educational institutions unless cleaning them or serving food. The radical redefinition of valid and formal knowledge can be achieved by sharing our research and its implications with persons who exist outside our academic bubble (Bhambra 2015).

Africana Demography's acute focus on Black American lives, awareness of African American cultural history and norms, acceptance of Black subjects as authorities of their own stories, and ease of understanding for those outside the academy distinguishes it from other areas of demographic and African American scientific inquiry. With Africana Demography's commitment to the highlighting of and solution building to the social and demographic problems and inquiries of peoples of the Africana diaspora, it creates the space for the study of a process that greatly impacts Black Americans and their communities of origin. This chapter will cover the ways post-release movements mimic a migratory pattern for returning citizens and the ways Africana Demography allows for new directions in both reentry and demographic scholarship to better address and analyze the needs and movements of returning citizens.

4 Migration

Demography, as a field, widely recognizes three major sources of population change: birth, death, and migration. In a report published by the Population Reference Bureau in 1991 migration is described as "a social process involving social networks that connect the place of origin to the place of destination" (McFalls, 21). Migrations can be voluntary as in the case of labor migrants who move across a city, state, or national boundary for job purposes or young adults who leave their homes to pursue college, or it can be involuntary as in the case of West African slaves brought to the Americas to build and maintain the Western societies that exist today (Brown and Bean 2005). Migration can occur internally (within national borders) or internationally (immigration) and is most successful when chain and step migrations occur (White and Lindstrom 2005).

Everyone is born and eventually dies but not everyone must migrate from one residence to another. Migration serves as the more socially influenced and nuanced demographic shift (Zuberi et al. 2003), in comparison to its counterpart population processes birth, death, and morbidity—making it an apt process to define reentry and the movements of returning citizens. The study of migration is important because it tells us about the push and pull factors which contribute to the movement of populations to and from respective locations. Reintegration to the community impacts the formerly incarcerated and soon-to-be released population of America, is a highly socially influenced voluntary movement, and is improved by methods similar to step and chain migration. These similarities justify the reframing of reintegration as part of a carceral migration with returning citizens acting as carceral migrants back to their communities.

5 An Introduction to Carceral Migration and the Import of Reintegration

Carceral migration is a pre-, during, and post-incarceration movement comprised of forced and voluntary progressions throughout the prison system. Though carceral migration refers to all parts of a citizen's interaction with the carceral system from arrest to return to the community this chapter will focus on the reintegration aspect of the carceral migratory process. Outside of the physical change of permanent residence, reintegration is a social process that corrections and pre-release/transition programs try to improve via pre-release education applicable to the non-incarcerated world (Shand 1996). Before describing the parallels between carceral migration and traditional migratory processes it is necessary to emphasize the importance of studying post-release community reintegration.

Within the last two years, thousands of formerly incarcerated persons in the United States (Louisiana Department of Public Safety and Corrections Louisiana Commission on Law Enforcement 2019; Travis 2014) have made the move from their incarceration facility across carceral boundaries to their home neighborhoods. There are a variety of opinions about what specifically comprises the reentry process with some defining it as starting once an inmate is physically released from prison while others believe one's sentence should be spent mostly preparing for her return to society (White et al. 2012). Some argue the initial entry one makes to a prison or jail is a part of the reentry process as one should start preparing for ones exit from the carceral system the day that he or she begins his or her sentence (Shand 1996). This perspective of reintegration places incarceration not as the final destination for the incarcerated but as stop on the road to ultimate release and reintegration back into society. There is not a definitive answer on when reentry begins and ends for an incarcerated person, yet most agree the ultimate goal of the correctional system is to rehabilitate and foster reintegration amongst formerly incarcerated citizens (Shand 1996). One significant marker of the correctional system's progress toward that goal is the recidivism rates.

Reentry literature supports that a returned citizen's avoidance of reincarceration is not the sole mark of successful reintegration into the community (Cooke 2005), but it is a significant indicator recognized almost universally by community members, national and state governments, and correctional agencies about the progress or regression of our correctional system. In their paper critiquing common interpretations of recidivism rates, Rhodes et al. stress the import of accurate reporting in this area as recidivism is the number one indicator of whether a correctional facility or system has been effective (2016). Powers, Kaukinenn, and Jeanis (2017) reinforce this idea in their examination of the recidivism rates of private facilities compared to state correctional facilities in Colorado where they acknowledge that reintegration failures can and do influence public policy and funding opportunities for the facilities being judged.

Frequently, recidivism statistics are taken at face value as proof the U.S. incarceration system is not working, yet researchers have acknowledged issues with recidivism data analysis (White et al. 2012) and problematized the notion that our incarceration system is failing since the majority of returned citizens are not reincarcerated (Rhodes et al. 2016). Rhodes et al. critique common measures of reporting recidivism rates and the samples they select from as they may suffer from an overrepresentation of high-risk reoffenders (2016). Other analysts state that recidivism is still too high to consider our carceral system successful at reintegrating the formerly incarcerated (Alper, Durose, and Markman 2018). Studies have suggested that a better investigative inquiry regarding post-release reintegration may be to ask what makes successfully reintegrated citizens successful as they represent the majority of the formerly incarcerated population in many states as opposed to studying what makes the reincarcerated fail at reintegration. Both of these inquiries are important, and this chapter will not declare which research pathway is best for addressing the problem. Referencing this tension is for the purpose of showing the multitude of issues and outcomes which are related to the study of carceral release and reintegration and the significance of investigating citizens' journeys upon release from prison. Community reintegration is valuable to study because improving this process could help thousands of American men and women (a significant portion whom are Black) better reintegrate back into their communities. There are multiple ways the difficulty and nuance that makes up reintegration mimics the difficulties and nuances present in 'traditional' migratory movements. The first of which is the stigma both migrants may face due to perceptions about their places of origin.

Reintegration into society after incarceration—particularly after significant amounts of time spent removed from the community—is difficult, and a significant number of formerly incarcerated persons do not successfully reintegrate (Alper, Durose and Markman 2018). Returned persons who do successfully reintegrate still experience challenges tied to their status as 'formerly incarcerated'. As formerly incarcerated persons attempt to reintegrate, they navigate a sometimes-invisible web of choices and networks to avoid returning to prison or jail and to achieve a sustainable life outside of prison. Yet, this navigation is mediated by a migrants' ability to overcome the challenges to successful reentry which include challenges acquiring resources and finding acceptance within their community, both which are linked to the stigma many non-incarcerated persons attach to the status of 'felon' or 'formerly incarcerated' (Keena and Simmons 2015).

International migrants and low-wage labor migrants face stigmas within their country of destinations that are many times tied to xenophobic myths about their country of origin (Campbell 2015). In a similar way some Americans have particularly strong and overwhelmingly conservative attitudes about carceral migrants. Narratives about their threats to our safety, regardless of the validity or nature of their conviction, and questions about formerly incarcerated persons' character and morality drive policy and legal decisions made in our country (Hagan and Coleman 2001). The hyper-criminalization of drug use in the 80s resorted in what some have deemed a "prison boom," in which the prison population grew by exponential percentages, which resulted in a rise in the age of arrest of the male prison population (Porter et al. 2016). The stigmas and the impact that stigmas can have for both immigrants and carceral migrants can create very real barriers to their successful in-migration. Felon stigma can disqualify the formerly incarcerated from employment opportunities long before their personal qualifications and ability to complete the job are examined. Carceral migrants' inability to secure gainful employment is a major cause of their reincarceration as financial demands may lead returned citizens to seek illegal means of income to make ends meet. Related to this stigma is the temporal nature of migrants' stay in their communities of destination, which is the second area of overlap between post-incarceration carceral migrants and international migrants.

In the pre-incarceration to incarceration phase of carceral migration, an incarcerated persons' home neighborhood is their community of origin while their penal home is their place of destination outside of their own will. In the incarceration to post-incarceration phase of the carceral migration flow a returning citizens' facility of detainment is their place of origin while their pre-incarceration environment is their community of destination. In international migration until one obtains citizenship rights within their country of destination, they run the risk of being sent back to their country of origin, or a holding place between the two places, if found to be without the proper paperwork. Carceral migrants run a consistent risk of returning to their place of origin—jail or prison—if they do not adhere to the rules and regulations determined by the correctional body of their respective state or city (Powers et al. 2017).

One of the external factors present in the journey back to one's pre-incarceration community is the penal system's judgment that one has served their time and is fit to return to society. Whether mediated by the authorities of the incarceration facility itself or judges in the sentencing courtroom prior to serving time, carceral migrants' release to the non-incarcerated world is many times in the hands of the institutions that hold them. The study of migration is useful within an Africana context because Black American movements have many times been instigated by systemic factors (Hunt, Hunt, and Falk 2013) such as racism, sexism, or governmental force with minimal regard to the value they bring to the places they inhabit or the community value lost due to their absence. Turning to the more positive areas of overlap between the two groups, a third parallel is the means by which both groups of migrants can improve and ensure successful integration into their communities of destination.

One way that international migrants attempt to achieve a successful migration to their place of origin is through chain migration. Chain migration is the following of guidelines and norms of migrants who have gone before them in order to reduce and avoid pitfalls and hang-ups in the migration process (White and Lindstrom 2005). Mentorship from successfully reintegrated men or faith-based volunteers has been shown to improve returning citizens chances of succeeding once released (Abrams et al. 2014; Stacer and Roberts 2018). Knowledge about what to expect once returned to their communities and how to effectively begin the pursuit of reintegration can be useful in absorbing some of the cultural and psychological shock some migrants experience when returning home while also informing them on when and how to best prepare to face the stigma and other barriers formerly incarcerated citizens face in their pursuit of reintegration.

Another contributor to successful reintegration is the opportunity to engage a form of step-migration in the transition back into the community. Step migration allows migrants to "moderate the financial and psychic costs of migration between dramatically different types of places by allowing for gradual adjustment and the collection of information about" their place of destination (White and Lindstrom 2005). Spaces such as hallway houses, post-release transition programs, and work-release allow carceral migrants the ability to slow down the transition back into non-incarcerated life (Keena and Simmons 2015; Pompoco et al. 2017). If migrants are able to successfully (re)integrate into their communities of destination they can have significant impacts on their communities of origin.

One community effect carceral migrants can have is their potential impact on the voting and political issues pertaining to their home communities. Many carceral migrants do not immediately receive their right to vote upon release which silences and limits their ability to civically engage in their neighborhoods. Even with recent legislation to grant interested returned citizens the ability to register to vote, this option can only be exercised after a set period of 'good behavior such as five years with no parole violations. Migrants of all kinds have impacts on their places of origin (whether sending money back to family left behind or leaving an economic absence) and their place of destination (usage of resources, potential ability to contribute politically or economically). Carceral migration impacts more than the incarcerated. It is well documented in criminological literature that imprisonment significantly impacts the communities, partners, and children that prisoners leave behind (Cooke 2005). In a similar vein returning citizens also impact the ecosystems of the neighborhoods they return to and the families they have been removed from for any number of years (Hagan and Coleman 2001). The reintegration of black formerly incarcerated citizens to their home community represents potential for rebuilding previously strained or severed family structures due to incarceration.

The subjugation to stigma—and reduced access to opportunity due to it—related to their communities of origin (jail or home countries), temporality of their residence in their place of destination, improvement of success at integration through chain and step migration, and significant civic impact their presence has on the communities they integrate are four of many similarities between carceral migrants and traditional migrants. Carceral migrants potentially have much more in common with international and domestic migrants than stated above because migration is a long-term process as is movement throughout the carceral system. Engaging reintegration as carceral migration invites new solutions or revised old ones to be employed when addressing all aspects of this process, specifically the most pertinent to a correctional system's success—a migrant's reintegration.

6 Why Is Carceral Migration an Africana Demography Problem?

Reentry, like migration, is not simply a physical movement across boundaries but a psychological and situational transition that can begin at varying points prior to and after one's physical release from prison. Carceral migrants' return to their pre-incarcerated communities inherently impact Black American neighborhoods as Black men represent the group most likely to be sent to prison for most violations (Gross, Possley, Stephens 2017). Turning back to the components of Africana Demography stated earlier in this chapter, the study of carceral migration is one of many ways the Black population's presence in the prison/jail system can be studied as a Black American movement which acknowledges Black persons' humanity and cultural background.

Africana Demography assesses black populations as well as the structures that move them as a whole. Carceral migration is engaged by thousands of Black persons in this country and the reintegration leg of migration is the future of thousands of other soon-to-be releasees. Analysis of carceral migration addresses the systems which have contributed to Black representation in American penitentiaries and the raced and gendered factors which affect black men's and women's rate of reintegration successes or failure. There is the acknowledgement that black incarceration is as much a result of personal choice and action as it is the result of structural factors such as over policing, disproportionate sentencing, and disinvestment in African American communities. Africana demographic analysis of carceral migration considers the social, emotional, and psychological causes and effects of the physical changes in residence between one's penal residence and their community. Carceral migration acknowledges the causes and the effects of these social processes which have persisted to the detriment of many black lower-income communities and neighborhoods.

Africana Demography's emphasis on black personhood ensures that the study of carceral migration can occur without the pathologizing of black peoples. Prior sociological commentary on the Black family pointed to Black persons' moral deficiencies (Moynihan 1965) as opposed to systemic forces as the root of inequalities in black life. Contradictory to government and academic inquiries which assign moral and ethical values to African American group behavior, an Africana-centered demographic analysis of carceral migration focuses on the systems, structures, and stories which inform post-release choices and outcomes removed from the assumption of dysfunctional or marginalized ways of being. An empirical study of carceral migration makes room for Black Americans to be the center of demographic inquiry with minimal comparison to their white counterparts or assumptions of their inherent deviance.

It is not lost that descendants of the African Diaspora have a centuries old history with forced migration in the Western World especially in the United States, a country long described as 'built on the backs of African slaves.' The forced migration of many Black Americans into carceral facilities—and the jarring effects those absences have on the communities they are removed from—represents to many a continuation of the initial forced migration that brought them to the shores of North and South America so many centuries ago. Africana Demography holds this history alongside the political and scholarly possibilities for improving the criminal justice system and its hold on black populations.

A key possibility within Africana Demography is its scholarly advocacy for the improvement of black lives like its Black sociological predecessors. Research on carceral migration can be used to advocate for the improvement of post-incarceration systems to reduce recidivism if rooted in the experiences of formerly incarcerated persons. More information about flaws and imminent progress within carceral systems can be to the benefit of thousands of American citizens who can better reintegrate into their home communities. Reduction in recidivism and alternatives to incarceration can potentially mean there are more free Black persons able to contribute to their communities and families (Alexander 2012).

Carceral migration is not a demographic phenomenon unique to Black Americans yet their overrepresentation in the carceral process makes it well worth the attention of demographers and social scientists as an Africana inquiry. With Black persons comprising such a significant minority of the incarcerated population it is within reason to believe that improvement in carceral migrants' reentry process, and even in their pre-incarceration preparation, would amount to an improvement in the quality of Black lives—a central goal of Africana Demography. Acknowledging the systemic factors and historical legacies that bear upon the relationship between African Americans and the criminal justice system without demonizing or misrepresenting the presence of Black persons in the carceral process is Africana Demography in practice.

7   Implications for Research

Reintegration is a process that causes major movements in rural and urban populations throughout the United States (as does its predecessor incarceration). Accurate counts of residential inhabitants must also account for the millions or people leaving correctional facilities and entering the community (Muller and Wilderman 2016). Many studies have found that if a carceral migrant is going to return to prison it happens within the first 6 months to a year after release (Dias et al. 2018; Bullis and Yovanoff 2006). If this holds true thousands of people are moving to and being removed from urban and rural communities with minimal record of them having been there and the impacts their entrance or exit has those communities. Better capturing, both quantitatively and qualitatively, of carceral migrants' movement can inform areas for needed funding in the neighborhood migrants leave in order to best serve their post-release needs.

Within this reframing of returning citizens as carceral migrants there is also room for the expansion of demography to involve non-traditional methodologies and analysis for the field such as interview data and qualitative analysis which seeks to explain and discover more about the migration process. Qualitative inquiry is in the minority in the field of demography. Though increasing in size, demography has traditionally been and continues to be a quantitative scholar's game. Morgan and Lynch describe demography's reliance on numbers or "ease of measurement" as one of the major contributors to the field's success thus far (2001, 40). Yet, as most fields progress there becomes greater need to describe and explain a phenomenon rather than to simply establish relationships. The field of demography is no different due to its basic commitment to explaining and studying populations regardless of the way in which it is studied. As demography concerns itself with the study of a population and predictability of phenomena impacting the respective population, it understandably leans toward the valuing of statistical methodologies and quantitative inquiries, yet it does not exclude the usage of qualitative methods or analysis to infer or describe populations of interest.

As Africana Demography concerns itself with the context of black subjects it inherently validates qualitative study of demographic movements. There are conclusions that can only be arrived via qualitative inquiry due to its emphasis on the quality of a phenomenon (Randall and Koppenhaver 2004) as opposed to simply establishing a relationship or verifying that a process occurs. The study of Black American migrations and the external factors which cause them requires more than just a validation of connections. They deserve the depth of investigation and situational contact that qualitative inquiry can provide. Africana Demography recognizes that the Black experience is more than just numbers and identification of trends, but also the narratives and oral histories which situate our current ways of being. Qualitative demography is a small but growing number within the field which can and should be a part of Africana demographic study.

Acknowledgment of incarceration and release as parts of a migratory movement can help further define and identify the phases of reintegration in an effort to better help the formerly incarcerated know what lies ahead upon release. A newly released citizen who has just begun his journey to pursue reintegration has different needs from a citizen who has acquired employment but still needs housing or other resources to avoid reincarceration. These differences need be acknowledged and targeted for intervention if releasees are consistently required to prove the case for their continued living outside a correctional facility.

The reframing of reintegration as carceral migration may also have a social benefit for the formerly incarcerated by perceiving community return as a demographic shift as opposed to a demonized process In line with the Africana Demographic tenet of documenting Black behavior and living without stigmatizing or further marginalizing Black subjects, the phrase 'carceral migration' may appeal more to supporters of harsh correctional policies. Demonized for their presence in a prison or jail, carceral migrants many times find themselves losing a game they cannot possibly win due to the social attachments many non-incarcerated place on their personhood. Viewing reintegration as a migratory process comparable to that of millions of others both international and domestic who seek better lives through movement may reframe and readjust some of the negative perceptions releasees may encounter.

Finally, reintegration represents an opportunity for healing and strengthening in these neighborhoods if carceral migrants are given the appropriate tools to successfully navigate the migration process. One of the major effects of the removal of carceral migrants from their communities is the severing of social and familial ties that can occur due to the physical distance from their neighborhoods and the loss of time and familiarity that comes with an extended absence (Hagan and Coleman 2001). On the other hand, the communities that carceral migrants return to are crucial to their success or failure at reintegration. Literature has found the community and families carceral migrants return to provide most of the social, financial, and emotional labor needed to successfully support their reintegration. Better distribution of resources to support this intangible labor could greatly improve reincarceration avoidance. Since these families and neighbors are the first line of support for the formerly incarcerated it is necessary that they receive proper financial support to best help the reintegration process. Referencing back to Yosso's community capital (2005), many of the types of cultural capital (familial, navigational, and resistant) that help carceral migrants survive incarceration and succeed post-incarceration are devalued or overlooked by systemic carceral entities. Save for a few initiatives in recent years, holistic community support for returning systems has not been the top priority of many post-release programs. Better examination of post-incarceration pathways and needs can provide support for such initiatives.

8 Future Research

The probation and parole system is an ever-present companion to all carceral migrants' reintegration voyage and represents their most tangible post-release interaction with the correctional entity that initially incarcerated them. This chapter did not touch upon this aspect of post-release, yet further research should investigate how P&P's goals and interactions with carceral migrants contributes or works against their successful reintegration. Probation and Parole is many times discussed as a proxy or secondary mediator of the criminal justice system (Bullis and Yovanoff 2008). Even when successfully reintegrated, a carceral migrant is still in danger of returning to a state of incarceration depending on the terms of their probation. Carceral migrants may not truly be "released" or "reintegrated" until they are off parole and able to move through the world as their non-incarcerated selves. Investigations into the reintegration process must expand past the movement of persons from their incarceration facilities and look at the ways the probation and parole system contribute to either reintegration or reincarceration.

Another area for exploration in the reintegration phase of carceral migration is jail reentry. State prisons are generally more resourced and are able to provide pre-release programming due to the length of stay of their inmates (Jung, Spjeldnes, Yamatani 2010). Jails generally don't have that same luxury since their inmates are there for significantly shorter times. Literature has shown that incarceration, regardless of holding space, is a traumatic process (Anderson, Geier, and Cahill 2016) that requires support for reintegration. Another way to service carceral migrants would be to learn more about the specifics of the jail pre-and post-release process.

Though this chapter only focuses on the reentry phase of carceral migration there are multiple movements which occur through that migratory process which should also be investigated. The pre-incarceration process is one of interest which can be improved and is understudied. Block and Ruffalo (2015) describe the anxieties of pre-incarcerated citizens and the need for accurate information to be shared with pre-incarcerated migrants so they may best optimize their carceral experience.

9 Conclusion

Black Americans represent a population of United States citizens who are oft highly studied yet misrepresented in the social sciences. Some of these misrepresentations are due to the researcher's lack of shared experience with Black American subjects, political narratives and agendas which benefit from the subjugation of African Americans for any variety of pro-capitalist, patriarchal reasons (Guy-Sheftall 1995), or an investigators' over-reliance on the existence of a monolithic Black experience. Whatever the reasons for the misrepresentation, informed social research by and/or about Black Americans is still a nascent and underserved body of literature. As academic journals, professional associations, and scholarly disciplines continue to expand their understandings and characterizations of valid Black research there is no reason demography cannot be a part of that progression. As the forefront of inquiry about populations, demography represents an opportunity to engage and define Black populations by the indicators and processes that are most relevant to their migrations, births, and deaths. Carceral migration is only one of many ways new narratives can be created about existing Black populations in America, and Africana Demography serves as the sojourner into the new sub-field of the demographic and sociological traditions.

Ideally, the criminal justice system will continue with its current focus on reform and rehabilitation. Understanding reintegration as a migratory movement establishes space for the standardization of measures of community re-entry. Incarcerated persons are a population whose movements greatly impact our neighborhoods and our society. Viewing returning citizens as migrants within an Africana demographic study focuses on the social aspects of this movement of Black men and women into the neighborhoods, job economies, and families they left behind. Carceral migration also welcomes non-traditional forms of demographic inquiry due to complex processes present in the move from a carceral facility to a neighborhood and vice versa. Lending voice to the experiences of those who navigate this maze of reintegration pursuit and reincarceration avoidance also empowers the stories of the formerly incarcerated. Many of whom have their rights as citizens stripped and altered due to their interaction with the criminal justice system. Carceral migration also has potential impacts for the realm of political science as carceral migrants many times do not have the right to participate in the democratic voting practice.

As Africana Demography continues to reframe and revive Black American migrations—such as black men's and women's journey to and through incarceration, Black family's residential movements once class barriers have been permeated, or influences on Black adults' residential migratory decisions when pursuing job opportunities across state lines—more understudied inquiries specific to the Black experience will become apparent. This book is not the summation of Black American demographic inquiries, but only a starting point for conversations and revised understandings of what is validly demographic and what is demographically Black. As states and federal authorities continue to try and fix what some would argue is a 'broken' criminal justice system it is important to learn as much as possible about the migrants who experience that system in this country. Africana Demography compiles a spectrum of opinions and inquiries focused solely on the Black American life cycle. With contemporary headlines that focus on the relationship between black women's mortality during childbirth, black men's overwhelming struggle to progress through the U.S. public and higher education systems, and the mortality of Black males at significantly younger ages than their white counterparts, America is acutely aware of the issues which uniquely impact Black citizens. We are in a space socially, scholastically, and politically where we can confirm and proclaim the truths of our community in and outside of the Ivory Tower of Academia.

Bibliography

Abrams, Laura S., Matthew L. Mizel, Viet Nguyen, and Aron Shlonsky. 2014. "Juvenile Reentry and Aftercare Interventions: Is Mentoring a Promising Direction?" *Journal of Evidence-Based Social Work* 11 (4): 404–22. https://doi.org/10.1080/10911359.2014.897115.

Alexander, Michelle. 2012. *The New Jim Crow : Mass Incarceration in the Age of Colorblindness*. Revised ed. New York: New Press. http://libezp.lib.lsu.edu/login?url=https://search.ebscohost.com/login.aspx?direct=true&db=cat00252a&AN=lalu.4592318&site=eds-live&scope=site&profile=eds-main.

Alinia, Minoo. 2015. "On Black Feminist Thought: Thinking Oppression and Resistance through Intersectional Paradigm." *Ethnic and Racial Studies* 38 (13): 2334–40. https://doi.org/10.1080/01419870.2015.1058492.

Alper, Mariel, Matthew R Durose, and Joshua Markman. 2018. "2018 Update on Prisoner Recidivism: A 9-Year Follow-up Period (2005–2014)." Bureau of Justice Statistics, Special Report, NCJ 250975.

Anderson, RaeAnn E, Timothy J Geier, and Shawn P Cahill. 2016. "Epidemiological Associations between Posttraumatic Stress Disorder and Incarceration in the National Survey of American Life." *Criminal Behaviour & Mental Health* 26 (2): 110. http://libezp.lib.lsu.edu/login?url=https://search.ebscohost.com/login.aspx?direct=true&db=edb&AN=114191064&site=eds-live&scope=site&profile=eds-main.

Bhambra, Gurminder K. 2015. "Black Thought Matters: Patricia Hill Collins and the Long Tradition of African American Sociology." *Ethnic and Racial Studies* 38 (13): 2315–21. https://doi.org/10.1080/01419870.2015.1058497.

Block, Steven, and Lyndsay Ruffolo. 2015. "An Exploratory Content Analysis of Offender Concerns Before Incarceration." *The Prison Journal* 95 (3): 309–29. https://doi.org/10.1177/0032885515587464.

Brown, Susan K, and Frank D Bean. 2005. "International Migration." In *Handbook of Population*, edited by Dudley L. Poston and Michael Micklin, 918. New York: Springer.

Bullis, Michael, and Paul Yovanoff. 2008. "Idle Hands: Community Employment Experiences of Formerly Incarcerated Youth." *Journal of Emotional and Behavioral Disorders* 14 (2): 71–85. https://doi.org/10.1177/10634266060140020401.

Campbell, Kristina M. 2015. "A Dry Hate: White Supremacy and Anti-Immigrant Rhetoric in the Humanitarian Crisis on the U.S.-Mexico Border." In *2015 Mid-Atlantic People of Color Conference*, 36.

Collins, Patricia Hill. 1992. "Transforming the Inner Circle: Dorothy Smith's Challenge to Sociological Theory." *Sociological Theory* 10 (1): 73–80.

Collins, Patricia Hill. 2000. *Black Feminist Thought: Knowledge, Consciousness, and the Politics of Empowerment*. 2nd ed. New York: Routledge Classics.

Cone, James H. 1975. *God of the Oppressed*. New York: Seabury Press.

Cooke, Cheryl L. 2005. "Going Home: Formerly Incarcerated African American Men Return to Families and Communities." *Journal of Family Nursing* 11 (4): 388–404. https://doi.org/10.1177/1074840705281753.

Cross, William E. 1991. *Shades of Black: Diversity in African-American Identity*. Philadelphia, PA: Temple University Press. https://eds-b-ebscohost-com.libezp.lib.lsu.edu/eds/detail/detail?vid=3&sid=c6907d47-b160-4c83-adb2-b4dae3806102%40sessionmgr103&bdata=JnNpdGU9ZWRzLWxpdmUmc2NvcGU9c2l0ZQ%3D%3D#AN=lalu.1034202&db=cat00252a.

Dias, Shannon, Stuart A Kinner, Ed Heffernan, Geoffrey Waghorn, and Robert Ware. 2018. "Identifying Rehabilitation Priorities among Ex-Prisoners Vulnerable to Mental Ilnesses and Substance Abuse." *Journal of Rehabilitation* 84 (3): 46–56. http://search.ebscohost.com/login.aspx?direct=true&db=ccm&AN=131658828&site=ehost-live.

Doyle, Otima, Ifrah Magan, Qiana R. Cryer-Coupet, David B. Goldston, and Sue E. Estroff. 2016. "'Don't Wait for It to Rain to Buy an Umbrella:' The Transmission of Values from African American Fathers to Sons." *Psychology of Men and Masculinity* 17 (4): 309–19. https://doi.org/10.1037/men0000028.

Frazier, E. Franklin. 1939. *The Negro Family in the United States*. Chicago, Ill.: The University of Chicago Press. https://eds-b-ebscohost-com.libezp.lib.lsu.edu/eds/detail/detail?vid=2&sid=2b8bb561-4cfe-47b3-ae37-a85acb1310f3%40sessionmgr103&bdata=JnNpdGU9ZWRzLWxpdmUmc2NvcGU9c2l0ZQ%3D%3D#AN=lalu.513536&db=cat00252a.

Gorga, Allison. 2017. "'Kinda Like a Man and a Woman Thing': The Construction and Reification of Gender Hegemony in a Women's Prison." *Social Currents* 4 (5): 413–28. https://doi.org/10.1177/2329496516686617.

Gross, Samuel R, Maurice Possley, Senior Researcher, Klara Stephens, and Research Fellow. 2017. "Race and Wrongful Convictions in the United States." National Registry of Exonerations. Irvine: Newkirk Center for Science and Society, University of California.

Guy-Sheftall, Beverly. 1995. *Words of Fire: An Anthology of African-American Feminist Thought*. New York: The New Press. https://eds-a-ebscohost-com.libezp.lib.lsu.edu/eds/detail/detail?vid=18&sid=b5ffd08c-4ccb-4f9f-ac8b-b8a7238830ad%40session mgr4009&bdata=JnNpdGU9ZWRzLWxpdmUmc2NvcGU9c2loZQ%3D%3D#AN=l alu.1433657&db=cat00252a.

Hagan, John, and Juleigh Petty Coleman. 2001. "Returning Captives of the American War of Drugs: Issues of Community and Family Reentry." *Crime & Delinquency* 47 (3): 352–67.

Harris-Perry, M V. 2013. *Sister Citizen: Shame, Stereotypes, and Black Women in America*. New Haven: Yale University Press. https://doi.org/10.1057/fr.2012.31.

Hirschman, Charles, and Stewart E. Tolnay. 2005. "Social Demography." In *Handbook of Population*, edited by Dudley L. Poston and Michael Micklin, 419–449. New York: Kluwer Academic.

Horton, Hayward Derrick, and Lori Latrice Sykes. 2008. "Critical Demography and the Measurment of Racism: A Reproduction of Wealth, Status, and Power." In *White Logic, White Methods: Racism and Methodology*, edited by Tukufu Zuberi and Eduardo Bonilla-Silva, 239–50. Lanham, MD: Rowman & Littlefield.

Hunt, Matthew O, Larry L Hunt, and William W Falk. 2013. "Twenty-First-Century Trends in Black Migration to the U.S. South: Demographic and Subjective Predictors." *Social Science Quarterly* 94 (5): 1398–1413. https://doi.org/10.1111/ssqu.12012.

Johnson, Walter. 2007. "Slavery, Reparations, and the Mythic March of Freedom." *Raritan* 27 (2): 41–67.

Jung, Hyunzee, Solveig Spjeldnes, and Hide Yamatani. 2010. "Recidivism and Survival Time: Racial Disparity among Jail Ex-Inmates." *Social Work Research* 34 (3): 181–89. http://content.ebscohost.com/ContentServer.asp?T=P&P=AN&K=54651225&S==R&D=a9h&EbscoContent=dGJyMNXb4kSep7A4yOvsOLCmr1GeqK9Srqe4SbKW xWXS&ContentCustomer=dGJyMPGuslGvr7VMuePfgeyx44Dt6fIA.

Keena, Linda, and Chris Simmons. 2015. "Rethink, Reform, Reenter: An Entrepreneurial Approach to Prison Programming." *International Journal of Offender Therapy and Comparative Criminology* 59 (8): 837–54. https://doi.org/10.1177/0306624X14523077.

Kozlowska, Hanna. 2017. "One in Three Prisoners Serving a Life Term Anywhere Is in the US." *Quartz*. 2017. https://qz.com/974658/life-prison-sentences-are-far-more-common-in-the-us-than-anywhere-else/.

Lawrence-Webb, Claudia, Melissa Littlefield, and Joshua N Okundaye. 2004. "African American Intergender Relationships: A Theoretical Exploration of Roles." *Journal of Black Studies* 34 (5): 623–639. https://www.jstor.org/stable/3180920.

Louisiana Department of Public Safety and Corrections Louisiana Commission on Law Enforcement. 2019. "Louisiana's Justice Reinvestment Reforms 2019 Annual Performance Report."

Mahon, M. 2015. "Sisters with Voices: A Study of the Experiences and Challenges Faced by Black Women in London Baptist Association Church Ministry Settings." *Black*

Theology: An International Journal 13 (3): 273–96. https://doi.org/10.1179/147699481
5Z.00000000063.
McDonald, Katrina Bell, and Caitlin Cross-Barnet. 2018. *Marriage in Black: The Pursuit of Married Life among American-Born and Immigrant Blacks.* New York: Routledge. https://eds-b-ebscohost-com.libezp.lib.lsu.edu/eds/detail/detail?vid=10&sid=6df2b9d7-fdb4-4ac1-a0e1-f3ee9b10d878%40pdc-v-sessmgr02&bdata=JnNpdGU9Z WRzLWxpdmUmc2NvcGU9c2l0ZQ%3D%3D#AN=lalu.5341221&db=cat00252a.
McFalls, Joseph A. 1991. "Population: A Lively Introduction." *Population Bulletin* 46 (2): 4–16.
Morgan, S Philip, and Scott M Lynch. 2001. "Success and Future of Demography The Role of Data and Methods." *Annals of the New York Academy of Sciences* 954 (1): 35–51.
Moynihan, Daniel. 1965. "The Negro Family: The Case for National Action." Washington, DC: Office of Policy Planning and Research. http://hdl.handle.net/2027/mdp.39015038910553.
Muller, Christopher, and Christopher Wildeman. 2016. "Geographic Variation in the Cumulative Risk of Imprisonment and Parental Imprisonment in the United States." *Demography* 53 (5): 1499–1509. https://doi.org/10.1007/s13524-016-0493-7.
Nam, Charles B. 1979. "The Progress of Demography as a Scientific Discipline." *Demography* 16 (4): 485–492. https://www.jstor.org/stable/2060930?seq=1.
NeMoyer, Amanda, Ye Wang, Kiara Alvarez, Glorisa Canino, Cristiane S. Duarte, Hector Bird, and Margarita Alegría. 2019. "Parental Incarceration During Childhood and Later Delinquent Outcomes Among Puerto Rican Adolescents and Young Adults in Two Contexts." *Law and Human Behavior* 44 (2): 143–156. https://doi.org/10.1037/lhb0000354.
Oris, Michel, Guy Brunet, and Alain Bideau. 2005. "The Social and Cultural Demography of Minorities." *History of the Family* 10 (1): 1–5. https://doi.org/10.1016/j.hisfam.2004.03.001.
Pompoco, Amanda, John Wooldredge, Melissa Lugo, Carrie Sullivan, and Edward J. Latessa. 2017. "Reducing Inmate Misconduct and Prison Returns with Facility Education Programs." *Criminology and Public Policy* 16 (2): 515–47. https://doi.org/10.1111/1745-9133.12290.
Porter, Lauren C., Shawn D. Bushway, Hui Shien Tsao, and Herbert L. Smith. 2016. "How the U.S. Prison Boom Has Changed the Age Distribution of the Prison Population." *Criminology* 54 (1): 30–55. https://doi.org/10.1111/1745-9125.12094.
Powers, Ráchael A, Catherine Kaukinen, and Michelle Jeanis. 2017. "An Examination of Recidivism Among Inmates Released From a Private Reentry Center and Public Institutions in Colorado." *The Prison Journal* 97 (5): 609–27. https://doi.org/10.1177/0032885517728893.
Randall, Sara, and Todd Koppenhaver. 2004. "Qualitative Data in Demography: The Sound of Silence and Other Problems." *Demographic Research* 11 (3): 57–94. https://doi.org/10.4054/DemRes.2004.11.3.

Rhodes, William, Gerald Gaes, Jeremy Luallen, Ryan Kling, Tom Rich, and Michael Shively. 2016. "Following Incarceration, Most Released Offenders Never Return to Prison." *Crime & Delinquency* 62 (8): 1003–25. https://doi.org/10.1177/0011128714549655.

Shand, Rebecca A.S. 1996. "Pre-Release/Transition: Inmate Programs and Support Upon Entry, During Incarceration, and After Release." *Journal of Correctional Education* 47 (1): 20–40.

Stacer, Melissa J., and Melinda R. Roberts. 2018. "'Reversing the Trend': The Role of Mentoring in Offender Reentry." *Journal of Offender Rehabilitation* 57 (1): 1–21. https://doi.org/10.1080/10509674.2017.1416439.

Travis, Jeremy. 2014. "Assessing the State of Mass Incarceration: Tipping Point or the New Normal?" *Criminology and Public Policy* 13 (4): 567–77. https://doi.org/10.1111/1745-9133.12101.

van Dooren, Kate, Stuart A. Kinner, and Simon Forsyth. 2013. "Risk of Death for Young Ex-Prisoners in the Year Following Release from Adult Prison." *Australian and New Zealand Journal of Public Health* 37 (4): 377–82. https://doi.org/10.1111/1753-6405.12087.

White, Michael D, Jessica Saunders, Christopher Fisher, and Jeff Mellow. 2012. "Exploring Inmate Reentry in a Local Jail Setting: Implications for Outreach, Service Use, and Recidivism." *Crime & Delinquency* 58 (1): 124–46. https://doi.org/10.1177/0011128 708327033.

White, Michael J, and David P. Lindstrom. 2005. "Internal Migration." In *Handbook of Population*, edited by Michael Micklin, 918. New York, NY: Springer.

Yosso, Tara J. 2005. "Whose Culture Has Capital? A Critical Race Theory Discussion of Community Cultural Wealth." *Race Ethnicity and Education* 8 (1): 69–91. https://doi.org/10.1080/1361332052000341006.

Zuberi, Tukufu, Amson Sibanda, Ayaga Bawah, and Amadou Noumbissi. 2003. "Population and African Society." *Annual Review of Sociology* 29 (1): 465–86. https://doi.org/10.1146/annurev.soc.29.010202.100126.

CHAPTER 2

Child Support Enforcement as Social Control: Black Fathers and Multi-partner Fertility

Maretta McDonald

The family—a social institution, a social bond, a system of support—fills many material and social needs. When it functions properly, everyone within the family thrives. When it does not, everyone involved suffers. The nuclear family is the model by which all other family structures are compared. Ignoring potential interpersonal conflicts between its members, society idealizes the nuclear family as the foundation for a successful life. In contrast, families that exist outside of the nuclear family structure are viewed as pathways that end at a myriad of negative outcomes for children. One of these forms is the single-parent female-headed household; another is multiple partner fertility. Multiple partner fertility (MPF) is defined as a mother or father having children with more than one partner. There is an abundance of research about the outcomes of single parenthood. Although research on MPF exists, it is much less abundant. Due to lack of nationally representative data, gaps exist in the knowledge of MPF and how it shapes the outcomes of those involved.

American society also understands the normative nuclear family as white and middle class. Black families in the United States have historically been composed in diverse patterns. These diverse family forms include nuclear families, single parent female-headed households, as well as, MPF (Collins 2009; Davis 2011; W. Du Bois 2001; Frazier 1966 [1939]). Scholars of race cite the influence of social and economic constraints of racism as a factor in the variation of Black family structure. Even though evidence supports these structural explanations of variation, family researchers and demographers are hesitant to consider racism as a possible mediator influencing the relationship between family and various outcomes.

Conventional demography analyses lack a framework that illuminates how systemic racism shapes trends in family formation or outcomes of Black family members. Family scholars and demographers, methodologically, approach research from a Eurocentric frame that privileges the benefits of nuclear family forms (Geronimus 2003). The utility or function of diverse routes to family formation is not approached. Simultaneously, the influence of societal sanctions for nonconformity in this realm is not often addressed. Lastly, predicting family outcomes without a critical analysis of the influence of racism underestimates the ways discriminatory access to resources and/or increased surveillance and social control in Black communities influence the outcomes of Black families. Using the white heterosexual middle class Christian household as the ideal, the findings of studies within the discipline of demography that pathologize alternate family structures are then used to justify the development and enforcement of social policy, like the Child Support Enforcement System, that punishes difference and reproduces inequality.

The Child Support Enforcement (CSE) program, as a social policy, was created to disrupt the pathway from single headed household status to raising a child in poverty. CSE collects money from nonresident parents (mostly fathers) and uses it to reimburse the state for providing assistance to resident parents (mostly mothers). However, I argue that CSE also acts as a form of social control to sanction alternate family structures. Additionally, race plays a major role in the way this institution operates. Black fathers -both historically and contemporarily- are structurally constrained from fulfilling the normative father role, as the breadwinner, which makes them more vulnerable to negative outcomes of their involvement with CSE as an organization. Many studies that examine CSE outcomes find that Black fathers are over represented on the case lists and in courtrooms (Brito, Pate Jr, and Wong 2015; Pate 2016). However, little has been theorized about why this phenomenon exists. The variation in CSE outcomes across race is an important social phenomenon that demographers and family scholars should examine as these disparities can exacerbate existing racial inequality.

In this chapter, I argue that racism is an important factor in explaining variation in family structure and outcomes of Black families as a unit and their individual members. I examine how the laws and policies that govern CSE system are used to punish Black fathers who do not conform to conventional norms of fertility and family structure. Using Fragile Families and Child Wellbeing study data, I explore how multi-partner fertility is associated with the harshness of the penalties doled out to nonresident Black fathers who are delinquent in their child support payments. I focus on this relationship because Black fathers' multi-partner fertility as a family formation practice is linked to stereotypical troupes of the absent Black father and the Hypersexual Violent Black Man (Collins 2009). Demography and research on families argues that MPF is a predictor of negative social and economic outcomes (Furstenberg and King 1999; Guzzo and Furstenberg 2007; Harknett and Knab 2007; Monte 2011a, 2011b). Taken together, stereotypes of the Black father and discourse on MPF help form the expectation that Black fathers' multi-partner fertility status makes them most vulnerable to carceral punishments for nonpayment of child support.

I also make the case for Africana Demography as a framework to expand knowledge on how racism embedded in social programs can shape life chances. The lack of methods within conventional demography that integrate the influence of racism into the study of trends and the life course begs for a new framework designed for these types of analyses. The tenets of Africana Demography speak to an analysis of Black nonresident fathers, a forgotten and racialized group. Africana Demography tasks researchers, primarily Black scholars, with conducting research that centers Black people. It is interdisciplinary and emphasizes drawing from "the cultural databank of Black Americans" to develop methodology and conduct analyses (Martin, forthcoming). Lastly, Africana Demography advocates for research dedicated to improving the lived experiences of the Black people by requiring the studies to have social policy implications and the findings to be disseminated outside of academia (Martin, forthcoming). Africana Demography allows for a deeper analysis of these relationships by understanding variation within Black fathers as a group to uncover latent consequences of policy decisions.

1 Conventional Demography: Study of Families

Conventional demography framework determines how research questions are framed, methodologies chosen, and the groups under study. When studying variation in family structure, female-headed household with children is the most heavily studied. Most examine this less socially accepted type of family as existing at a deficit. Female headed household status is cited by demographers and family scholars as the major predictor of child poverty, various children's cognitive and behavior issues, and low educational attainment (McLanahan 2009). Likewise, when examining single parent households, demographers and family scholars center their research on the outcomes of women and children. Studies about fertility look at mothers as their group of interest; whereas, studies on the life course place an emphasis on the outcomes of children. Most recently, researchers began to examine couples' childbearing and the influence of their family structure. However, far fewer researchers examine mens' fertility, as well as, fathers' life course trajectory. When fathers are the center of an analysis, the discourse revolves around the impact of absent fathers on family outcomes and mothers' and children's lives. Studies of nonresident fathers, the counterpart of the female household head mother or resident mother is increasingly important as this group increases with the increase of family dissolution and nonmarital births. Of particular interest should be research concerning men's fertility and the impact of their status as fathers on their lived experiences and outcomes.

Most conventional research on the family, using a multitude of methods and data, suggests that living and growing up in a single parent households make mothers' and more importantly children vulnerable to a long list of adverse outcomes (Barnhart and Maguire-Jack 2016; Cairney et al. 2003; McLanahan 2009). Interestingly, research finds that single parent household status has a smaller impact on Black families than their white counterparts on a number of indicators. Little is understood about why the relationship is different across race. Recently, researchers began to examine this relationship outside of the deficient model analysis. Research by Cross (2019) sought to explain between-group differences in the influence of single parent household status on educational outcomes. She found evidence that the negative effects of single parent household status are "less impactful for racial/ethnic groups already facing many socioeconomic advantages" (1). Her research suggests that public policies that funnel tax dollars into programs focused on promoting the nuclear family structure and penalizing non-conventional pathways to parenthood among the Black people, should be replaced with programs dedicated to addressing racialized economic inequality, a phenomenon connected with racism in America.

Demographers have recently turned their attention to examining MPF. Because of data and methodological constraints, little is understood about its prevalence, the characteristics of this segment of the population, or how this fertility behavior shapes outcomes. Of late, Monte (2019) used United States Census data to estimate the prevalence of multi-partner fertility and the characteristics of those who experience it. Because of the lack of consistency of estimates of multi-partner fertility in previous research, Monte used data from the Survey of Income and Program Participation (SIPP), a nationally representative data source to provide baseline parameters. The author found that about 10 % of all adults and roughly 15% of all parents experience multi-partner fertility. Additionally, multi-partner fertility is found in about 20% of parents with more than one biological child. Women are more likely than men to experience MPF. Lastly, parents who experience multi-partner fertility, compared to single partner fertility families, are more likely to be Black/Brown people and less likely to have bachelor's degree or higher.

Other family scholars and demographers estimate that the makeup of the multi-partner fertility subpopulation are primary poor families (Monte 2011a), unmarried parents (Cancian, Meyer, and Cook 2011), unmarried mothers who were young at first birth (Guzzo and Furstenberg 2007), and living in an urban setting (Carlson and Furstenberg 2006). Similar to the nation's relationship with single parent household, the increased prevalence of MPF does not mean it is unconditionally culturally accepted. Formal and informal social control are used to sanction and punish this behavior. The demonization of single parent households led to the more punitive and restrictive policies of welfare reform (Brito 2000). One very prominent public policy that emerged from welfare reform is Child Support Enforcement.

2   Child Support Enforcement: Anti-poverty or Anti-black

The Child Support Enforcement system (CSE) is a state institution that impacts the lived experiences and life trajectories of increasing numbers of children, custodial parents (primarily resident mothers), and noncustodial parents (primarily nonresident fathers). The federal government promotes CSE as a poverty reduction social program created to increase the economic resources available to parents in single parent households (OSCE 2019). As divorce, cohabitation, and procreation outside of marriage increased the number of single parent households, the population impacted by and the influence of CSE also increases. 2018 performance estimates from the United States Office of Child Support Enforcement (OSCE) report that over $32 million was collected. The reports also estimate that, on average, there were nearly 15 million children involved in child support cases nationwide during the 2018 fiscal year (OCSE 2019). This is equivalent to one in five American children. In comparison, roughly two million children were in families that received Temporary Assistance to Needy Families (TANF)—commonly known as welfare—during the same period (OCSE 2019).

CSE operates as a federally legislated locally administered program. The mission of child support enforcement at its inception was to decrease child poverty and welfare dependence by ordering nonresident parents to pay a set monthly amount to the resident parent. However, research is mixed on whether child support has or can accomplish this. For example, Bartfeld (2000) focused on the economic well-being of families with child support ordered found, using SIPP data, that families in which child support was received reduced the poverty levels of these families by six to seven percent. Meyer and Hu used the 1995 Current Population Survey (CPS) data to compare the effectiveness of child support as income to social insurance and welfare benefits. Their study showed that between six and seven percent of poor women who started receiving child support where brought out of poverty by the receipt of child support only (Meyer and Hu 1999). A Wisconsin study conducted by Park, Cancian, and Meyer (2005) looked at the effects of child support and poverty. They found that child support income received into families closes the fissure between income levels and the poverty line; especially in poor families where child support helped close this gap by forty-four percent.

In contrast, other scholars find that child poverty is not affected by child support. Using Wisconsin administrative data, Cancian and Meyers (2006) posit that mothers who are poor are more likely to have children with fathers who are also poor which limits child support's potential to elevate a family out of poverty. Sorenson and Oliver (2002) used 1999 National Survey of America's Families to assess the constraints poor fathers encounter to paying their child support. They found that thirty-three percent of these fathers are poor, 2 out of 5 have less than a high school education and their median annual income level in 1999 was $5000. With these types of situations, child support is not seen as the cure for single parent household poverty

Despite lack of clear evidence that points to child support being an effective strategy to combat child poverty, CSE laws and policies have become increasingly punitive. Critical legal scholars Tonya Brito and Ann Cammett both point to racialization of poverty and negative stereotypes about Black families as the impetus of more restrictive child support laws. Brito (2000) argues that US individualism and ideology about work ethic has been used to justify changes to welfare laws and the "welfarization" of family law. Assumptions about poverty, the deserving and undeserving poor, and morality are written into welfare reform which includes enhanced surveillance and the increasingly punitive nature of child support enforcement. Brito (2010) also asserts that the demographic shift of welfare recipients from primarily white women to nearly half Black women was the impetus for the change of ideology about helping poor families, resulting in tough child support laws. These laws "create a revolving prison door for many disadvantaged noncustodial fathers" (634).

Aligning with the arguments of Brito (2000; 2010) Cammett (2014) asserts that deadbeat dads have also been racialized as the counterpart to the Black welfare queen stereotype as a broader narrative about the dysfunctional Black family. Based on the perceptions of Black mothers who received welfare as lazy, the deadbeat dad would be the Black father who abandoned his children and it is he that caused poverty in the Black community. Cammet posits that the child support enforcement narrative became increasing more punitive without separating fathers who cannot pay child support due to poverty from those who refuse to financially support their children. She goes on to argue that support for more punitive child support enforcement policies are driven by this narrative that intertwines the racialized welfare queen troupe with the deadbeat dad metaphor creating an image of a dysfunctional Black family formation that creates its own poverty.

Demographers and family scholars fail to consider the impact of race and racism when analyzing the effectiveness of CSE and the impact of punitive policies. Legal researchers examine the racialize subtext of CSE policies. However, they lack the methodologies to analyze statistical data to provide empirical evidence to support their claims that racial stereotypes influence the way

CSE policies are written and enforced. Additionally, understandings of race and empirical evidence that support the racialized nature of CSE policies adds a different lens to debates in why CSE continues its punitive course when its effectiveness as an anti-poverty strategy is debatable.

3   The Nuclear Family as the Correct Family

Family formation in the United States, and the ideology that institutionalized it, has long been a site of interest for demographers. Privileging the nuclear family as the ideal, family scholars study changes away from this hegemonic—the only socially and morally accepted—family structure. Studies examine the changes in the marriage rates and non-marital births looking for trends and seeking to understand why these changes are occurring. They also look at how non-traditional family forms operate in comparison to the traditional family. Although the nuclear family is promoted by academics and politicians as an anti-poverty strategy, the return for marriage is not the same for a Black low-income couple with children as it is for white middle-class families (Pate 2010). Therefore, the social policy and social research of the family are also sites of inequality.

Commitment to preserving the nuclear family as the ideal type of family structure is illuminated by the way demographers and family scholars situate their research. For example, the era deemed the second demographic transition has been highly researched within conventional demography. Scholars outlines the characteristics of this era that began in the 1950s as sub-replacement fertility, varying living arrangements (cohabitation and single persons), the disconnection between marriage and procreation, the instability of the population (lack of age-specific fertility and mortality), declining native-born population sizes in western nations, and gains in longevity (Lesthaeghe 2010). Demographers and sociologists look at this at the demise of the social institution of the family (Bennett 2001) and marriage (Cherlin 2004).

Multi-partner fertility is also studied as part of the new reality of families as a result of the shifts inherent in SDT by demographers and family scholars. The increase of divorces, cohabitation, remarriages, and procreation outside of the marital context is directly linked to the increase of multi-partner fertility (Bohannan 1970; Andrew J. Cherlin and Furstenberg 1994; Furstenberg 1987; Johnson 1988). Most research on multi-partner fertility emphasizes its ills. Researchers argue that multi-partner fertility leads to less social support to mothers from family and fathers (Harknett and Knab 2007; Manning and Smock 2000) and increased financial hardship for mothers (Cancian, Meyer, and Park 2003; Meyer, Cancian, and Cook 2005; Sinkewicz and Garfinkel 2009).

The way multi-partner fertility is studied is another example of the centralization of the nuclear family in American society.

However, the theoretical debate about family and population change does not take into account race, gender, inequality, or other structural contexts. Most of the explanations used to understand the changing levels and variations characterized as the second demographic transition lean toward a rational choice or higher order needs argument (Lesthaeghe 2010). Some of these arguments include changes in the economic structure, the development of a welfare state, and women's liberation (Sweeney 2002; Willis 1973). This description of, what is often framed as the "second demographic transition" (SDT), does not explain family formation in the Black community nor do they help predict how policies created to address these changes will impact Black families. For example, Black women have always worked outside of the "home" (Collins 2009; Furstenberg 2007). Additionally, Black people lacked the freedom to conform to the hegemonic family structure per legislation and other structural constraints (Collins 2009; DuBois 2001). In fact, some scholars find that fertility practices seen in Black communities—which are demonized—are adaptive as a result of shorter life spans and adverse physiological stress responses experienced within this population due to racial discrimination (Burton 1990; Geronimus 2003).

Conventional demography studies of the family make invisible the influence of systemic racism on the development of Black family structure. As the racial gap of the prominence of various non-traditional family structures close, the narrative about these family forms became more situational. More energy is given to individual failing instead of inherent immoral character. Interestingly, these explanations do not provide insight into the lived experiences of Black families because they lack a discussion of the influence economic, political and social oppression has on the way social institutions operate. The framing of all other family structures outside of the nuclear family archetype as a social problem, automatically points to Black families as deviant. This points to the necessity for Africana Demography as a framework that allows centering of the Black family without judgment, in the historical tradition of analyses conducted by Black scholars.

4   The Black Family: Lessons from Du Bois and Frazier

In light of the structural constraints that shaped the experiences of Black families, Black scholars took up the helm of examining family formation and fertility in the Black community. These studies on the Black family began in the

1800s with W.E.B. DuBois (1994 [1903], 2014). Early Black social scientists goal was to combat narratives of deviant biological explanations for racial inequality. DuBois conducted research in urban and rural areas examining Black families and their progress since Emancipation. DuBois found evidence that racism was a major predictor of social position and the legacy of slavery impacted Black families' ability to improve their lives in urban Philadelphia and in rural Georgia. He argued that the bleak conditions that Black people within cities experienced were the result of lack of training which prevented Black men from working in factories, the threat felt by whites and white immigrants at the large influx of Black migrants from the rural south, and the continued support for slavery during the period. He pointed out that Black rural families lacked access to asset ownership and worked under conditions that mimicked slavery. Because of racially discriminatory laws including lack of voting rights to change them, Black people in the rural south lived lives influenced by lack of education and servitude. DuBois also argued that these material conditions and the residual effects of slavery in the rural south resulted in the breakup of families, delayed marriage for women, and cohabitation—all of which are different from the revered nuclear family structure.

DuBois also found a large number of female-headed households in the Black community. He theorized that there were more economic opportunities for Black women as domestic workers in addition to the discrimination against Black men. He also reasoned that Black families existed on a continuum of laxed morality created during slavery and strict morality cultivated by the Quaker tradition. DuBois posited that those on both sides of the spectrum attributed to the large female-headed households. He points to Black men deserting their families (due to early marriage) and promiscuity as central to the explanations of this form of family formation. DuBois's research centered the lived experiences of Black families instead of using the nuclear family model as a way to demonize differences in family structure he observed in the Black community.

E. Franklin Frazier (1966 [1939]) followed with another Black centered analysis of family. He agreed that historical elements of slavery—like the breaking up of Black families by selling its members—shaped contemporary family formation of Black folks. Frazier argued that female-headed households reflect the primacy of enslaved mothers in slave family structure. Unlike DuBois, he posited that children had stronger attachments to their mothers than their fathers because mothers were more integral to children's survival. Frazier goes on to argue that most enslaved fathers were unable to build an attachment to their wives and children, thereby influencing the absence of Black fathers in the household.

Nearly 40 years after the work of Dubois, Frazier still found that Black people in rural areas lacked education and property ownership. He also found that female-headed households were a prominent family structure, a relic of slavery. Frazier goes on to suggest that this type of family configuration and lack of education is not as detrimental in rural areas as it is in urban settings. He wrote, "family traditions and social distinctions that had meaning and significance in relatively simple and stable southern communities have lost their meaning in the new world of the modern city" (1966 [1939]:485). Advocating for assimilation, Frazier argued that this non-American societal form of family construction is the cause of the increase in juvenile delinquency in cities. Frazier, like DuBois, blamed "immorality, delinquency, desertions, and broken homes" for the lack of development of Black families in America during his era.

Both of these early scholars are cited as the pioneers of an Africana Demography. They used both qualitative and quantitative methods to compare Black families social position against the times' ideas of racial progress while giving attention to the structural constraints and historical legacies of racism in the United States. Though the methodological techniques used to analyze families continue to evolve, it is important to note that from the beginning of Black centered analyses, issues of race and racism are essential to explaining the outcomes of Black families and predicting the impact of social structure on its trajectory.

5 The Moynihan Era and Beyond

By the mid-1900s, more demographers and family researchers studied the Black family. The Moynihan report can be considered one of the most influential studies of the period leading to the transformation of social policy in the United States. Daniel Moynihan's (1965) report on the "Negro Family" was used as justification to leave the Black community on the side lines of the war on poverty. The high number of female-headed households was blamed on Black womens' unwillingness to allow Black men to lead. Black poverty, juvenile delinquency, and the high number of female-headed households were blamed for higher crime rates. Even though Moynihan later wrote that his report was meant to be a starting point to design comprehensive social policy to bolster the economic status of Black men and Black families (Moynihan, Smeeding, and Rainwater 2004), his report was used to justify more punitive actions against members of the Black community (Western and Wildeman 2009). Although he attributed the state of the Black family to years of oppression, his diagnosis of a "tangle of pathology" was taken as an irreversible disease of deviant subculture that could not be cured.

Furstenberg (2009) and Burton and Tucker (2009) both hinge off of the discussion of the consequences of the Moynihan report of the 1960s. The report has been held responsible for a legacy of social policies that penalized Black communities for their lack of morality, particularly Black women bearing children outside of marriage. Furstenberg discusses that a lot of the findings were accurate but the packaging of the issues as social problems inherent to deviant Black culture was irresponsible and damaging to the Black community. He asserts that economic factors are responsible for the plight of Black communities and poor white communities have similar trajectories, like increases in nonmarital childbearing, but they are occurring more slowly and not studied. Burton and Tucker look at how the Moynihan report seems to place the brunt of Black community conditions on the backs of Black women, especially mothers. Burton (1990) argues that uncertainty in the realm of time, like anticipated life expectancy, as well as, time constraints in dealing with the many pressures of everyday life while economically disadvantaged, can be used to explain the differences across race in marriage and romantic relationships. She advocated for contextual understanding of Black women and how their responses to oppression were reflected in their family formations.

Sarkisian and Gerstel (2004) article made a compelling argument that the separation of structural and cultural explanations in research on Black families does not fully explore the ways in which Black families are different from the families that society sees as the norm. They encourage analyses free from moral judgment of the practices. Everything is compared to the Eurocentric ideology of how families should look and behave as though their way is the right way. Also, negative outcomes may not be just due to the construction of the family but due to penalizing alternate families for not embodying the accepted family formation. The authors used quantities data from the NSFH to examine the relationship between family integration—measured by kin support—and racial, structural, and cultural factors. They found that in most forms of kin support (except financial support), there is no difference in men's participation in kin support across race. There were significant differences in women across race. They forward that an intersectional approach is required to study race and family integration to gather empirical evidence and construct theories that incorporate the multiplicative effects of gender, race, and class inequality.

Geronimus (2003) discusses how social policies are used to penalize those who do not conform to social norms. "Social support becomes a vehicle for social control that is offered or withheld to realize beliefs about appropriate ages and circumstances for child bearing in a self-fulfilling way." Geronimus also argues that the "historical relationship (between white and Black people) can be seen in the public racial coding of behaviors that are deemed irresponsible or even threatening by European Americans" (888). She goes on to assert, "The entrenchment of European American and African Americans selects African Americans as the primary target of moral condemnation and also sets up African Americans to pay a particular price in response to racial inequality." Assigning positive traits to whiteness and negative traits to people of color operates to maintain systems of oppression in the United States (Feagin 2013; Winant 2001).

6   Black Men in America: Stereotyped and Gendered

Black men have been the object of social control in many forms in the United States. Hooks (2004) asserts that Black men are stereotyped historically as "animals, brutes, natural-born rapists and murderers" and because of these stereotypes Black men are victimized using these depictions as justification. She also cites the "gendered politics of slavery" as the mechanism that prevented Black men from being able to perform with in the white defined role of manhood. During slavery, they were not allowed to marry or act as the heads of household in an effort to control their masculinity and maintain their subservient status (Staples 1970). After emancipation, Black codes, Jim Crow laws, and lynching were used as mechanisms to control the masculinity, sexuality, and labor of Black men (Alexander 2012; Wells-Barnett 2014). For example, fear of interracial sexual relationships between Black men and white women were the impetus for anti-miscegenation laws and lynching. More contemporarily, the state uses hyper-surveillance and increased policing to control Black masculinity resulting in the disproportionate incarceration of Black men (and Black women) removing them from their families, decreasing their "marriageability," and controlling their reproduction (Alexander 2012; Western and Wildeman 2009).

When kidnapped Africans were brought to this continent, slave owners were not discriminate in the conditions in which they worked or lived viewing them as disposable. When enslaved African men and women died, rich landowners quickly replaced them from a new lot of imported human beings. However, when the international slave trade was abolished, slave owners became invested in maintaining their current enslaved laborers as well as securing future free labor (Davis 2011). This continued demand for slaves facilitated the slave breeding system. Slaveholders forced enslaved Black men to indiscriminately have sex with enslaved Black women in order to increase their stock of slaves via Black reproduction (Davis 2011). Familial and marital relationships were not respected or acknowledged as valid. Through the use of violence toward them or threats of violence toward their loved ones, Black men's sexuality and reproduction was controlled during slavery.

During Jim Crow, white anxiety around miscegenation between Black men and white women was the impetus for many laws and violent acts. Most southern states created anti-miscegenation laws to prevent interracial relationships that included Black men (Alexander 2012). Lynchings of Black boys and black men, like that of Emmett Till, occurred with alarming frequency based on the allegations of white women of improper behavior of Black men and boys (Alexander 2012). These laws and acts of murder and mutilation reflect broader attempts to control Black male heterosexuality and reproduction.

More contemporarily, new color blind racism (Bonilla-Silva 2018) moved social control of Black male sexuality and reproduction to the ideological realm with real world consequences. For example, in the media, Black men are portrayed as absent fathers. Hooks (2004) argues that the absent Black father is a combination of ideology that fathers are not important and the societal constraints of Black men as breadwinners and patriarchs. They are presented as uncaring men who have multiple children among multiple families that they fail to financially and emotionally support. They are blamed for the increases in welfare expenditures as an extension of the welfare queen (Cammett 2014). The real world consequences may be experienced by Black fathers through CSE.

Social control comes in various forms, as mentioned above. Systems of stigma and shaming are integral parts of formal and informal social control. Battle (2019) finds that CSE policy and practice uses shaming as a mechanism to separate good fathers from bad ones—deadbeat dads. Logically, punishment actions follow to address the deviant behavior of deadbeat dads because CSE does not exist only in the ideological realm. Child support enforcement "brings together the welfare and criminal justice systems" (Battle 2019: 23). Historically, the system of informal and formal social control create disparate outcomes for Black men compared to white fathers as illustrated by the overrepresentation of Black men in rates of poverty and incarceration. As a system that merges the two, Black men are also overrepresented on the case logs of CSE. Additionally among Black fathers, those who are deemed further from the societal norms of childbearing and family formation are vulnerable to harsher punishments in an effort to deter or penalize the behaviors deemed more deviant. One of these behaviors is multi-partner fertility.

Within demography, critical demography is presented as a framework that lends itself to examining how racism can be examined at the macro level

(Horton and Sykes 2008). However, the authors advocate for more analyses that examine racism at a more medial level. Examining how transitions into multi-partner fertility status within a state/local level institution answers this call and Africana Demography provides a paradigm with which to frame it. Using an Africana Demography framework, I use literature from criminology, Black cultural studies, and sociology to understand how perceptions of Black men as a group influence the outcomes of their involvement with CSE. This chapter seeks to examine the relationship between stigmatized child-bearing behavior of multi-partner fertility and harshness of punishment for non-payment of child support.

7   Methodology

Building on the historical relationship between race, social control, and hegemony, this chapter examines the relationship between the types of enforcement actions used by Child Support Enforcement (CSE) and Black fathers' multi-partner fertility status. Through the lens of industrialized racism and previous research, I expect that Black fathers receive more punitive sanctions when they have children with more than one woman. The experiences of fathers will be measured by the type of enforcement action taken against fathers for non-payment of child support.

8   Data

The data used in this analysis are drawn from the Fragile Families and Child Wellbeing Study (FFCWS) conducted by Princeton University's Center for Research on Child Wellbeing (CRCW), the Columbia Population Research Center, and The National Center for Children and Families (NCCF) at Columbia University. The purpose of this study was to collect data from families of unwed parents at the time of their child's birth. This was done to assess the impact of this family structure on the well-being of the children. This longitudinal study collected data on approximate 4,700 births of children born to 3,600 unwed mothers and 1,100 married mothers between 1998 and 2000. The researchers used a stratified random sampling method to obtain respondents from 75 hospitals located in 20 U.S. cities with populations of over 200,000. Researchers over sampled from births of unwed mothers at a ratio of three to one. Data collection occurred in stages. The initial interview (referred to as the baseline interview) was conducted soon after the birth of the child. Follow up interviews were conducted at the child's age of one, three, five, and nine. The first follow-up interviews began in 1999 after the child was a year old in the same sequence with each subsequent follow-up interview cycle being conducted using the same method. (For more information about the sample design, see Reichman, et al. 2001). This study analyzed pooled data from the mothers' and fathers' responses in the most recently available data that still conducts a separate father interview, which is the fifth wave of the study that administered the surveys from 2007 to 2010.

9 Operationalized Measures

9.1 CSE Penalties

The type of child support enforcement action taken by CSE against fathers to collect arrears is the outcome variable for this analysis. This variable was derived from the responses to several questions used to describe the child support enforcement actions that have been taken in an effort to collect delinquent support. The responses included wage garnishments, interception of income tax refunds, driver's license suspension, freeze and seize of liquid assets, professional and occupational license suspension, criminal probation, and jail sentence. Both the respondent mothers and respondent fathers for each focal child were asked these questions.

Four CSE penalty action categories were created to capture the different levels of harshness of these sanctions: 1. No enforcement actions; 2. economic penalties, which includes wage garnishment and income tax intercept; 3. coercive penalties, which include driver's, professional, and occupational license suspension, as well as moveable and moveable asset liens; and carceral penalties, which includes placing the father on probation and remanding fathers to jail. The responses to the individual questions were combined into one child support action variable with four categories. The responses from the mother's and the father's survey supplemented missing values. If the father and the mother had different responses, the mother's response was given preference due to address potential social desirability bias of the father as well as previous research that found that mothers are more knowledgeable about their child support cases and child support policies in general than fathers (Pate 2016). Additionally, I included respondents who have may have been skipped in the current wave but were surveyed in previous waves to maximize my sample. In this analysis as reflected in Table 2.1, the most common sanction type is no action at all (88.94%). Followed by economic sanctions (6.05%), suspension-type sanctions (2.84%), and carceral sanctions (2.17%), respectively.

TABLE 2.1 Descriptive statistics of sample

Enforcement type	Mean/Percentage
No enforcement actions taken	88.94
Economic sanctions	6.05
Suspension-type sanctions	2.84
Carceral sanctions	2.17
Multi-parent fertility	72.40
Multiple child support cases	24.95
Employment status	56.99
Father's education	
Less than high school	22.00
High school or equivalent	33.18
Some college or above	46.79
Arrears	$2579.00
Household income	$41731.17
Mother ever received welfare	20.70

SOURCE: FRAGILE FAMILIES AND CHILD WELLBEING STUDY AND THE NATIONAL CENTER FOR CHILDREN AND FAMILIES.

9.2 *Multi-partner Fertility*

Multi-partner fertility is defined as a father having at least one child outside of the focal child under study with a different mother. In this analysis, I measured this two ways. The first measure operationalized as a dichotomous variable of constructed by respondent nonresident Black father's number of biological children not living with him including the focal child and number of biological children living with him not including the focal child. The next multi-parent fertility variable analyzes whether the father also has more than one child support obligation. This is also a dichotomous variable. Seventy-two percent of fathers in the sample experience multi-partner fertility and 25 percent have at least two legal child support obligations (see Table 2.1).

9.3 *CSE-related Factors*

Arrears are defined as the amount of child support that has not been paid on the month it was due. Many assume that the amount of unpaid child support would be a strong predictor of the type of enforcement action is taken against a father who is delinquent in his child support payments; the more

CHILD SUPPORT ENFORCEMENT AS SOCIAL CONTROL   63

child support may be related to the severity of the punishment. To measure child support delinquency, I use the amount of the arrears. The arrears were determined using the responses of the mother and the father on the amount of delinquent child support is owed for the child in the case. The response of the mother is given priority when both parties answer differently for the same reasons as with enforcement actions The arrears amount is a continuous variable that was capped at $50000 to address issues of skewness and converted to $100s. Also reflected in Table 2.1, the mean arrears in this sample is about $2,500.00.

Involvement in the welfare system is the next concept in the model estimate. One of the major precepts of the CSE system is to shift financial responsibility for impoverished children from the state on to parent. If a mother is now receiving or previously received monetary benefits from the TANF program, a least a portion of the child support obligation is now owed to the state as reimbursement for money disbursed to the custodial parent. This would provide an increased incentive to CSE to take enforcement actions against the father. The mother's welfare status is whether the mother has ever received financial assistance through the state's Temporary Assistance to Needy Families (TANF). Whether the mother has ever been involved in the welfare system is measured by combining mothers' responses to two questions; 1) are you currently receiving welfare or TANF and 2) have you ever received welfare or TANF. These responses are recoded into a dichotomous variable that reflects whether the mother has ever received welfare/TANF (1) or not (0). Less than a quarter of the mothers in the analyzed sample ever received TANF benefits for the focal child, shown in Table 2.1.

9.4   Sociodemographic Characteristics

Father's economic characteristics include survey items reporting his employment status, household income, and educational attainment, all of which are used as indicators of his economic status.

Employment status consisted of the pooled response to questions about activities that the father participated in last week: fathers' question—Did you do regular work for pay last week? and, mothers' question—What was the father doing most of last week—working at a regular job, going to school, or something else? The father's response was prioritized when the mother and father gave different responses because it is assumed that he would have more intimate knowledge about his employment status. The measure is a dichotomous variable with (1) coded to represent the father was employed the week before the interview. Also displayed in Table 2.1, nearly two-thirds of fathers were currently employed.

Household income is measured using the father's household income in the last 12 months. Household income is a continuous variable that was capped at $120,000 due to outliers that skewed the data. The mean income in this sample is $41,731 as reflected in Table 2.1.

Fathers' educational attainment measures the highest level of education completed. This is a multinomial variable with three categories: less than high school completion, high school diploma or equivalent, and at least some college. Referring to Table 2.1, 80 percent of the respondent fathers have at least a high school diploma.

10 Analytic Strategy

The outcome variable, different types of enforcement penalties, is nominal with four discrete groups of alternate types of actions. These categories can be ordered based on presumed severity of the enforcement action type, ordered according to harshness from no action taken, to economic, to coercive, and ending with carceral penalties, then estimated with ordered logit regression. However, the exploratory nature of this study makes it important to estimate the differing effects of the independent variables on each outcome of the dependent variable. Therefore, multinomial logistic regression was more appropriate for this analysis. The baseline category in the model is "no action taken" and it is coded 0. The other categories of this variable are coded 1 for economic type actions, 2 for coercive type actions, and 3 for carceral type actions.

Based on the literature, the following hypotheses were developed and tested using the data outlined above.

> H1: Black fathers' experience multi-partner fertility will receive harsher sanctions than fathers who do not.
> H2. This relationship will be robust after considering multi-partner fertility that is known and reacted to by CSE.
> H3: Other socioeconomic and CSE case-relevant factors will not fully explain this relationship.

11 Results

Table 2.2 includes the abbreviated results from the multinomial logit model predicting Black fathers' outcomes on the dependent variable, "type of

TABLE 2.2 Multinomial regression coefficients predicting child support enforcement sanction type of black fathers by multi-parent fertility status

Enforcement type		Model 1	Model 2	Model 3
1 Economic sanctions				
	Multi-partner fertility	0.091(0.231)	-0.013(0.250)	-0.117(0.301)
	Multiple child support cases	—	0.833***(0.044)	0.792*** (0.058)
	Constant	-2.754***(0.091)	-2.939***(0.107)	-3.061*** (0.325)
2 Coercive sanctions				
	Multi-partner fertility	0.460(0.491)	0.425(0.542)	0.247(0.434)
	Multiple child support cases	—	0.319(0.474)	0.331(0.482)
	Constant	-3.795***(0.297)	-3.853***(0.209)	-3.852*** (0.697)
3 Carceral sanctions				
	Multi-partner fertility	1.425***(0.207)	1.239***(0.205)	1.095*(0.439)
	Multiple child support cases	—	1.372***(0.277)	1.404*** (0.282)
	Constant	-4.894***(0.500)	-5.273***(0.405)	-5.227*** (0.585)
	N	1058	1058	1058
	Pseudo R2	0.01	0.03	0.15

Standard errors in parentheses.
+ p <0.10 * p<0.05 ** p<0.01 *** p<0.001
Note: The baseline comparison in each equation is No enforcement action taken.
The controls used in Model 3 not included in the table are: Educational attainment, Employment status, Household income, Arrears amount, Mother's welfare status.
SOURCE: FRAGILE FAMILIES AND CHILD WELLBEING STUDY AND THE NATIONAL CENTER FOR CHILDREN AND FAMILIES.

enforcement action taken." The comparison group for this set of models is "no action taken," however, I also examined all other combinations of outcome pairs against different base categories. The results were the same.

In all three models displayed in Table 2.2, MPF is a significant predictor of receiving a carceral sanctions action type for being delinquent in child support payments. For example, in Model 1, the baseline model that only includes the focal independent variable of MPF as the predictor, the log odds of being jailed or placed on probation is 1.425 (p<.001). In other words, in comparison to no action being taken by CSE, Black fathers' MPF status makes then 3 times more likely to be subjected to carceral sanctions than their fathers who do not. The results of this model also make clear that Black fathers' MPF status is not a significant indicator of whether CSE will use economic or coercive sanctions. The results of Model 1 provide evidence to support hypothesis one: Black fathers' experience multi-partner fertility will receive harsher sanctions than fathers who do not.

Directing attention to Model 2, I modeled the relationship between CSE action type and both MPF status and whether Black fathers have multiple child support orders managed by CSE. After controlling for multiple child support cases, the results show that Black fathers' MPF status is still a significant predictor of carceral types of sanctions (b=1.239 p<0.001); the effect was reduced by about 13 percent between models (1.425 to 1.239). However, in comparison to no action at all, Black fathers' multi-partner fertility significantly increases their odds of going to jail or being placed on probation by almost 250 percent. The results from this model also show that after controlling for MPF status, having multiple child support cases significantly increases the probability CSE instituting economic sanctions to 77 percent (b=0.833, p<.001). Similarly, having multiple CSE managed delinquent child support orders significantly increases the likelihood of carceral sanctions by nearly 300 percent (b=1.372, p<.001). The results of Model 2 provide empirical evidence to support hypothesis two: This relationship will be robust after considering multi-partner fertility that is known and reacted to by CSE.

Lastly, we see that the relationship between CSE sanctions and Black father's multi-partner fertility is still significant after controlling for additional case related and demographic factors: educational attainment, employment status, household income, arrears amount, and mother's welfare status. Multiple child support cases increase the chances of experiencing income diversion strategies and carceral punishments. The effect of multiple child support orders overseen by CSE on the likelihood of economic sanctions being used changed a little over 5 percent between Models 2 and 3 (0.833 to 0.792 respectively). Interestingly, controlling for other predictors in Model 3 increased the odds of experiencing carceral sanction for Black fathers who have multiple child support cases by two percent.

Returning to the focus of this analysis, Model 3 shows that after controlling for case related factors such as arrears amount and welfare status, as well as, demographic factors like level of education, whether the father is employed, and household income, Black fathers' MPF is still a significant predictor of carceral punishments. Even after controlling for all other measures in the model, Black fathers' MPF status increases the odds of going to jail or being placed on probation by nearly 200 percent. The addition of other factors did, however, reduce the effect of MPF between Models 2 and 3 by approximately 13 percent (1.239 to 1.095).

Figure 2.1 shows that after controlling for all other factors Black fathers with multi-partner fertility probability of all other outcomes are not significantly different from their single partner family counterparts. However, a significant difference in reflected in the experiencing of carceral sanctions. Black fathers who do not have multiple families have almost no chance of going to jail even with the same amount of arrears. In contrast, about 1 percent of the Black fathers will go to jail or be placed on probation just based on the non-case related characteristic of having children with more than one mother. The results of Model 3, as displayed in Figure 2.1, provide support for hypothesis three: Other socioeconomic and CSE case-relevant factors will not fully explain this relationship.

12 Discussion and Conclusion

The purpose of this chapter was to engage Africana Demography as a paradigm to illuminate the underpinnings of racism in social policy application. Based on the literature, I hypothesized that Black fathers' MPF is a predictor in the harshness of CSE punishment. I also expected that CSE's management of multiple child support orders per Black father would not fully explain this relationship. Lastly, based on the literature of the social control of Black men's masculinity and racialized social policy, I hypothesized that case related factors like welfare status of the mother and the amount of delinquent child support or fathers' sociodemographic characteristics would not sever the relationship between Black fathers' MPF and the harshness of the CSE sanctions they received. The results of the analysis support all three of these assertions. Additionally by using an African Demography framework, this study examined the experiences of Black fathers in the CSE system without comparing them to white fathers or using a deficit model to uncover how racism impacts how Black people interact with the state.

The analysis found evidence inferring that child support policy is a racialized as punishment for the stereotypical assumption about Black families,

TABLE 2.3 Multinomial regression coefficients predicting child support enforcement sanction type of black fathers by multi-parent fertility status

Enforcement type	Model 1	Model 2	Model 3
Least harsh—Economic sanctions			
Multi-partner fertility	0.091(0.231)	-0.013(0.250)	-0.117(0.301)
Multiple child support cases		0.833***(0.044)	0.792***(0.058)
Employment status			-0.301+(0.165)
Education (less than HS)			
High school or equivalent			0.053(0.209)
Some college or better			0.327***(0.094)
Arrears			0.010***(0.002)
Household income			-0.000(0.000)
Mother ever received welfare			0.282(0.245)
Constant	-2.754***(0.091)	-2.939***(0.107)	-3.061***(0.325)
Moderately harsh—Coercive sanctions			
Multi-partner fertility	0.460(0.491)	0.425(0.542)	0.247(0.434)
Multiple child support cases		0.319(0.474)	0.331(0.482)
Employment status			-0.898**(0.330)
Education (less than HS)			
High school or equivalent			0.236(0.817)
Some college or better			0.109(0.568)
Arrears			0.012***(0.001)
Household income			-0.000(0.000)
Mother ever received welfare			0.300(0.569)
Constant	-3.795***(0.297)	-3.853***(0.209)	-3.852***(0.697)
Most harsh—Carceral sanctions			
Multi-partner fertility	1.425***(0.207)	1.239***(0.205)	1.095*(0.439)
Multiple child support cases		1.372***(0.277)	1.404***(0.282)

TABLE 2.3 Multinomial regression coefficients predicting child support enforcement sanction type of black fathers by multi-parent fertility status (cont.)

Enforcement type	Model 1	Model 2	Model 3
Employment status			-0.283(0.392)
Education (less than HS)			
High school or equivalent			-0.418(0.435)
Some college or better			-0.166(0.335)
Arrears			0.014*** (0.003)
Household income			-0.000(0.000)
Mother ever received welfare			-0.944(1.344)
Constant	-4.894*** (0.500)	-5.273*** (0.405)	-5.227*** (0.585)
N	1058	1058	1058

Standard errors in parentheses.
+ p<0.10 * p<0.05 ** p<0.01 *** p<0.001
SOURCE: FRAGILE FAMILIES AND CHILD WELLBEING STUDY AND THE NATIONAL CENTER FOR CHILDREN AND FAMILIES.

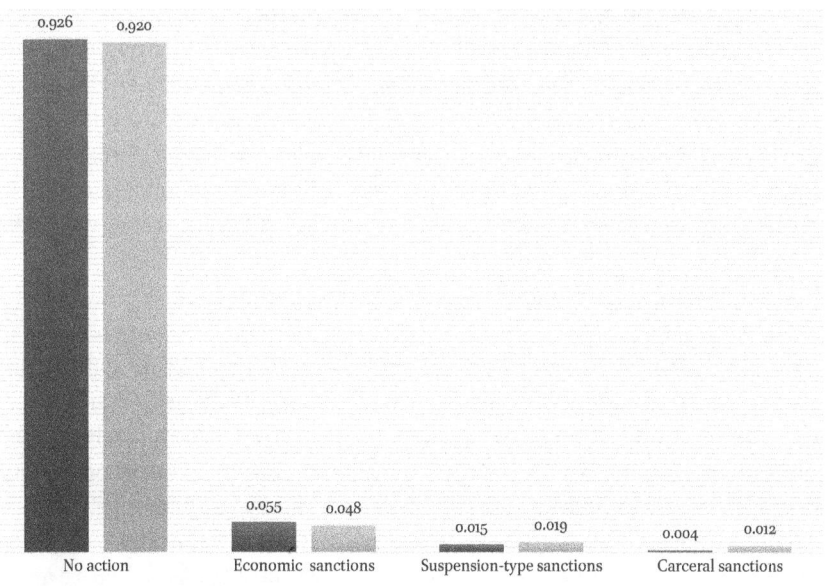

FIGURE 2.1 Predicted probability of child support enforcement type by multi-partner fertility

particularly Black fathers. Black men who have children with more than one woman are more likely to experience differential types of enforcement actions against them than fathers who do not. The stated goal of CSE is to end child poverty; however, the indicators of child poverty like whether a single mother receives welfare did not mediate this relationship. Additionally, the severity of the CSE sanctions for delinquency is associated with nonpayment. However, this analysis shows that the amount of arrears owed did not disestablish the relationship between MPF and the harshness of CSE sanctions. Therefore, the empirical findings of this study support Cammett's (2011) assertion that the creation of child support as an institution was founded on the racialization of Black men as irresponsible and hypersexual individuals that have sex with multiple women, producing children they do not plan to financially support, and plunging Black women into poverty.

13 Limitations and Suggestions for Future Research

One of the limitations of this study is the exclusion of mothers as nonresident parents and payers of child support. Mothers are increasingly becoming the nonresident parent who pays and owes child support. Future research should move away from the father-as-breadwinner assumptions and begin to ask child support collection questions to both women and men to capture data on this growing group of parents impacted by CSE policies. Another limitation is the lack of information on the ordering of CSE sanctions for payment delinquency. For a better understanding of how and when CSE uses carceral solutions to the problem of nonpayment, especially for Black fathers with MPF status, examining if different groups of fathers experience a different progression on the increasing harshness of CSE sanctions can reveal important nuances within the system.

Additionally, more research is needed to analyze where the mechanisms are located that differentiate enforcement actions between different groups of fathers. CSE is a multi-level system internally with many external stakeholders that may have influence on whether CSE takes a specific type of action to collect past due child support. In law enforcement research, scholars found that most differentiation is located in areas where discretion was utilized to make decisions like who to arrest, who to prosecute, and what sentence to render and race impacts these decisions (Cole 2009). There are many areas where discretion is to make enforcement decisions used within CSE. A qualitative analysis is needed to locate the nuanced ways that racial discrimination influences policies and enforcement of these policies.

14 Policy Implications

This study found support for the hypothesized relationship between perceptions about Black families and public policy considerations. Some may attempt to re-interpret this relationship as a byproduct of strained resources and how increasing numbers of children may impact the ability to pay. However, measures to control for class (educational attainment and household income) as well as delinquency in child support payments (arrears) did not moderate this relationship in this analysis. Also, Black fathers with multiple child support cases may be more vulnerable to carceral punishments because they may be seen more often. However, the increased interaction caused by having multiple child support cases did not explain the relationship between Black fathers' MPF and the increased likelihood of going to jail or being placed on probation.

The results show that MPF status, like poverty and living in urban areas, may be yet another pathway to incarceration for Black men. This finding is consistent with Haney (2018) research of the lived experiences of fathers who are entangled in the both the criminal justice and child support enforcement systems. She found the link between child support and incarceration is not only by the arrears that accumulate while fathers are in prison, but incarceration because of child support arrears is another pathway to incarceration for some that would not have otherwise been in jail. Similarly, increased surveillance in the administration of social support programs and increased pressure to eliminate the dependency on welfare create a net-widening of fathers who may not have otherwise entered the CSE system (Brito 2000). Cooperation requirements to receive TANF, Medicaid, and Supplemental Nutrition Assistance Program (SNAP) coerced poor resident parents to provide information needed to pursue nonresident parents for child support. However, resident parents entangled in CSE because of participation in other social welfare programs would rather handle child support informally with the fathers of their children (Waller and Plotnick 2001). This disjuncture between the practices of CSE and the desires of their targeted population calls into question the justification for CSE policies, especially among poor and working class Black families.

It is important to consider that this is an exploratory study and the findings are preliminary. However, there are a number of implications that should be considered. First, this chapter reflects the influence of race on seemingly race-neutral public policy. Perceptions of Black women as welfare queens influenced support for restrictive welfare reform policies (Gilens 1995, 1996). Likewise, stereotypes about Black men's sexuality and fathering practices undergird the increased punitive nature of CSE policies. West suggests that "white fear of black sexuality is a basic ingredient of white racism" (cited in hooks 2004). In this same way, white supremacy uses public policy to control what it fears.

Additionally, the harshness of CSE policies may influence the prevalence of the absent father within the Black community. Collins (2004) argues that the inability of Black men to fulfill the breadwinning role encourages them to leave their families. She suggests that Black fathers' absence is "in the name of saving male pride" (204). Therefore, penalizing Black fathers for their MPF status within the shaming and stigmatizing nature of CSE (Battle 2019) can push fathers further away from their families, indirectly increasing the number of truly absent Black fathers.

Ultimately, this chapter attests to the strength of using an Africana Demography worldview in creating research projects that allow for the analysis of racism's influence of a growing demographic, nonresident Black fathers. Using quantitative methods, I demonstrated how statistical models that operationalize hypothesized relationships between race- and gender-neutral public policies and cultural stereotypes of Black people. This framework can also be used to analyze how perceptions of other racialized groups impact public policy creation and administration.

Africana Demography allows for the centering of Black fathers without the obligatory inclusion of a white comparison group. As a group marginalized by race and gender, it is important to bring these experiences to the forefront of the analysis (Wright and Wallace 2015). By understanding how CSE reproduces racial inequality, policy recommendations that aim for a more equitable system for all parties can be suggested. CSE policymakers should be concerned with the economic and social impact of their decisions on fathers, as well as, mothers and children.

Bibliography

Alexander, Michelle. 2012. *The New Jim Crow: Mass Incarceration in the Age of Colorblindness*. New York: The New Press.

Barnhart, Sheila, and Kathryn Maguire-Jack. 2016. "Single Mothers in their Communities: the Mediating Role of Parenting Stress and Depression between Social Cohesion, Social Control and Child Maltreatment." *Children and Youth Services Review* 70: 37–45.

Bartfeld, Judi. 2000. "Child Support and the Postdivorce Economic Well-Being of Mothers, Fathers, and Children." *Demography* 37 (2): 203–213. https://doi.org/10.2307/2648122. http://www.jstor.org/stable/2648122.

Battle, Brittany Pearl. 2019. "'They Look at You like You're Nothing': Stigma and Shame in the Child Support System." *Symbolic Interaction* 42 (4): 640–668.
Bennett, William J. 2001. *The Broken Hearth: Reversing the Moral Collapse of the American Family.* New York: Doubleday.
Bohannan, Paul, ed. 1970. *Divorce and After.* New York: Anchor Books.
Bonilla-Silva, Eduardo. 2018. *Racism without Racists: Color-blind Racism and the Persistence of Racial Inequality in America.* Lanham, MD: Rowman & Littlefield.
Brito, Tonya L. 2000. "The Welfarization of Family Law." *University of Kansas Law Review* 48: 229–284. https://heinonline.org/HOL/P?h=hein.journals/ukalr48&i=241.
Brito, Tonya L. 2012. "Fathers behind Bars: Rethinking Child Support Policy toward Low-Income Noncustodial Fathers and Their Families." *Journal of Gender, Race & Justice* 15: 617–674. https://heinonline.org/HOL/P?h=hein.journals/jgrj15&i=625.
Brito, Tonya L., David J. Pate Jr, and Jia-Hui Stefanie Wong. 2015. "'I Do for My Kids': Negotiating Race and Racial Inequality in Family Court." *Fordham Law Review* 83 (6): 3027–3052. http://libezp.lib.lsu.edu/login?url=http://search.ebscohost.com/login.aspx?direct=true&db=lft&AN=102415070&site=eds-live&scope=site&profile=eds-main.
Burton, Linda M. 1990. "Teenage Childbearing as an Alternative Life-course Strategy in Multigeneration Black Families." *Human Nature* 1 (2): 123–143. https://doi.org/10.1007/bf02692149. https://doi.org/10.1007/BF02692149.
Burton, Linda M., and M. Belinda Tucker. 2009. "Romantic Unions in an Era of Uncertainty: A Post-Moynihan Perspective on African American Women and Marriage." *The Annals of the American Academy of Political and Social Science* 621 (1): 132–148. https://doi.org/10.1177/0002716208324852. https://journals.sagepub.com/doi/abs/10.1177/0002716208324852.
Cairney, John, Michael Boyle, David R. Offord, and Yvonne Racine. 2003. "Stress, Social Support and Depression in Single and Married Mothers." *Social Psychiatry & Psychiatric Epidemiology* 38 (8): 442. http://libezp.lib.lsu.edu/login?url=http://search.ebscohost.com/login.aspx?direct=true&db=pbh&AN=10759427&site=eds-live&scope=site&profile=eds-main.
Cammett, Ann. 2011. "Deadbeats, Deadbrokes, and Prisoners." *Geo. J. on Poverty L. & Pol'y* 18: 127.
Cammett, Ann. 2014. "Deadbeat Dads & Welfare Queens: How Metaphor Shapes Poverty Law." *Boston College Journal of Law and Social Justice* 34: 233–266.
Cancian, Maria, Daniel Meyer, and Hwa-Ok Park. 2003. *The Importance of Child Support for Low-Income Families.* Institute for Research on Poverty University of Wisconsin (Madison).
Cancian, Maria, and Daniel R Meyer. 2006. "Child Support and the Economy." In *Working and Poor: How Economic and Policy Changes are Affecting Low-wage Workers,*

edited by Rebecca M. Blank, Sheldon Danziger and Robert F. Schoeni, 338–65. New York: Russell Sage Foundation.

Cancian, Maria, Daniel R. Meyer, and Steven T. Cook. 2011. "The Evolution of Family Complexity from the Perspective of Nonmarital Children." *Demography* 48 (3): 957–982. www.jstor.org/stable/41237819.

Carlson, Marcia J., and Frank F. Furstenberg. 2006. "The Prevalence and Correlates of Multipartnered Fertility Among Urban U.S. Parents." *Journal of Marriage and Family* 68 (3): 718–732. https://doi.org/10.1111/j.1741-3737.2006.00285.x.

Cherlin, Andrew J. 2004. "The Deinstitutionalization of American Marriage." *Journal of Marriage and Family* 66 (4): 848–861. https://doi.org/doi:10.1111/j.0022-2445.2004.00058.x. https://onlinelibrary.wiley.com/doi/abs/10.1111/j.0022-2445.2004.00058.x.

Cherlin, Andrew. 2014. *Labor's Love Lost: The Rise and Fall of the Working-Class Family in America*. New York: Russell Sage Foundation.

Cherlin, Andrew J., and Frank F. Furstenberg. 1994. "Stepfamilies in the United States: A Reconsideration." *Annual Review of Sociology* 20 (1): 359–381. https://doi.org/10.1146/annurev.so.20.080194.002043. https://www.annualreviews.org/doi/abs/10.1146/annurev.so.20.080194.002043.

Collins, Patricia Hill. 2004. *Black Sexual Politics: African Americans, Gender, and the New Racism*. New York: Routledge.

Collins, Patricia Hill. 2009. *Black Feminist Thought: Knowledge, Consciousness, and the Politics of Empowerment*. 2nd Edition ed. New York: Routledge.

Cross, Christina J. 2019. "Racial/Ethnic Differences in the Association Between Family Structure and Children's Education." *Journal of Marriage and Family* n/a (n/a). https://doi.org/10.1111/jomf.12625. https://onlinelibrary.wiley.com/doi/abs/10.1111/jomf.12625.

Davis, Angela Y. 2011. *Women, Race, & Class*. New York: Vintage Books.

Du Bois, W.E.B. 1994 [1903]. *The Souls of Black Folk. Dover Thrift Editions*. New York: Dover.

Du Bois, W.E.B.. 2014. *The Philadelphia Negro: a Social Study*. New York: Oxford University Press.

Du Bois, W.E.B. 2001 [1935]. *Black Reconstruction in America, 1860–1880*. New York: The Free Press.

Feagin, Joe R. 2013. *The White Racial Frame: Centuries of Racial Framing and Counter-framing*. New York: Routledge.

Frazier, E. Franklin. 1966 [1939]. *The Negro Family in the United States*. Chicago: Phoenix Books.

Furstenberg, Frank F. 1987. "The New Extended Family: The Experience of Parents and Children after Remarriage." In *Remarriage and Stepparenting: Current Research and Theory*, 42–61. New York: Guilford Press.

Furstenberg, Frank F. 2009. "If Moynihan Had Only Known: Race, Class, and Family Change in the Late Twentieth Century." *The Annals of the American Academy of*

Political and Social Science 621 (1): 94–110. https://doi.org/10.1177/0002716208324866. https://journals.sagepub.com/doi/abs/10.1177/0002716208324866.

Furstenberg, Frank F. 2007. "The Making of the Black Family: Race and Class in Qualitative Studies in the Twentieth Century." *Annual Review of Sociology* 33 (1): 429–448. https://doi.org/10.1146/annurev.soc.33.040406.131727. https://www.annualreviews.org/doi/abs/10.1146/annurev.soc.33.040406.131727.

Furstenberg, Frank F, and Rosalind Berkowitz King. 1999. "Multi-partnered Fertility Sequences: Documenting an Alternative Family Form." Annual Meeting of the Population Association of America, Chicago, IL.

Geronimus, Arline T. 2003. "Damned if You Do: Culture, Identity, Privilege, and Teenage Childbearing in the United States." *Social Science & Medicine* 57 (5): 881–893. https://doi.org/https://doi.org/10.1016/S0277-9536(02)00456-2. http://www.sciencedirect.com/science/article/pii/S0277953602004562.

Gilens, Martin. 1995. "Racial Attitudes and Opposition to Welfare." *The Journal of Politics* 57 (4): 994–1014. https://doi.org/10.2307/2960399. http://www.jstor.org.libezp.lib.lsu.edu/stable/2960399.

Gilens, Martin. 1996. "'Race Coding' and White Opposition to Welfare." *American Political Science Review* 90 (3): 593–604.

Grall, Timothy. 2006. *Custodial Mothers and Fathers and their Child Support: 2003.* Current Population Reports. Washington, DC: US Government Printing Office.

Guzzo, Karen Benjamin, and Frank F. Furstenberg. 2007. "Multipartnered Fertility among Young Women with a Nonmarital First Birth: Prevalence and Risk Factors." *Perspectives on Sexual and Reproductive Health* 39 (1): 29–38. https://doi.org/10.1363/3902907. https://onlinelibrary.wiley.com/doi/abs/10.1363/3902907.

Harknett, Kristen, and Jean Knab. 2007. "More Kin, Less Support: Multipartnered Fertility and Perceived Support Among Mothers." *Journal of Marriage and Family* 69 (1): 237–253. https://doi.org/10.1111/j.1741-3737.2006.00356.x.

Hooks, Bell. 2004. *We Real Cool: Black Men and Masculinity*. New York: Routledge.

Horton, Hayward D, and Lori L Sykes. 2008. "Critical Demography and the Measurement of Racism." In *White Logic, White Methods: Racism and Methodology* edited by Tukufu Zuberi and Eduardo Bonilla-Silva, 239–50. Lanham, MD: Rowman & Littlefield.

Huang, Chien-Chung, Richard L. Edwards, and Robert B. Nolan. 2008. "State Performance on Child Support Enforcement under CSPIA." *Journal of Policy Practice* 7 (4): 280–297. https://doi.org/10.1080/15588740802258516. https://doi.org/10.1080/15588740802258516.

Johnson, Colleen Leahy. 1988. *Ex Familia: Grandparents, Parents, and Children Adjust to Divorce*. Piscataway, NJ: Rutgers University Press.

Lesthaeghe, Ron. 2010. "The Unfolding Story of the Second Demographic Transition." *Population and Development Review* 36 (2): 211–251. https://doi.org/10.1111/j.1728-4457.2010.00328.x. https://doi.org/10.1111/j.1728-4457.2010.00328.x.

Manning, Wendy D., and Pamela J. Smock. 2000. "'Swapping' Families: Serial Parenting and Economic Support for Children." *Journal of Marriage and the Family* 62 (1): 111–122. https://doi.org/10.1111/j.1741-3737.2000.00111.x.

Martin, Lori Latrice. Forthcoming. "African Demography: Lessons from Founders E. Franklin Frazier, W.E.B. Du Bois and the Atlanta School of Sociology." *Issues in Race and Society*.

McLanahan, Sara. 2009. "Fragile Families and the Reproduction of Poverty." *The Annals of the American Academy of Political and Social Science* 621 (1): 111–131. https://doi.org/10.1177/0002716208324862. https://journals.sagepub.com/doi/abs/10.1177/0002716208324862.

Meyer, Daniel R, Maria Cancian, and Steven T Cook. 2005. "Multiple-partner Fertility: Incidence and Implications for Child Support Policy." *Social Service Review* 79 (4): 577–601.

Meyer, Daniel R., and Mei-Chen Hu. 1999. "A Note on the Antipoverty Effectiveness of Child Support among Mother-Only Families." *The Journal of Human Resources* 34 (1): 225–234. https://doi.org/10.2307/146309. www.jstor.org/stable/146309.

Monte, Lindsay M. 2011a. "The Chicken and the Egg of Economic Disadvantage and Multiple Partner Fertility: Which Comes First in a Sample of Low-Income Women." *Western Journal of Black Studies* 35 (1): 53–66. http://libezp.lib.lsu.edu/login?url=https://search.ebscohost.com/login.aspx?direct=true&db=a9h&AN=59733264&site=eds-live&scope=site&profile=eds-main.

Monte, Lindsay. 2011b. "Multiple Partner Maternity Versus Multiple Partner Paternity: What Matters for Family Trajectories." *Marriage & Family Review* 47 (2): 90–124. https://doi.org/10.1080/01494929.2011.564526. https://doi.org/10.1080/01494929.2011.564526.

Monte, Lindsay. 2019. "Multiple-Partner Fertility in the United States: A Demographic Portrait." *Demography* 56 (1): 103–127. https://doi.org/10.1007/s13524-018-0743-y. https://doi.org/10.1007/s13524-018-0743-y.

Moynihan, Daniel P. 1965. *The Negro Family: The Case for National Action*, Edited by Office of Palnning and Research. Washington, D.C.

Moynihan, Daniel Patrick, Timothy Smeeding, and Lee Rainwater. 2004. *The Future of the Family*. New York: Russell Sage Foundation.

Nepomnyaschy, Lenna, Katherine A. Magnuson, and Lawrence M. Berger. 2012. "Child Support and Young Children's Development." *Social Service Review* 86 (1): 3–35. https://doi.org/10.1086/665668. https://www.journals.uchicago.edu/doi/abs/10.1086/665668.

Office of Child Support Enforcement. 2019. 2018 Child Support: More Money for Families, edited by Administration of Children and Families. Washington, DC: U.S. Government Publishing Office.

Park, Hwa-Ok, Maria Cancian, and Daniel R Meyer. 2005. *The Role of Child Support in the Economic Well-being of Custodial Mothers.* Madison, WI: Institute for Research on Poverty.

Pate, David J. 2010. "Fatherhood Responsibility and the Marriage-Promotion Policy: Going to the Chapel and We're Going to Get Married?" In *The Myth of the Missing Black Father*, edited by Roberta Coles and Charles Green, 351–365. New York: Columbia University Press.

Pate, David J. 2016. "The Color of Debt: An Examination of Social Networks, Sanctions, and Child Support Enforcement Policy." *Race and Social Problems* 8 (1): 116–135.

Reichman, Nancy E, Julien O Teitler, Irwin Garfinkel, and Sara S McLanahan. 2001. "Fragile Families: Sample and Design." *Children and Youth Services Review* 23 (4–5): 303–326.

Sarkisian, Natalia, and Naomi Gerstel. 2004. "Kin Support among Blacks and Whites: Race and Family Organization." *American Sociological Review* 69 (6): 812–837. https://doi.org/10.1177/000312240406900604. https://journals.sagepub.com/doi/abs/10.1177/000312240406900604.

Sinkewicz, Marilyn, and Irwin Garfinkel. 2009. "Unwed Fathers' Ability to Pay Child Support: New Estimates Accounting for Multiple-partner Fertility." *Demography* 46 (2): 247–263. https://doi.org/10.1353/dem.0.0051. https://doi.org/10.1353/dem.0.0051.

Sorensen, Elaine, and Helen Oliver. 2002. *Policy Reforms are Needed to Increase Child Support from Poor Fathers.* Washington, DC: Urban Institute.

Staples, Robert. 1970. "The Myth of the Black Matriarchy." *The Black Scholar* 1 (3–4): 8–16. https://doi.org/10.1080/00064246.1970.11430667. https://doi.org/10.1080/00064246.1970.11430667.

Sweeney, Megan M. 2002. "Two Decades of Family Change: The Shifting Economic Foundations of Marriage." *American Sociological Review* 67 (1): 132–147.

Waller, Maureen R., and Robert Plotnick. 2001. "Effective Child Support Policy for Low-income Families: Evidence from Street Level Research." *Journal of Policy Analysis and Management* 20 (1): 89–110. https://doi.org/10.1002/1520-6688(200124)20:1<89::AID-PAM1005>3.0.CO;2-H. http://dx.doi.org/10.1002/1520-6688(200124)20:1<89::AID-PAM1005>3.0.CO;2-H.

Wells-Barnett, Ida B. 2014. *On Lynchings.* Mineola, New York: Dover Publications.

Western, Bruce, and Christopher Wildeman. 2009. "The Black Family and Mass Incarceration." *The Annals of the American Academy of Political and Social Science* 621 (1): 221–242. https://doi.org/10.1177/0002716208324850. https://journals.sagepub.com/doi/abs/10.1177/0002716208324850.

Willis, Robert J. 1973. "A New Approach to the Economic Theory of Fertility Behavior." *Journal of Political Economy* 81 (2, Part 2): S14–S64. https://doi.org/10.1086/260152. https://www.journals.uchicago.edu/doi/abs/10.1086/260152.

Winant, Howard. 2001. "White Racial Projects." In *The Making and Unmaking of Whiteness*, edited by Birgit Brander Rasmussen, Eric Klinenberg, Irene J. Nexica and Matt Wray, 97–112. Durham: Duke University Press.

Wright, Earl, and Edward V Wallace. 2015. "Black Sociology: Continuing the Agenda." In *The Ashgate Research Companion to Black Sociology*, edited by Earl Wright II and Edward V Wallace, 3–14. New York: Routledge.

PART 2

Africana Demography and Policing

∴

CHAPTER 3

Us versus Them: "We Are More Fearful of the Police than the Actual Criminals"

Melinda Jackson-Jefferson

1   Introduction

"We are more fearful of the police than the so-called actual criminals," this is a repetitive account made by Black inner-city residents who are devastated by the deaths and injuries of many unarmed Black and Brown bodies at the hands of local police officers. Police brutality has been a serious social problem among the African-American experience dating back to the early 1900s. Outrageously, people of color continue to be overrepresented as victims of racial profiling, stop and frisk and excessive use of force. For decades, research has consistently shown that Black communities have disproportionately experienced mistreatment, abuse and racial bias (Fagan and Davies 2000; Kane 2002; Terrill and Reisig 2003; Ingram 2007) at the hands of powerful social forces, particularly in criminal justice realm. Consequently, an enormous number of Black residents are more fearful of criminal victimization by a police officer than any other racial group.

The crises facing today's criminal justice system are closely intertwined in Black communities. In American society, it is the Black population that is strongly portrayed as violent criminals (Alderman 1994; Pain 2001; Welch 2007), not only is this true in the south but in the United States in general. Blacks, who make up 12% of the general population in the United States, are accounted for more than half of all arrests for violent crimes, and almost half of all inmates in state and federal correctional facilities. Without even trying to investigate the causes behind such data (Meier 1994; Hacker 1995), it is fair to assume that the Black communities provide some of the best evidence that we are not living in a post-racial society. It is the Black community in which crime is high, poor social services and dilapidated housing exists, as well as an area frequently viewed as dangerous and unsafe to the general public (Woldoff 2006). Subsequently, it is only right to examine fear of crime within the environments it is likely to occur. The key findings indicate that the overwhelming majority of residents do not report feeling afraid of the so-called criminals within their community; conversely, they are more fearful of the police officers themselves. This experience is at the core of #BlackLivesMatter, an international activist movement that has pushed the media and politicians to consider the issue of police brutality as a matter of racial injustice and systemic racism towards Black people. The movement was not created as a belief that Black lives are more important than others but that lives of Blacks have been historically mistreated and endangered and as a result, Black lives matter too.

The police use of force is used as a tool to reinforce systems of racial inequity. Given the disturbing history of racism in the United States, this was never a farfetched notion. The variations of police brutality across time and space are intense and thus, upsetting. To tackle the pressing issues supported by unjust policies and practices that criminalize and dehumanize African Americans, residents' marginalized voices are placed at the center of this chapter. By creating this space, residents can tell their own stories and share their experiences as Black inner-city residents.

Baton Rouge represents some of the poorest, uneducated, high violent, segregated areas in Louisiana. Baton Rouge, therefore, serves as an important area to study fear and give voice to the voiceless. The city itself is a representation of racial inequality and is symbolic of the unequal opportunities made available to Black residents and the challenges associated with racial disparities among social institutions. Similar to the U.S. in general, the high-crime areas represent the continuing racial divide, particularly concerning the criminal justice system.

This chapter raises many inquiries and issues that some scholars may not be willing to acknowledge or tackle. However, we will never make improvements unless these issues and problems are at the forefront and tackled with the truth-the "New Normal." The new normal is the same practices that were allegedly left behind that are reconfigured in ways that are often hidden, unspoken and distorted. The new normal is the same "New Jim Crow," that Michelle Alexander discusses. It is a "system" that focuses on locking up Black and Brown bodies not only behind actual bars in actual prisons but also behind walls that are infrequently unrecognizable (Alexander 2012). The system serves as an overarching racial caste system that validates discrimination. The "New Normal" is a reality that must be confronted by doing more with less. These include, for example, understanding the interest of the dominant group, teaching and educating our children of color how to live and survive within a system that is designed to benefit the affluent and powerful groups of society and ways we can move forward as a community of color.

This chapter reflects Africana Demography in that it brings light to the disparities that exist between Black and white people in the United States by putting Black Americans at the forefront and addressing racism. This chapter is important given that the data speaks for itself by giving voice to the disadvantaged and thus, uses theory to provide a deeper understanding of the relationships between race, fear, crime and policing. An important purpose of this chapter is to effectuate positive social changes, which is critical for Africana Demography.

2   What Is Fear?

There are several definitions for fear of crime that occurs in the literature; however, a clear-cut definition is an unending dispute (Reid and Konrad 2004). There are, however, categories of fear of crime that many scholars would agree on. Generally speaking, fear of crime is associated with a wide range of emotions, anxieties, concerns, opinions, and attitudes (Ditton and Farall 2000; Mawby, Brunt and Hambly 2000; Warr 2000). Therefore, fear is possibly best described as a multidimensional practice that represents individuals' feelings, behaviors and thought processes about being physically harmed by criminal victimization (Roundtree 1998). This definition is related to the concern about being outside one's home, most likely in an urban area, unaccompanied and possibly susceptible to personal harm (Stanko 1995). In this chapter, fear is referred to as a multifaceted concept of crime where fear becomes an everyday practice based on three interlinked categories of experience: emotional (such as worrying or anxiety), behavioral (such as avoiding certain areas and purchasing equipment for protection) and cognitive (such as thinking one is at risk and vulnerable to crime) (Roundtree 1998; Gabriel and Greve 2003). All of these features are related to a person's fear of becoming a victim of a crime (Gabriel and Greve 2003).

3   Who Are Most Fearful and Why? A Historical Perspective of Police Killings

Fear of crime, as a research topic has been an evolving social issue dating back to the mid-1960s when President Lyndon Johnson told lawmakers "the most damaging of the effects of violent crime is fear, and that fear must not be belittled." That statement suggested that fear of crime had grown into a public illness (Warr 2000). Research shows that an enormous number of Black residents are more fearful of criminal victimization by police officers than any other racial group (Frankovic 2019). In every city in America, Blacks are more likely to experience deadly force by the police than their White counterparts (Mock 2019).

"Violent and brutality have become a recognized part of police work" (Quinney 1980, 58). To begin addressing the issue at large, one must first understand the history of police killings on many nonviolent unarmed Black and Brown bodies. The criminal justice system has deep historical roots in policing, prosecuting, imprisoning, and executing people of color (Brewer and Heitzeg 2008). For centuries, white police officers have targeted Black inner-city residents- as they are perceived as a threat to civil society (Alexander 2012) and are not entitled to civil rights. Beginning with the Thirteenth Amendment that abolished slavery, except during the event of incarceration, to the Fourteenth Amendment granting due process, except for when engaging with law enforcement officials and the Fifteenth Amendment that guarantees the right to vote, except for when you've been incarcerated and then branded a felon, African Americans in the United States have been reminded that their constitutional rights can be called into question at any given moment.

The brutal, often fatal, attacks of African American residents by police are nothing new in America. African Americans have been viewed as inferior and powerless since they arrived as slaves in the 16th century. Slavery mandated a violent policing apparatus that protected Whites and brutalized Blacks (Jones 1977). A historical account provides evidence that Black lives never mattered and how the criminal justice system participates in and rationalizes the deaths of African Americans.

In 1955, Emmett Till, a 14-year old Black male was taken from his great uncle's house in Money, Mississippi. He was brutally beaten and killed by two white men, Roy Bryant and John William Milam for allegedly whistling at Bryant's wife and may have uttered bye baby. His killers were freed.

In 1999, 23-year-old Amadou Diallo was shot and killed by four NYPD officers. According to the officers he was an alleged rape suspect whom they thought he was holding a gun. The officers fired 41 shots, hitting Diallo 19 times. The public learned that Diallo was holding his wallet. The four officers were acquitted.

In 2004, Timothy Stansbury Jr., an unarmed 19-year-old, Black male was shot and killed by a New York Police Department officer. The officer was patrolling the rooftop of a housing project and claimed he was "startled" by Stansbury. Stansbury was shot in the chest while taking a short-cut to a birthday party. The officer was not indicted on his murder charges.

In 2009, Oscar Grant, a 22-year-old Black man, was fatally shot by a Bay Area Rapid Transit (BART) officer in Oakland, Calif., on New Year's Day. This incident occurred after earlier allegations that a fight had occurred on a transit train from San Francisco. Upon arrival, Oscar Grant and several of his friends were immediately detained. The BART officer insisted that an unarmed man was resisting and that more force was needed. While lying face down, with his hands behind his back, the officer shot Grant in his back.

In Kimani Gray, a 16-year-old Black male was shot four times in the front and side of his body and three times in the back. Gray was leaving a friend's birthday party in Brooklyn, New York when he was killed by two NYPD officers. The eyewitness stated that Gray was empty-handed at the time of his murder.

In 2012, 19-year-old Kendrec McDade was shot and killed in California by two police officers. He was unarmed with no criminal record. During the same year, officer Michael Brelo was found not guilty on all counts in the shooting of deaths of two Black, unarmed suspects-Timothy Russell and Malissa Williams in Cleveland, Ohio. Also in 2012, Ervin Jefferson was shot and killed by a security guard in Decatur, Georgia and Rekia Boyd, an innocent bystander was fatally shot in Chicago, Illinois by an off-duty Chicago police detective.

Fear of police violence and unjust treatment by the criminal justice system has also increased in the aftermath of countless others including but not limited to, Orlando Barlow in Las Vegas, Nevada, Sean Bell in Queens, New York; Jordan Davis in Jacksonville, Florida; Trayvon Martin in Miami Gardens, Florida; Tamir Rice in Cleveland, Ohio; Michael Brown in Ferguson, Missouri; Eric Garner in New York City, Freddie Gray in Baltimore, Maryland; and Alton Sterling in Baton Rouge, Louisiana at the hands of local police officers on Black Americans. When a vigilante kills a Black body, it is commonly considered justifiable due to the socially constructed danger it possesses. These stories are evidence that all lives do not matter, specifically, Black lives.

The hashtag #BlackLivesMatter was created by three community organizers and activists on social media after the acquittal of George Zimmerman in the Trayvon Martin case. The social movement was formed with hopes of bringing communities together to fight against racism and police violence, racial profiling, and racial inequality in the criminal justice system. The social movement went viral in 2014 following the killing of Michael Brown, an unarmed African American teenager.

The Black body for decades has been viewed and treated as something unworthy of humanity and threatening. However, research argues that African Americans tend to be more fearful and vulnerable than other groups because they are more likely to reside in disadvantaged neighborhoods where violent crime is more common (St. John and Healdmoore 1995; Skogan 1995; Day 1999; Franklin, Franklin and Fearn 2008). Studies have shown that when fear of crime is considered, individuals belonging to higher income statuses had the lowest level of fear than those residents who are poor in all areas (Will and

McGrath 1995; McGarrell, Giacomazzi and Thurman 1997) given that they are more equipped and have more resources to protect themselves (Biderman 1967). Citizens who reside in low-income neighborhoods are normally considered to be more fearful, since they are more likely to be challenged by certain community characteristics, such as ethnic heterogeneity and residential mobility (Taylor and Covington 1993). Often time ignored in the research on fear of crime is an understanding of who the actual criminals are that African Americans are most fearful of.

4 A Broader Social Problem: Whites Gets Richer and Blacks Gets Prison

In incidences where Blacks are not fatally shot and killed by police, they are arrested and sentenced at a higher rate. The probability of being incarcerated as an African American is not random or isolated events. Nevertheless, it is a broader social problem. A large number of Blacks are convicted of felony offenses in state and federal courts (Gabbidon and Greene 2019) than any other racial group. Both the school-to-prison pipeline and the prison-industrial complex reinforces racial injustice.

With the "tough on crime" policies, the criminal justice system facilitates a school to prison pipeline by transferring students of color out of educational institutions, mainly through "zero tolerance" techniques (Heitzeg 2009). These policies and practices have increased the probability of students of color being suspended, expelled, and/or arrested at school (Heitzeg 2009). Many of these students have learning disabilities, comes from impoverished communities, and have been abused or neglected and would benefit from additional educational and counseling services. Instead, they are isolated, pushed out and imprisoned (American Civil Liberties Union). Many schools have also authorized the use of drug-sniffing dogs, hired private security, increased police presence with officers patrolling the perimeter of school grounds and installed metal detectors and surveillance cameras (Kupchik 2010). Minor nonviolent behaviors, such as disruption, increasingly become criminalized and offer a punishment approach rather than a rehabilitative tactic. The punishment, therefore, does not fit the crime and shows that those in positions of power are corrupt, unfair and unreformed. All of these security measures create a pipeline from the classroom to juvenile detention facilities and eventually to prisons.

According to the American Civil Liberties Union, children should be educated, not incarcerated; however, instead of financing education in poor communities, elected politicians have chosen to fund incarceration—for corporate profit and political gain (Heitzeg 2009). While under-resourced schools struggle to provide updated resources for students, policymakers' rather spend thousands annually to send that same child to prison (Kozol 2005). Through prisons, the power of white and blue privileged groups are preserved and prolonged as the criminal justice institution receive huge proceeds from private organizations. To continue functioning, jails and prison cells are overflowing with vulnerable men of color. Thousands of prisoners are employed in the prisoners by producing goods for private sector companies. As a result, Black men are highly subject to exploitable labor, which many multinational industries benefit from, just as they have been doing throughout American history (Alexander 2012). As alleged solutions to economic, social and political problems, the overlapping interests of government continue to build prisons for profit.

The prison system is often misconstrued as a means to create more jobs and remove violent criminals off the streets; however, it has troubled many families, reduced funds for education, and produced, many times unwarranted, fear of crime amongst Black communities. The prison-industrial-complex has developed into this massive living organism that must be fed constantly while threatening the wellbeing of equality in America (PCARE 2007).

Due to the interest of the dominant group and increased spending on imprisonment, the United States has become dependent upon incarceration. The U.S. has the highest incarceration rate in the world and sadly, this rate continues to rise. Much like we see today, Edwin Sutherland (1947) first noted that Blacks were "arrested, convicted, and committed to prisons approximately three times as frequently as white persons" (121). Additionally, Sutherland (1947) also states that the statistics "probably reflect a bias against all of the minority races but especially against the Negro" (121). Once released from prison, Black men have a small chance of successful integration back into their communities and incarceration leaves a negative impact on their families (Wooldredge et al. 2015). Research shows that children of incarcerated parents experience more upheaval in their lives—they are more likely to live with a caregiver who abuses drugs, experience sexual and physical maltreatment, and live in poverty than those whose parents are not (Phillips, Costello, and Angold 2007). Once labeled a felon, they are excluded from employment, housing, voting and educational opportunities which thus perpetuate and enable crime.

5 We Are More Afraid of the Police than the So-called Actual Criminals

Drawing upon thirty in-depth semi-structured interviews and 100 hours of ethnographic research over three years, this chapter seeks to understand the fear of crime within the Black population, a group that is disproportionately entangled, scrutinized, and confined by the system (Lawrence 2011). The city of Baton Rouge serves as an interesting case study for fear of crime research for a few reasons. First, crime statistics showed that the city was one of the most violent cities on America's 25 murder capitals' list (Thomas 2017). Second, the city is a highly segregated metropolitan area, which is important because research found that high crime areas are frequently populated by racial and ethnic minorities, and thus may impact fear of crime responses for African Americans differentially (Franklin and Franklin 2009). The developing violent crime problem in the city has been widely acknowledged by the state and local law enforcement, the local government, and the mass media. The city has been gaining an unsavory reputation as being one of the most dangerous cities in the country. Examining fear of crime within these areas allows a way to fully understand how residents identify, construct and describe fear based on their own direct and indirect knowledge and experiences.

Fear has been a dominant concern in high crime urban neighborhoods for decades (Toet and van Schaik 2012). To understand residents' fear of crime in this urban area, participants were asked *"Are you afraid to walk in your neighborhood at night?"* This particular question has been criticized for being limited to nighttime, failing to mention crime and only measuring intensity; however, it is most practiced by social scientists and has been used to measure fear since the 1960s. I was able to address some of these points of contention by asking residents to elaborate on the responses provided to gain additional information. The residents acknowledges that crime is a serious problem within their neighborhood; however, it was not the criminals that they were most afraid of; nevertheless, it was the police. African-Americans within this urban area were more fearful that they or a family member would be a victim of police violence than they were about becoming a victim of a violent crime by someone else.

Sixty percent of women reported being afraid to walk alone in their neighborhood at night due to police presence. For instance, Ann, a fifty-four- year-old, Black woman states: "Yes there are several areas around here that I would be afraid to walk alone at night. I don't feel safe inside this neighborhood at all. The residents within the community are close-knit. It's not so much of the people who are committing the crimes I am afraid of. It's the law enforcement." Alice, a thirty- five-year-old resident, similarly acknowledges:

> Yes, not only am I afraid to walk alone in this area, but a lot of areas in the city because of the color of my skin. I try not to go anywhere alone and I try not to go anywhere by myself too late at night. I know the police are out. They are everywhere just looking for something. You just can't trust anyone these days. The ones that are supposed to serve and protect are

killing too. It's obvious that blue and white lives matter more, but Black lives matter too.

On the other hand, forty percent of women reported that they were not afraid to walk alone in their neighborhood at night but would not do so because of precautionary reasons. Illustrating this point, Betty-Ann, a fifty-six-year-old, female minister in the community stated:

> Well no, I'm not afraid to walk alone but I wouldn't just walk around here late at night. When I'm on the street ministering with my church, we are off the street by 8 p.m. and then we go home. We don't want any unnecessary problems. I don't think it's real safe to just walk around the neighborhoods at night. I do not want to be a target or stereotyped by the police just because I'm walking.

Mary, a fifty-six-year-old resident, described how violated she felt when she called the police for help. She stated:

> I used to think I was safe but now I don't know. I feel traumatize. One day someone had broken into my home. I called the police and they took forever to come. When they did come, they made me feel even more violated. They talked to me like I was nobody. Like my property did not matter. Questioning me like I was the criminal. Abusing their power because they could. All you hear on the news are police abusing their power and brutality. That's, that's hard to deal with, especially when you have kids, nieces and nephews growing up in an area targeted by law enforcement. You can't sleep good cause you're listening for something, thinking something bad is going to happen to your kids. Who can I call if I can't call the ones who job is to serve and protect. You just feel violated, and I feel like my life has been violated. I am not the criminal.

Jada, a thirty-five-year-old resident, similarly explains:

> Most people who live here are African Americans and the perceptions of the police officers are bad because of the way they handle crime and treat people. People have different experiences in other areas where resources are plentiful. The media views our neighborhood as crime hot spots but it's really the police hot-spots.

Renee, a fifty-five-year-old resident shared with me the following narrative:

> This area needs more resources and better patrolling, not just any patrolling. We need good officers. Police officers that comes from the area. Someone who knows the people in the community. Someone who understand the community needs. Someone who understands us and the unethical system. Someone who has been discriminated against and understand the problems of our community. We need someone we can trust.

Collectively, women responses revealed that regardless of whether or not they were afraid to walk along in their neighborhoods at night, clearly they were concerned and afraid about being mistreated by local law enforcement. All of the men in the study reported not being afraid to walk along at night, but similar to women, acknowledge how they avoid police presence for precautionary reasons. The narratives suggest that they are more terrified of police presence than the crimes that occur in their respective neighborhoods. For instance, AJ justifies:

> I'm not afraid to walk alone at night. I avoid police presence though at all times. Many of them are really disrespectful and inconsiderate. I just want them to be more involved, not just with the law but be a mentor type so that we the people in the neighborhood can see them differently. They need to start showing us and teaching us that they are not all about locking you up and throwing away the key, that they can be your friends too. They need to be a mentor for the young adults. Having a conversation with us and referring us to something positive like an educational program or some sort of extracurricular activity instead of just locking us up and treating us like animals. Hell, even some animals are treated better.

A local pastor in the community stated:

> The local officers are never going to know anything around here. They are very rude, have a lack of respect for the members of the community and have a nasty attitude with people. One day I stopped to tell them I was glad to see someone parked on the corner and they asked me what I wanted, told me to get away, what I was looking for? I was treated so unworthy. I'm afraid to say anything to them now or even be in their presence.

Buddy, a fifty-four-year-old male respondent stated:

> The police need to address real crime. They are the real criminals. The corrupt system itself is the criminal. It's bigger than this neighborhood.

> I do not trust them; they never come on time when you call them and when they are around they are racially profiling. We need officers who grew up in the community they are patrolling. We need officers who are mentors. We need officers who are not scared to get out of their patrol cars and walk the streets. We need someone who understands the struggle and the lack thereof in our community. We need real police and police reform.

As the narrative implies a majority of the residents (eighty percent), stated, that they had no trust in their local officers and their neighborhood needed better patrolling. The community needs someone who knows the community and the community can trust. The community's perception of their local police officials was influenced by the amount of trust they had with them based on previous experiences, which were fueled by mistreatment and disrespect. For instance, Billy, for example, made the following statement:

> Residents will see something going on and not report it because they don't trust the police department because they don't come on time and in many instances the victims is treated as criminals. The community is actually more afraid of the police than they are of the actual criminals. Now that's sad to say, but it's true. We are scared for our life. In today's society, we are still segregated and treated unequally. I know for a fact they do not treat those people in the other neighborhoods this way.

The accounts also illustrated that some of the women of the high crime population have some faith in the police department. For example, Erica stated:

> I do have some faith. I have family members on the force but they are sent to other areas. If they start patrolling a little more and getting in the community instead of hiding behind a badge they could build a better relationship. Instead of making this community feel like they are looking down on us, they should let us know that they are here to protect and serve us. Even when you call about something minor they have attitudes.

Elaine explained:

> I do believe there are very few good officers. It's hard to acknowledge those when the majority are corrupt. You know one bad apple spoils the entire barrel. I feel like it's "us against them." I have faith in some of the police officers but our overall views are negative because of the historical

mistreatment of Black and Brown people. They need to get out the cars and build relationships with the people in the community. Ride bikes and talk to people and get their perspective of their neighborhood. If they start doing that then people may view them differently and may have a little trust in them.

Many residents also believe their area is a major focus of law enforcement because of the racial makeup. For example, Betty Ann stated: "You want to believe that the police are not focusing on this area because of race, but that's hard to believe. That's why we are fearful of them. We love our families too. We want to see our sons and daughters grow up too. There are both good and bad people in the police force, just like in every organization. You just never know who is which. Who are the ones that care and who just don't give a damn."

As these narratives illustrate some of the residents want police in their neighborhoods. However, they want the police to know the community by developing relationships with the members of the community and treat the residents with respect and dignity. In economically disadvantaged communities, residents are likely to experience neglect and rudeness at the hands of the police (Fagan and Davies 2000; Kane 2002; Terrill and Reisig 2003; Ingram 2007). As a result of negative encounters with local police officers, residents tend to construct an undesirable perception (Tyler and Wakslak 2004; Brunson and Miller 2006; Gau and Brunson 2010). These unconstructive evaluations of the police are more usual amongst residents of communities with high levels of poverty and crime (Sampson and Bartusch 1998; Weitzer and Tuch 2004; Weitzer, Tuch and Skogan 2008). When the police procedures become severe and unfair, residents lose faith in the system and question the legitimacy of both the patrolling practices and the punishments and as a result, they openly challenge a system they view as unjust. Overall, residents' responses indicate that the local officials are both over- and under-policing in their communities. The community experience under-policing when officers dismiss certain calls for service or refuse to make arrests for crimes that they believe would have been harshly punished in better-off neighborhoods. On the other hand, residents' responses indicate that the local officers are over-policing when they are riding around looking for criminal activities and racially profiling. Numerous residents made it very transparent that some of the residents in the neighborhood are more afraid of the presence of the police than they are of the actual crime rates.

Taken together, existing research confirms that when it comes to crime and the criminal justice system, Black and Brown Americans remain at the forefront. As Sampson and Wilson (1995) noted, "the evidence is clear that African

Americans face dismal and worsening odds when it comes to crime in the streets and the risk of incarceration." These dismal odds continue to exist in today's society. Research shows that African Americans are six times more likely to be killed than their White counterparts; nonetheless, homicide continues to be the leading cause of death amongst young African American teens. Police reports and self-reported surveys both reveal how a disproportionate number of Blacks continue to be involved in serious violent crimes, and how roughly one in three Black men are likely to be incarcerated during his lifespan in comparison to less than 5 percent of White men (Sampson and Wilson 1995). Although crime rates have been declining since the 1990s, African Americans are still at a greater risk of being incarcerated as well as having a weak attachment to the labor market which reinforces the marginalization of Blacks and their attachment to crime (Sampson and Wilson 1995; Saad 2011). As Crystal, one of the resident's explains, "it's a continuous cycle and Black lives matter too."

6 Black Lives Matter Too: Promoting Critical and Innovative Approaches to Address the Multifaceted Needs of Black Communities

Despite some historical gains, Black lives never truly mattered amongst the "systems": education, healthcare, social service and the criminal justice system. The fact that African-Americans are more fearful that they or someone in their families will be a victim of police use of deadly force than they are to becoming a victim of violent crime is quite distasteful. Therefore, I offer three strategies to address the multifaceted need of Black communities:
(1) Understanding the Interest Convergence Nature of the "System,"
(2) Teaching and Educating Our Children of Color, and
(3) Fight The Power: Us versus Them

7 Understanding the Interest Convergence Nature of the "System"

Understanding the interest of the dominant group requires that Blacks must first understand that the "system" could never fail us if it was never redesigned to protect us. The longevity of bigotry in this nation has not survived in the same form; instead, discrimination has and will always shift, change, and form into often-unrecognizable entities (Alexander 2012). As Crystal, one of the residents, explains, "it's a continuous cycle." We (the word we in this paragraph and the subsequent paragraphs are referring to we as African/Black Americans) are living in a society where powerful stakeholders are unwilling to give up the financial benefit of locking up Black and Brown bodies that have been derived from the slave trade. We are living in a society where the fundamental purpose of prisons is not to rehabilitate its prisoners but to exploit them for cheap labor. We are living in a society where police officers falsely prejudge African Americans as aggressive and hostile, and the government passes laws that punish them more severely. We are living in a society where Blacks are swept into the criminal justice system by local police officers who conducts drug operations primarily in impoverished communities of color. We are living in an oppressive society that uses the police force as its mercenaries. We are living in a society where police officers are acquitted for killing unarmed Blacks. Rather than rely on the color of one's skin, the criminal justice system labels people of color as "criminals" and then it engages in all the practices that we allegedly left behind (Alexander 2012). Once labeled as a felon, the old forms of discrimination in employment, housing, and education are surprisingly legal. African American men are part of a growing under-caste in which they are locked up and locked out of mainstream society, which in turn has a devastating impact on African American communities.

Though the criminal justice system is a major piece of the puzzle; we must also diagnose the evil that exists within the entire social system. Blacks lag behind the dominant group in terms of educational attainment, occupational prestige, income, and health outcomes (Martin, Fasching-Varner and Jackson 2016). While African-Americans have made significant growth since slavery, there are still major disparities that continue to exist amongst Blacks and Whites (Bertrand and Mullainathan 2004; Pager and Quillian 2005). Not only do Blacks struggle with their own poverty, but their surrounding communities have fewer job opportunities, lower-performing schools, higher crime rates, and more public health problems. Being poor in an underprivileged community makes it that much harder to get out of poverty (Ward 2011). In other words, being taught in a poorly performing public school means that many low-income residents often enter the job force lacking the basic skills needed (Wilson 2009). Research has shown that African American high school graduates are 70% more likely to experience job loss than their White counterparts, and when they do find a job they are often in job sectors with few benefits (Wilson 1996; Smith 2002). The unemployment rate for African Americans is consistently twice that of Whites (Wellers and Fields 2011). Consequently, this affects their ability to gain jobs, political power, wealth, and police protection. The evidence is clear that African Americans face depressing and worsening odds when it comes to adequate resources, crime in the streets and the risk of incarceration.

The disparities that continue to endure provide some of the best evidence of the continuing significance of race and racism in our country. The practicality that our Black residents must understand and acknowledge is the system as it is and our inferior location inside it. The challenges that the communities of color faced, consist of, but are not limited to crime, poverty, under-resourced schools, crime-ridden neighborhoods, high unemployment rates, and racial profiling by police officers. As Curry (2008) states, "equality only serves as an imaginative allure—a fantasy, and this is the reality that must be conceptually disengaged" (42). Change only occurs when it is favorable to those in power. There must always be an inferior group in order for the dominant group, or those with power and wealth, to profit and make revenue. As a result, the dominant group continues to control, oppress and suppress large portions of the Black community (Martin et al. 2014).

8   Teaching and Educating Our Children of Color

Ultimately, the crisis of the system can only be truthfully addressed by first recognizing the undermining means of those in power and secondly, teaching and educating our children of color how to live within a society where race determines how they are perceived, treated, and evaluated as humans. Once one understands what the discrimination in social services can lead to, as African Americans parents, we must start the conversation on how to live and survive in a broken system with our children at a very early age. Poverty, community disorganization and the prevalence of drugs and crime in Black neighborhoods put them at a greater risk of being stigmatized and labeled. We have to teach our kids what it means to be "Black" in America and how the color of their skin unfairly marked them out to the criminal justice system. We must teach them the appropriate protocol on how to interact with the police to avoid being punished, apprehended, or even killed. We must teach them that just because the system says you have rights do not mean you have those rights. We must teach them how to behave and speak in a classroom that is taught by another racial being who does not understand the struggle and therefore, teach students of color. We must teach them how the school system is designed to usher Black students from the school system to the juvenile detention facilities with tough disciplinary policies in place. We must teach them how Black kids are more likely to be punished and expelled for behaviors that fall out of line than their White classmates. We must make sure that they are aware that the majority of incarcerated students never graduate from high school which consequently creates additional challenges for communities with limited resources (Mauer and Chesney-Lind 2002; Roberts 2004). We must teach them how both individual and institutional racism exists which has shaped the unlevel playing field amongst dominant and subordinate groups. We must teach them that living the American Dream is impossible because they are not given the same opportunities. We must teach them to do the same work as their ancestors once they too make a family of their own.

Additionally, it is equally important that Black educators continue to mentor, train and educate Black youth on how to succeed within the "system" where race does matter. African American residents face countless obstacles not experienced by their White counterparts. As a community of color, we can together teach our children how to recognize, evaluate and live in a society that is functioning in the way that it has always envisioned (Fasching-Varner, et al., 2014). With this mind frame we can together help children of color be aware of the system that has for decades decided who benefits, lives, dies, and who gets life in prison; otherwise we will continue to live in our blind spots and in fear. Educating our children about the nature of their inferior social position in society allows them to be conscious of the invisible walls that exist in virtually every social institution. Through teaching and facilitating, children of color acknowledge the racial realism ideology allows them to navigate and succeed in a world where they are viewed as undeserving. Through teaching allows racial prejudice and discrimination amongst the Black group more explicit and identifiable.

9   Fight the Power: Us versus Them

As parents, teachers, and mentors in the community, we must never stop fighting for justice. Once one understands how the system operates and start having conversations with our youth of color early on, we can together unite and fight the power. By continuing to give voice to marginalized groups and through continued social action, we can overcome yet another form of violence. We must learn how to free ourselves from the delusion that change is likely to occur without stopping our fight to change it. The fight by communities of color to overcome freedom, fairness, and justice in this country is as ancient as this country itself (Bell 1992) and there's still a lot more fighting that needs to take place. Since different groups' lives are valued more than others, the divide becomes a wide gap. As the subtitle alludes, "Us versus Them" denotes to the

Black community as a group against the criminal justice and the entire "system" at large.

The idea that we are living in a post-racial society has contributed to a number of issues, including the fear of the police. Individual and institutional racism, sexism, and classism all occur when individuals are disadvantaged when society itself legally classify people in a strictly structured system for the sake of exploitation by privilege groups. We fight the power by protesting and rallying for change. The entire system (i.e. criminal justice, education, labor and housing market, healthcare, and countless other social services) must be held accountable, eradicated and reconstructed. We must lobby that the system serves and protects African Americans in the same way it serves and protects the dominate group. We must lobby for police officers to wear cameras and be held accountable for their unfair actions. We must lobby for equitable resources in the school system. We do not want textbooks that are outdated and passed down to Black schools once white schools have received updated resources. We must lobby for equal pay and benefits in the labor market. We must demand shared accountability amongst stakeholders. We must demand and accept nothing less than a substantive change in policy, legislation, and practices. When only a small change takes place that's advantageous to all, we must continue to lobby.

Eradication is not just about eliminating buildings full of cages. The entire social system is broken. It's about undoing the whole society we live in. We live in a society that feeds on and maintains oppression and inequalities through punishment, brutality, and unfair treatment. An abolitionist vision means being aware of our unique status as African Americans in every aspect of our daily lives and developing practical strategies that move us toward making our goals factual. It means giving voice to the voiceless. Eradication is both a practical tool for eliminating racial inequality and a long-term goal. We fight the power by continuing our fight for equality.

The response that "all" lives matter is a response that does not want to recognize the hatred and unequal treatment experienced by Blacks. In reality, some lives matter more than others. Scholars, if "all" our lives truly matter, then we must take the idea that we are living in a post-racial society off the table for discussion. For those of us who are aware of the "system" and how it operates, we cannot afford to be silent but we must unite our voices. For those who are oblivious, it is time to start having a meaningful, honest and open dialogue. By engaging in effective discourse may start closing the gap between the well-known and unknown of racial disparities. This platform allows us to utilize our voices that will eventually create more spaces for active dialogue. Clearly, everyone doesn't understand the struggle faced by Blacks within the subsystems;

therefore, more conversation is needed to highlight the disparities and unfair treatment of people of color. By giving voice to the Black population who are marginalized by their social constructed identities helps fight the power. No agency or scholar alone can succeed in addressing the multifaceted needs of Black communities. I invite scholars to engage in uncompromising honesty because unconsciously, people ignore how the social construction ideology of race has real and severe implications. With this honesty, we can fight the power. Educators and police officers need to submerge and educate themselves in the communities they serve. Fighting the powerful means fighting efforts to dehumanize and criminalize Black individuals. Fighting the powerful—the government, private industries, and other social services, gives us hope for a better future (Bell 1992).

This chapter has provided the theory and data that supports the actions that are the source for policing tactics that target certain neighborhoods, which lead to the criminalization and incarceration of Black bodies. Fighting the powerful means coming together to communicate, rallying for a revolution and sharing the responsibility for the consequences. This togetherness will bring about positive changes that would lead to the liberation of Black Americans, which is important for Africana Demography. Centering race gives Black Americans, including Sociologists and Demographers, a voice to fight the power by engaging in debates about a topic that has alarmed the entire nation.

Bibliography

Alderman, Jeffrey. 1994. "Leading the Public: The Media's Focus on Crime Shaped Sentiment." *Public Perspective* 5 (3): 26–27.

Alexander, Michelle. 2012. *The New Jim Crow: Mass Incarceration in the Age of Colorblindness*. New York, NY: The New Press.

American Civil Liberties Union. n.d. "The School to Prison Pipeline." Accessed October 2019. http://www.aclu.org/racial-justice/school-prison-pipeline.

Bell, Derrick. 1992. "Racial Realism." *Connecticut Law Review* 24: 363–379.

Bertrand, Marianne and Sendhi Mullainathan 2004. "Are Emily and Greg More Employable than Lakisha and Jamal? A Field Experiment on Labor Market Discrimination." *American Economic Review* 94 (4): 991–1013.

Biderman, Albert. 1967. *Report on a Pilot Study in the District of Columbia on Victimization and Attitudes Towards Law Enforcement*. Washington, DC: Government Printing Office.

Brewer, Rose M., and Nancy A. Heitzeg. 2008. "The Racialization of Crime and Punishment Criminal Justice, Color-blind Racism, and the Political Economy of the Prison Industrial Complex." *American Behavioral Scientist* 51 (5): 625–644.

Brunson, Rod K. and Jody Miller. 2006. "Gender, Race, and Urban Policing: The Experience of African American Youths." *Gender & Society* 20 (4): 531–552.

Curry, Tommy. 2008. "Saved by the Bell: Derrick Bell's Racial Realism as Pedagogy." *Ohio Valley Philosophy of Education Society* 39: 35–46.

Day, Kristen. 1999. "Embassies and Sancturaries: Women's Experiences of Race and Fear in Public Space." *Environment and Planning* 17 (3): 307–328.

Ditton, Jason and Stephen Farrall. 2000. *The Fear of Crime*. New York, NY: Routledge.

Fagan, Jeffrey and Garth Davies. 2000. "Street Stops and Broken Windows: Terry, Race, and Disorder in New York City." *Fordham Urban Law Journal* 28: 457–504.

Franklin, Travis W., Courtney A. Franklin and Noelle E. Fearn. 2008. "A Multilevel Analysis of the Vulnerability, Disorder, and Social Integration Models of Fear of Crime." *Social Justice Research* 21 (2): 204–227.

Franklin, Courtney A., and Travis W. Franklin. 2009. "Predicting Fear of Crime: Considering Differences Across Gender." *Feminist Criminology* 4 (1): 83–106.

Frankovic, Kathy. 2019. "More African-Americans Fear Victimization by Police than Fear Violent Crime." *YouGov Poll Politics*, December 12, 2019. https://today.yougov.com/topics/politics/articles-reports/2019/03/15/black-americans-police.

Gabbidon, Shaun and Helen Greene. 2019. *Race and Crime*. Thousand Oaks, California: SAGE Publications.

Gabriel, Ute and Werner Greve. 2003. "The Psychology of Fear of Crime: Conceptual and Methodological Perspectives." *British Journal of Criminology* 43 (3): 600–614.

Gau, Jacinta M. and Rod K. Brunson. 2010. "Procedural Justice and Order Maintenance Policing: A Study of Inner-city Young Men's Perceptions of Police Legitimacy." *Justice Quarterly* 27 (2): 255–279.

Hacker, Andrew. 1995. *Two Nations: Black and White, Separate, Hostile and Unequal*. 2nd ed. New York, NY: Ballantine Books.

Heitzeg, Nancy. 2009. "Education or Incarceration: Zero Tolerance Policies and the School to Prison Pipeline." *Forum on Public Policy Online*: 1–21.

Ingram, Jason R. 2007. "The Effect of Neighborhood Characteristics on Traffic Citation Practices of the Police." *Police Quarterly* 10 (4): 371–393.

Jones, Terry. 1977. "The Police in America: A Black Viewpoint." *The Black Scholar* 9 (2): 22-39.

Kane, Robert J. 2002. "The Social Ecology of Police Misconduct." *Criminology* 40 (4): 867–896.

Kozol, Jonathan. 2005. *Shame of the Nation: The Restoration of Apartheid Schooling in America*. New York, NY: Crowe.

Kupchik, Aaron. 2010. *Homeroom Security: School Discipline in an Age of Fear*. New York, NY: NYU Press.

Lawrence, Keith. 2011. *Race, Crime, and Punishment: Breaking the Connection in America*. Washington, D.C: The Aspen Institute.

Martin, Lori, Kenneth Fasching-Varner, Molly Quinn and Melinda Jackson. 2014. "Racism, Rodeos, and the Misery Industries of Louisiana." *The Journal of Pan African Studies* 7 (6): 60–83.

Martin, Lori Latrice, Kenneth Fasching-Varner and Melinda Jackson. 2016. "A Tale of Two Cities: Race and Wealth Inequality in the New South." In *After the Storm: Occupation, Militarization, and Segregation in Post-Katrina America*, edited by Lori Martin et al. Santa Barbara, CA: Praeger Publishers.

Mauer, Marc and Meda Chesney-Lind. 2002. *Invisible Punishment: The Collateral Consequences of Mass Imprisonment*. New York, NY: The New Press.

Mawby, Rob, Paul Brunt, and Zoe Hambly. 2000. "Fear of Crime Among British Holidaymakers." *The British Journal of Criminology* 40 (3): 468–479.

McGarrell, Edmund, Andrew Giacomazzi and Quint Thurman. 1997. "Neighborhood Disorder, Integration, and the Fear of Crime." *Justice Quarterly* 14 (3): 479–500.

Meier, Kenneth J. 1994. *The Politics of Sin: Drugs, Alcohol and Public Policy*. Armonk, NY: M.E. Sharpe, Inc.

Mock, Brentin. 2019. "What New Research Says About Race and Police Shootings." *CityLab*, December 12, 2019. https://www.citylab.com/equity/2019/08/police-officer-shootings-gun-violence-racial-bias-crime-data/595528/.

Pager, Devah, and Lincoln Quillian. 2005. "Walking the Talk: What Employers Say Versus What They Do." *American Sociological Review* 70 (3): 355–380.

Pain, Rachel. 2001. "Gender, Race, Age and Fear in the City." *Urban Studies* 38 (5–6): 899–913.

Phillips, Susan, Elizabeth J. Costello, and Adrian Angold. 2007. "Differences Among Children Whose Mothers Have a History of Arrest." *Women and Criminal Justice* 17 (2–3): 45–63.

Prison Communication, Activism, Research and Education (PCARE). 2007. "Fighting the Prison Industrial Complex: A Call to Communication and Cultural Studies Scholars to Change the World." *Communication and Critical/Cultural Studies* 4 (4): 402–420.

Quinney, Richard. 1980. Class, State, and Crime. New York: Addison-Wesley Longman.

Reid, Lesley W. and Miriam Konrad. 2004. "The Gender Gap in Fear: Assessing the Interactive Effects of Gender and Perceived Risk on Fear of Crime." *Sociological Spectrum* 24 (4): 399–425.

Roberts, Dorothy. 2004. "The Social and Moral Cost of Mass Incarceration in African American Communities." *Stanford Law Review* 56 (127): 1271–1305.

Rountree, Pamela. 1998. "A Reexamination of the Crime-fear Linkage." *Journal of Research in Crime and Delinquency* 35 (3): 341–372.

Saad, Lydia. 2011. "Most Americans Believe Crime in U.S. Is Worsening." *Gallup News*, November 30, 2014. http://www.gallup.com/poll/150464/americans-believe-crime-worsening.aspx.

Sampson, Robert J., Dawn J. Bartusch. 1998. "Legal Cynicism and (Subcultural?) Tolerance of Deviance: The Neighborhood Context of Racial Difference." *Law & Society Review* 32 (4): 777–804.

Sampson, Robert J. and William J. Wilson. 1995. "Toward a Theory of Race, Crime, and Urban Inequality." In *Crime and Inequality*, edited by John Hagan and Ruth D. Peterson, 37–56. Stanford, CA: Stanford University Press.

Skogan, Wesley. 1995. "Crime and the Racial Fears of White Americans." *Annals of the American Academy of Political and Social Science* 539: 59–71.

Smith, Ryan. 2002. "Race, Gender, and Authority in the Workplace: Theory and Research." *Annual Review of Sociology* 28: 509–542.

Stanko, Elizabeth A. 1995. "Women, Crime, and Fear." *Annals of the American Academy of Political and Social Science* 539: 46–58.

St. John, Craig and Tamara Heald-Moore. 1995. "Fear of Black Strangers." *Social Science Research* 24 (3): 262–280.

Sutherland, Edwin H. 1974. Principles of Criminology. 4th ed. Philadelphia: Lippincott.

Taylor, Ralph B. and Jeanette Covington. 1993. "Community Structural Change and Fear of Crime." *Social Problems* 40 (3): 374–395.

Terrill, William, Michael D. Reisig. 2003. "Neighborhood Context and Use of Police Force." *Journal of Research in Crime and Delinquency* 40 (3): 291–321.

Thomas, Rachael. 2017. "Baton Rouge Lands in Top 25 on America's 25 Murder Capitals List." *WAFB News,* September 19. https://www.wafb.com/story/36853780/baton-rouge-lands-in-top-25-on-americas-25-murder-capitals-list/.

Toet, Alexander and Martin G. van Schaik. 2012. "Effects of Signals of Disorder on Fear of Crime in Real and Virtual Environments." *Journal of Environmental Psychology* 32 (3): 260–276.

Tyler, Tom R. and Cheryl J. Wakslak. 2004. "Profiling and Police Legitimacy: Procedural Justice, Attributions of Motive, and Acceptance of Police Authority." *Criminology* 42 (2): 253–282.

Ward, Steven. 2011. "Report: Poverty high in Baton Rouge." *The Advocate,* May 2013. http://theadvocate.com/news/1231729-123/story.html.

Warr, Mark. 2000. "Fear of Crime in the United States: Avenues for Research and Policy." In *Measurement and Analysis of Crime and Justice: Criminal Justice*, edited by David Duffee, 451–489. Washington, DC: U.S. Department of Justice.

Weitzer, Ronald and Steven Tuch. 2004. "Reforming the Police: Racial Differences in Public Support for Change." *Criminology* 42 (2): 391–416.

Weitzer, Ronald, Steven Tuch, and Wesley Skogan. 2008. "Police–Community Relations in a Majority-Black City." *Journal of Research in Crime and Delinquency* 45 (4): 398–428.

Welch, Kelly. 2007. "Black Criminal Stereotypes and Racial Profiling." *Journal of Contemporary Criminal Justice* 23 (3): 276–288.

Weller, Christian and Jaryn Fields, J. 2011. *The Black and White Labor Gap in America The Black and White Labor Gap in America Why African Americans Struggle to Find Jobs and Remain Employed Compared to Whites.* Washington, D.C: Center for American Progress.

Will, Jeffry A. and John H. McGrath. 1995. "Crime, Neighborhood Perceptions, and the Underclass: The Relationship Between Fear of Crime and Class Position." *Journal of Criminal Justice* 23 (2): 163–176.

Wilson, William. J. 1996. *When Work Disappears: The World of the New Urban Poor.* New York: Vintage Books.

Wilson, William J. 2009. *More Than Just Race: Being Black and Poor in the Inner City.* New York: W.W. Norton.

Woldoff, Rachel A. 2006. "Emphasizing Fear of Crime in Models of Neighborhood Social Disorganization." *Crime Prevention and Community Safety: An International Journal* 8 (4): 228–247.

Wooldredge, John, James Frank, Natalie Goulette, and Lawrence Travis. 2015. "Is the Impact of Cumulative Disadvantage in Sentencing Greater for Black Defendants?" *Criminology & Public Policy* 14 (2): 187–223.

CHAPTER 4

Policing the Black Community: History, Reality, and the Rudiments of Change

Edward Muhammad and Jack S. Monell

In recent years the much-publicized deaths of Alton Sterling, Michael Brown, Tamir Rice, John Crawford, and Philando Castille at the hands of police continues to affirm the ongoing antagonism between the black community and law enforcement. The death of these men and countless others is emblematic of the potential for death associated with black encounters with police. The killing of blacks by police has become so prevalent that a recent analysis has concluded that, "for young men of color, police use of force is among the leading causes of death" (Edwards, Lee and Esposito 2019, 16793–16798). When you add to this the fact that, police being charged in these shootings is rare and convictions even rarer, (Stinson 2017) police use of violence, and especially police violence against black communities, is increasingly being seen as a threat to public health (American Public Health Association 2015).

In this chapter we analyze the history of policing, its impact in society, and its antagonistic relationship toward the black community. In line with the principles of critical demography in general, and Africana Demography specifically, this contribution offers a critical analysis of policing by scholars from the black community with recommendations emanating from the inherent resources and cultural sensibilities within the black community. We begin the analysis by framing our work within the traditions of critical and Africana Demography. From there we explore the history of policing as it relates to the black community. Next, we contextualize perceptions of police by discussing public opinion and support of police. Given the levels of public support for police, we then discuss the much-touted "War on Cops" that was purported to be raging focusing specifically on the year 2015 when the narrative was in full swing. Following this is a detailed discussion of the deadly consequences of black encounters with police in which we spotlight data from public databases of police shootings and closing this chapter, we discuss both policing based options for improving relations with the black community as well as a citizen-based, community option for policing that has been implemented in one city in particular.

1 Framing the Discussion: from Critical Demography to Africana Demography

Hayward Derrick Horton (1999) contrasted conventional demography with his conception of a of critical demography. Detailing this distinction, he informed us that, "critical demography is a paradigm that makes explicit the manner in which the social structure differentiates dominant and subordinate groups in society" (Hayward 1999, 363). Horton further pointed out that critical demography is specifically concerned with "how power both affects and is impacted by demographic processes and events" (Hayward 1999, 364). The oppressive, antagonistic, and deadly interactions between police and the black community detailed in this chapter "necessitates an open discussion and examination of the nature of *power* in society" (Hayward 1999, 364). Throughout this piece we examine the relationship between the police and the black community. In providing the history of, and data documenting this brutal relationship, our analysis will be descriptive in nature. But as Horton argued, critical demography is not just a data driven endeavor, it is also theory driven (Horton). Addressing the intransigence of racist police culture and practices and seeking to transform them calls not just for a recitation of data and facts but also for bold, theory driven, and innovative approaches to changing the power dynamic between the black community and police. The following analysis offers this and something more. In going a step further than the necessary steps involved in critical demography, this chapter embodies the tenets of Africana Demography as well.

Martin (n.d.), noting both the relevance and the limitations of critical demography, identified five key characteristics of Africana Demography. Building upon the foundation laid down by Horton, Martin saw Africana Demography as extending his work by
1) being led by black Americans;
2) focusing on research centered on issues impacting black Americans;
3) deriving its power from the reservoirs of black, cultural knowledge and experience;
4) generating research findings that can be generalized to other populations if appropriate; and
5) deriving social and policy implications from the work while at the same time proliferating findings to non-academic audiences.

This chapter, in keeping with this rich critical tradition, adds to the body of Africana Demography literature by having been produced by black scholars, by focusing on policing (an issue critically impacting the black community), by pulling from the lived experience of black Americans, and by producing findings that are generalizable, digestible to multiple audiences, and ripe with policy implications.

2   History of Policing Blacks: the Role of Slave Patrols

Conventional histories point out that U.S. police departments derived from various watch groups and militias that sprang up in cities like Philadelphia, Boston, New York, and Chicago from the 17th through the 19th centuries (French 2018). According to these histories, volunteer, citizen-manned groups gave way to metropolitan police departments in the North. While this version is no doubt the more popular rendition of police history, the infrequently discussed development of policing in the South has a darker history, one "deeply intertwined with the violence of racial oppression" (Carter 2015).

As pointed out by Walker and Katz, police departments in the South evolved from slave patrols. About these patrols they write,

> The slave patrol was a distinctly American form of law enforcement. In southern states where slavery existed, it was intended to guard against slave revolts and capture runaway slaves. In some respects, the slave patrols were the first modern police forces in this country. The Charleston, South Carolina, slave patrol had about 100 officers in 1837 and was far larger than any northern city police force (Walker and Katz 2002).

These slave patrols, or "paddyrollers" (Archbold 2013) operated with a clear purpose handed down to them from the clergy and planting classes of the antebellum south. A definitive account of this purpose was documented in the *Annual Report of the Missionary to the Negroes, in Liberty County, Georgia* in 1833. The report is comprised of progress reports and recommendations by members of The Association for the Religious Instruction of the Negroes in Liberty County, Georgia. The association was comprised of clergy and slave owners charged with bringing black slaves into "subordination" by means of converting them to and instructing them in Christianity. The association, in linking the role of the police with that of subordinating enslaved blacks, reminds slave owners that, "In connection with proper discipline on plantations, the *police of the County*, for the helping of your efforts, should be strict. The patrol should be *real*, not *nominal*, conducted so as… to maintain them in fear and order" (Association for the Religious Instruction of the Negroes in Liberty County 1834). Toward this goal of maintaining "fear and order," the slave patrols engaged in chasing, apprehending and returning escaped slaves to their owners, providing "organized terror" (Potter 2013) to deter slave insurrections, and doling out discipline to slaves who violated plantation rules. The brutality of the slave patrols was evidenced by the fact that "slave patrols were both feared and resented by slaves" (Reichel 1988) and many viewed the patrols as "the worst thing yet about slavery" (Reichel 1988). Seeking continued control of the newly freed slaves after the Civil War, the slave patrols quickly adapted by evolving into the various police departments of the American south. As a result, "the transition from slave patrols to publicly funded police agencies was seamless in the southern region of the United States" (Archbold 2013).

3   Public Support for Police

Despite this troubled history and the almost daily killings by police, many Americans still express unwavering support for the law enforcement community. A Gallup poll assessing the public's confidence in the institutions of American society found police garnered the third highest vote of the public's confidence, beating out public schools, television news, and even the church (Gallup). In addition, even after racially charged, highly publicized police killings like those of Tamir Rice, Eric Garner, John Crawford, and Walter Scott, a majority of white respondents still expressed either a "great deal" or a "fair amount" of trust in both local and national law enforcement (YouGov 2015). This unwavering support for police by white society is all the more peculiar given the belief shared among blacks and whites (69% and 54% respectively) that deadly black-police encounters, rather than being isolated incidents, are in fact signs of a broader problem (Pew research Center 2017).

What accounts for this seemingly unshakeable support of police in the face of their history and actions with respect to the black community? One possible explanation is the tacit approval that Whites seem to give to the brutality (both past and present) of police toward the Black community. Pew Research polling has consistently shown that Blacks and Whites diverge in their views of police (Drake 2015). While Blacks have always protested police actions and activities, Whites, as far back as slavery and as recent as now, have always sided with, sanctioned, and supported law enforcement's heavy handed and antagonistic approach to dealing with Blacks.

Another possible reason for the continued support of law enforcement is the popular notion promoted mostly by Right Wing politicians and police unions that law enforcement officers are under a greater threat of harm. But, is that the case? Is there really a "War on Cops" being waged? At the height of the most recent "War on Cops" narrative in 2015, despite a majority of Americans, both Black and White, believing that there was indeed a deadly war on cops being waged by criminals (Rasmussen Reports 2015), nothing could've been further from the truth.

4 The "War on Cops" That Wasn't

Relatively and statistically speaking, being a police officer is not as dangerous as one is led to believe. In fact, in terms of fatalities, the Bureau of Labor Statistics reported that in 2017 it was more dangerous being a grounds maintenance worker, a garbage collector (waste management and remediation), or working in sales related occupations than it was being a police officer (U.S. Department of Labor 2018). And, according to the most recent data, being a police officer doesn't even make the top 15 when compared with fatalities in other occupations (Sauter and Stockdale 2019). Digging deeper into the fatalities experienced by police officers is particularly instructive when viewed in light of the supposed "war on cops."

The most recent claim of a "war on cops" reached its zenith in late 2014 and 2015. On the heels of the racialized, heavily publicized deaths of Michael Brown, Freddie Gray, Tamir Rice, and others, police activities and police themselves, came under intense scrutiny and calls for police reform reverberated throughout society. Rather than using the incidents and public reactions as an impetus for review and reflection, police departments, their unions, and conservative pundits and politicians opted for a war footing. The reactionary response took the form of combative indictments of those who critiqued, criticized or questioned police practices. Their narrative was bolstered by books like law enforcement apologist Heather MacDonald's *The War on Cops* and by the high-profile killings of police in New York in 2014 and in Dallas and Baton Rouge in 2016. At one point, nearly two thirds of Americans believed that there was a "war on cops" waging in America (Etkins 2016). In light of this narrative, we turned to an analysis of law enforcement data sources to better understand the reality of police fatalities. In particular the analysis focused on the year 2015, the year in which the "war on cops" narrative was raging throughout society.

According to the FBI, 86 officers were killed in the line of duty in 2015 (U.S. Department of Justice 2016b). Of the 86 killed, the majority (52%) died as a result of accidents, with the leading cause of these accidental deaths in 2015 was automobile accidents (U.S. Department of Justice 2016b). The number of officers killed feloniously in the line of duty for 2015 is telling. According to the same FBI source, the 41 felonious officer deaths represented a 10% decrease from the 51 officers killed feloniously in 2014 (U.S. Department of Justice 2016b). Referencing the 41 felonious officer deaths in 2015, the FBI reported that, "The 5- and 10-year comparisons show a decrease of 31 felonious deaths compared with the 2011 figure (72 officers) and a decrease of 7 deaths compared with 2006 data (48 officers)" (U.S. Department of Justice 2016b). To reiterate, in 2015 the majority of cops killed on the job died as a result of automobile, motorcycle crashes, and being hit outside their vehicle by oncoming traffic. In that same year, the number of officers killed feloniously were among the lowest for the previous decade. Additionally, referencing the decrease in the number of firearm related officer deaths and adjusting for U.S. population growth, the right-leaning American Enterprise Institute reported that, "the years 2013 and 2015 will be the two safest years for police in US history" (Perry 2017). These statistical realities are a far cry from the "war on cops" alarm being sounded at the time.

5   "Black Identity Extremists" and Law Enforcement Threat Assessments

Further fueling the unsubstantiated claims of a "war on cops" was a new threat said to be aggressively and specifically targeting law enforcement. Spurred by fears of a reaction to the refusal to indict Darren Wilson for the killing of Michael Brown in Ferguson, Missouri, in November of 2014 the FBI issued its first of three reports on the presence of "Black Identity Extremists" (U.S. Department of Justice 2016b). Again, in a 2017 report entitled "Black Identity Extremists Likely Motivated to Target Law Enforcement Officers," the FBI noted that "it is very likely Black Identity Extremists (BIE) perceptions of police brutality against African-Americans spurred an increase in premeditated, retaliatory lethal violence against law enforcement and will very likely serve as justification for such violence" (U.S. Department of Justice 2016b, 2). Basing their assumptions on six separate and unrelated incidents of police attacks by black perpetrators in 2014 and 2016, and despite noting that "BIE violence has been rare over the last 20 years" (U.S. Department of Justice 2016b, 6), the FBI still went on to make that claim that "it is very likely that the BIE's perceptions of unjust treatment of African Americans and the perceived unchallenged illegitimate actions of law enforcement will inspire premeditate attacks against law enforcement over the next year" (U.S. Department of Justice 2016b, 7). Ironically, while black nationalists were responsible for zero deaths of law enforcement officers in 2017, white supremacists and white nationalists killed three law enforcement officers (Irby 2018) and, one week after the release of the FBI's 2017 report that invented BIEs, a white nationalist ran over and killed Heather Heyer, a protestor at the Unite the Right rally held in Charlottesville, Virginia.

The fact that the FBI's report of on a "fictional" BIE movement (Speri 2019) came just before an actual deadly attack by a white supremacist is fitting. While the FBI seems intent on fabricating an entire movement out of six cases that had only the race of the perpetrators and their anger at police violence in common, there have been nearly 300 attacks perpetrated by right-wing extremists that fit legal definitions of terrorism (Speri 2019). The FBI's decision to fabricate terror threats instead of focusing on legitimate threats not only flies in the face of sound policing, it at the same time disregarded who law enforcement officials across the country identified as the leading threat against their communities.

In 2015, Duke University's Triangle Center on Terrorism and Homeland Security in collaboration with the U.S. Department of Justice issued a revealing report. Detailing the threat assessments of nearly 400 law enforcement agencies nationwide, the report identified who law enforcement officials themselves deemed the most potent, violent threat. According to the report, the vast majority of law enforcement agents (74%) said that the mostly white anti-government groups posed the greatest violent extremist threat to their agencies (Kurzan and Schanzer 2015) Of note in the report are the absence of any mention of "Black Identity Extremists" and the repeated discussion of "Al Queda Inspired Violent Extremism," a group that only 39% of law enforcement agencies deemed a threat (Kurzan and Schanzer 2015). Here again we see that law enforcement data itself exposes the false narratives surrounding black extremists while corroborating the threat to police posed by white extremists.

6 Law Enforcement's "War on Blacks"

While government and law enforcement sources alike dispel the overblown and media hyped dangers *to* police, what remains all too real are the dangers posed *by* police to the Black community. According to the website Mapping Police Violence, these were the facts in 2015 during the height of the fictitious "War on Cops" narrative:

- There were 1152 people killed by police
- Blacks were 41% of victims despite making up only 20% of the population in cities
- Police killed 104 unarmed Blacks

- Unarmed blacks were 5 times as likely to be killed by police as unarmed whites
- Only 13 of the 104 cases of police killing unarmed Blacks resulted in criminal charges being filed and only 4 of those cases resulted in convictions
- In 14 of America's 60 largest police departments, Blacks accounted for 100% of those killed by police. Those cities include St. Louis (home of Mike Brown), Cleveland (home of Tamir Rice), and Baltimore (home of Freddie Gray). Forty-one of the 60 police departments killed Blacks in numbers disproportionate to their representation in the jurisdiction (Mapping Police Violence 2015).

These numbers are indicative of the steady increase seen in Blacks being killed by police since 2013. This increase, as well as the above numbers for 2015, is all the more startling for three very important reasons. First, according to the FBI, there has been a consistent decline in violent crime nearly every year since 1999 (U.S. Department of Justice 2018). Second, the Black community has witnessed more than a 78% drop in Black violent crime since 1994 (U.S. Department of Justice 2015). And last, even if Black criminality had risen (instead of drastically dropping), and even if the "War on Cops" myth were true, that still doesn't justify the disproportionate number of Blacks being killed by cops because as pointed out above, the group most responsible for murdering cops was and is white males.

7 Turning the Corner: Guiding Principles, Community Policing, and Busy Streets: a Return to the Peelian Principles of Policing

Perhaps the best way to address the restructuring needed in the police/black community relationship is to return to the principles that framed law enforcement from its beginning. In 1829, Sir Robert Peel is credited with the creation of the London Metropolitan Police, widely viewed as the world's first modern police department (Williams 2003, 97). As the "father" of modern policing, Peel was adamant that a properly functioning police force must be deemed credible and legitimate in the eyes of the public it served. To this end, he developed nine principles that, if followed, would foster the respect and dignity sought by the community and the police alike.

His principles were:

> *Principle 1*: The basic mission for which the police exist is to prevent crime and disorder;

Principle 2: The ability of the police to perform their duties is dependent upon public approval of police existence, actions, behavior and the ability of the police to secure and maintain public respect;

Principle 3: Police must secure the willing cooperation of the public in voluntary observance of the law to be able to secure and maintain the respect of the public;

Principle 4: The degree of the cooperation of the public that can be secured diminishes proportionally to the necessity of the use of physical force;

Principle 5: Police seek and preserve public favor not by catering to public opinion, but by constantly demonstrating absolute impartial service to the law;

Principle 6: Police use physical force to the extent necessary to secure observance of the law or to restore order only when the exercise of persuasion, advice and warning is found to be insufficient;

Principle 7: Police, at all times, should maintain a relationship with the public that gives reality to the historic tradition that the police are the public and the public are the police; the police being only members of the public who are paid to give full-time attention to duties which are incumbent upon every citizen in the interests of community welfare and existence;

Principle 8: Police should always direct their action strictly towards their functions and never appear to usurp the powers of the judiciary;

Principle 9: The test of police efficiency is the absence of crime and disorder, not the visible evidence of police action in dealing with them (Williams 2003, 100).

Highlighting a few of these principles identifies both the problems of modern law enforcement as well as the starting point for solutions. For example, principle 2 links the ability of the police to perform their duties to the degree of public approval of and respect for police. Principle 4 points out that the degree of cooperation from the public is directly correlational to the use of force by police. And perhaps the most groundbreaking of all, principle 9 establishes that the benchmark of efficient policing is the *absence* of crime and disorder rather than the police's response to crime and disorder. In these examples we find the common core of respect, the thing we find most lacking in police encounters with the black community, as the crux of a fruitful and successful partnership between police and the community they police. Simply returning to these foundational principles that mandate mutual recognition and respect would go a long way in addressing and correcting many of the errors police make when dealing with the Black community.

8 Community Policing

By the end of the 1960s, policing in black communities was in a state of crisis. The crisis involved a legitimacy issue stemming from the community relations problems in the 1960s, an undermining of traditional assumptions related to police management and reform, a limited focus on what constituted police work, and the failure to recognize citizens as coproducers of police services (Walker and Katz 2018, 325–326). In recognizing the need for a transformation in policing, the law enforcement community adopted what came to be known as community policing.

Originating in the 1970s and developed throughout the 1980s, community policing is defined as "a philosophy that promotes organizational strategies that support the systematic use of partnerships and problem-solving techniques to proactively address the immediate conditions that give rise to public safety issues such as crime, social disorder, and fear of crime" (U.S. Department of Justice 2014). There are three core components of community policing. Community partnerships refer to the "collaborative partnerships between the law enforcement agencies and the individuals and organizations they serve to develop to develop solutions to problems and increase trust in police" (U.S. Department of Justice 2014). Organizational transformation involves the "alignment of organizational, structure, personnel, and information systems to support community partnerships and proactive problem solving" (U.S. Department of Justice 2014). The third component, problem solving, is "the process of engaging in the proactive and systematic examination of identified problems to develop and evaluate effective responses" (U.S. Department of Justice 2014). These components have manifested in community policing practices such as "foot or bicycle patrols, establishing neighborhood police substations, identifying neighborhood problems, dealing with disorder, organizing community meetings, or conducting community surveys" (Walker and Katz 2018, 327). Despite the increased movement toward community policing, challenges still remain rampant. For example, although nearly 90% of police departments have implemented some form of community policing program, barely 50% of police chiefs and sheriffs understand what community policing means (Walker and Katz 2018, 327).

What can be said of the effectiveness of community policing? Empirical evidence to date is mixed. In one meta-analysis, community policing was found to have a positive impact on citizen satisfaction and perceptions of disorder but no effect on police legitimacy, crime, or the fear of crime (Gill et al. 2014). In light of these shortcomings, given the violent and antagonistic history of police in the black community, and informed by the inability of reform efforts to be fully embraced and implemented, other approaches have surfaced that focus on empowering communities to play a vital role in their own transformation and well-being.

9 Busy Streets

Empowerment theory is a framework that has several applications and definitions. In the context of policing and the black community as discussed in this work, a useful definition of empowerment theory casts it as "an intentional, ongoing process centered in the local community, involving mutual respect, critical reflection, caring, and group participation through which people lacking an equal share of valued resources gain greater access to and control over those resources" (Zimmerman 2000, 43). Out of this framework community upliftment can be crafted and applied in a way that allows for the community to guide its own development and subsequently its own safety. One such empowerment theory that seeks this kind of transformation is the Busy Streets theory.

The Busy Streets theory represents a framework for increasing the safety and desirability of impoverished neighborhoods (Aiyer et al. 2015, 137–147). Seeking to provide an alternative to the deficit based, criminogenic approaches of popular social disorganization theories like Broken Windows theory, Busy Streets theory instead focuses on ways to promote social organization and positive neighborhood change. Specifically, Busy Streets theory focuses on establishing "a positive social context where social cohesion, trust, social capital, and collective efficacy thrive" (Aiyer et al. 2015, 137). "Busyness" in the community is accomplished by "actively maintained, organized spaces, thriving businesses, and visible informal (and formal) social interactions" (Aiyer et al. 2015, 137).

There are three components to the Busy Streets theory seen as integral to promoting social organization of neighborhoods and positive social change. The intracommunity component involves relationships among members of the community itself. The interactional component involves the interactions between individuals and organizations that foster trust and social capital. Finally, the behavioral component represents collaborations between residents and organizations within the community that seek the overall improvement of the neighborhood (Aiyer et al. 2015, 140). Together these three components represent the merging of individual beliefs (intracommunity), social process (interactional), and collective action (behavioral) and through their merging the groundwork for more safer communities is laid. Describing how this process unfolds, Aiyer and colleagues suggest that

> Neighborhood street activity creates opportunities for informal interactions that ultimately foster deeper social connections. These social connections also increase residents' sense of accountability and responsibility, further strengthening social control. Thus, community vibrancy creates a context that encourages interactions and social connections among residents facilitating social control and reducing crime (Aiyer et al. 2015, 142).

In short, through a community empowerment framework, Busy Streets theory provides a blueprint for the improved conditions of a community, the fostering of cohesion among residents, and the reduction of crime. We argue that, in light of the racism, antagonism, and violence that is seemingly endemic to the police/black community relationship, this kind of community-based, citizen driven approach to community safety should be given considerable attention. In the next section we offer an examination of one such organization attempting to implement just such an approach and we further argue for the replication of their model on a broad scale.

10   The 10,000 Fearless Men and Women of Atlanta

The 10,000 Fearless "is a free, 24 hour conflict resolution center founded in the spirit of Love & Unity to provide resources and training that empowers families spiritually, physically and economically, promotes peace and ultimately transforms communities" (10,000 Fearless of the South). Located in an impoverished section of metropolitan Atlanta, Georgia known as "The Bluff," the organization offers several outreach programs to the residents of the community. Examples include a food pantry offered twice a week, a community patrol/neighborhood watch program, conflict resolution services, a barber initiative providing free haircuts to community residents, and various youth programs. The idea for the 10,000 Fearless came out of a lecture delivered by Minister Louis Farrakhan, leader of the Nation of Islam, in 2016. Citing the birth of the 10,000 Fearless organization, Ashahed M. Muhammad pointed out that "During the 'Justice or Else!' tour, Minister Farrakhan called for '10,000 fearless' willing to be trained in strategies and sacrifice their lives, if necessary, to make black communities safe and decent places to live" (Muhammad 2016). As an outgrowth of this call, the goal of the 10,000 Fearless is "to promote peace, resolve conflicts, empower families and transform communities. Ultimately, make our communities a decent place to live" (Muhammad 2016).

Viewed in the context of Busy Streets theory, the 10,000 Fearless provide a fitting example of community self-empowerment and policing by their cultivation of "actively maintained, organized spaces, thriving businesses, and visible informal (and formal) social interactions" (Aiyer 2015, 137). Documenting the early work organized out of the 10,000 Fearless headquarters in 2016, one news report described how "over 160 volunteers from 30 organizations" worked to beautify The Bluff "using paint and other supplies and equipment donated by Home Depot" (Muhammad, Muhammad and Muhammad 2016). In "beautifying the neighborhood by painting houses, improving landscaping and even fixing siding on homes" (Muhammad, Muhammad and Muhammad 2016, 36), the 10,000 Fearless, from its beginning, engaged in organizing and maintaining many of the dilapidated spaces throughout The Bluff.

The 10,000 Fearless, in addition to its beautification efforts also opened up businesses. Attempting to bring economic vitality and thriving businesses to The Bluff, the 10,000 Fearless opened Your Supermarket (Muhammad 2017), a dry cleaner, and the Blue Seas restaurant specializing in "offering fresh, healthy, affordable food for the neighborhood" (Primus). Attempting to foster visibility and social interaction, many of the 10,000 Fearless' activities in The Bluff are predicated on community involvement and social interactions. Examples include professional conflict resolution services offered to deter violent encounters between neighborhood residents, street patrols made up of 10,000 Fearless volunteers and community residents, and by locating the food and clothing giveaways right on the front porch of the headquarters house and the sidewalk out front. Several residents of the neighborhood also assist the 10,000 Fearless in dispersing food/clothing to other residents and on walking street patrols, which further fosters interaction between community members.

In referencing the street patrols, some attention must be given to the effectiveness of this activity in the way of crime reduction. Responding to the safety needs of not only the neighborhood but the local university as well, the 10,000 Fearless established voluntary patrols of both The Bluff and the university campus not far from The Bluff's neighborhood. Meetings with city and campus officials resulted in a welcomed and much-needed security support on both the campus and in the neighborhood. Adorned in either jeans, t-shirt and the obligatory black baseball cap with "10,000 Fearless" in white letters, or the customary and immediately familiar dark suit and bowtie uniform of the Fruit of

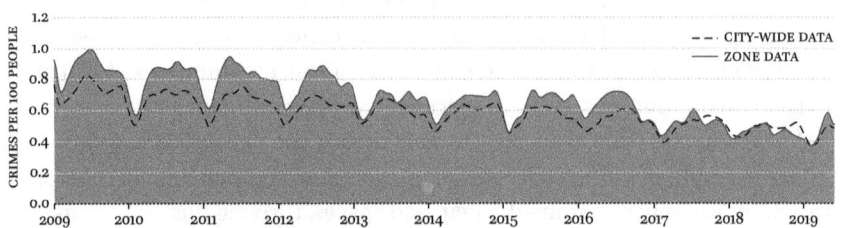

FIGURE 4.1 Crime rates for the zone containing Westside and the university center
SOURCE: AJC, CRIME IN ATL, ZONE 1. HTTPS://CRIME.AJC.COM/#ZONES/1.
THE ATLANTA JOURNAL-CONSTITUTION.

Islam (the male members of the Nation of Islam), the visibility of the men on patrol is said to have resulted in a decrease in crime over the years. While the specific impact of the 10,000 Fearless patrols is difficult to pin down, zone specific police data does indeed show a drastic decline in crime in the zone in which The Bluff is located (Zone 1). That decline coincides with the appearance and community patrols of the 10,000 Fearless in 2016 (see Figure 4.1). The noteworthy drop in crime that began in 2016 was not only a 50% decrease from 2009 levels, it subsequently gave way to levels of crime that, for the first time in a decade, were lower in The Bluff than they were for the entire city of Atlanta.

Through these and other ways the 10,000 Fearless are able to routinely engage in actions that empowered The Bluff through developing social cohesion among residents, opening businesses in the community, building trust and safety through their consistent presence, and fostering a "busyness" in the streets of Westside through their various beautification projects, food/clothing giveaways and street patrols.

11   Conclusion

From its beginnings in the slave patrols of the American south, there has been an antagonistic if not predatory relationship between the police and black Americans. This has manifested in the diverging conceptions of police between blacks and whites as well as the disproportionate, deadly actions of police toward blacks. While the dangers of policing are often overhyped, what is not overly inflated are the physical and psychological risks that law enforcement poses to the public health of marginalized groups in general and blacks specifically.

In pointing out the dire historic and current relationships with law enforcement, this article has sought to move from the data to the suggesting of theory-based alternatives toward community safety. In doing so, we've argued for an approach to community safety that draws from the time-honored principles of policing while at the same time implementing grassroots solutions based in the larger framework of community empowerment practices. By highlighting an organization currently implementing many of these community empowerment approaches, our contribution to the field of Africana Demography is one in which data informs the real-world, street level application of theoretical principles for the betterment of the lives of black people. In this way, we hope to be a catalyst for initiatives that rely less on a predatory and intransigent relationship with law enforcement and more upon the vitality, cohesion, and collective efforts of black people within their own communities.

Bibliography

10,000 Fearless Men and Women of the South. 2019. Accessed December 22, 2019. https://www.10000fearlessofthesouth.com/about-us.

Aiyer, Sophie M.; Zimmerman, Marc A.; Morrel-Samuels, Susan and Reischl, Thomas. 2015. "From Broken Windows to Busy Streets: A Community Empowerment Perspective." *Health Education & Behavior* 42 (2): 137–147.

American Public Health Association. 2015. *Addressing Law Enforcement Violence as a Public Health Issue*. Policy number 201811. https://www.apha.org/policies-and-advocacy/public-health-policy-statements/policy-database/2019/01/29/law-enforcement-violence.

Archbold, C.A. 2013. *Policing: A Text/reader*. Thousand Oaks, CA: SAGE Publications Inc.

Association for the Religious Instruction of the Negroes in Liberty County, Georgia, *Annual Report of the Missionary to the Negroes of Liberty County, Georgia*, 1834. Charleston, SC: Observer Office Press, 1834, 14.

Carter, S.L. 2015, October 29. "Policing and Oppression Have a Long History." *Bloomberg*. https://www.bloomberg.com/opinion/articles/2015-10-29/policing-and-oppression-have-a-long-history.

Drake, Bruce. 2015. "Divide Between Blacks and Whites on Police Runs Deep." *Pew Research Center* April 28, 2015. https://www.pewresearch.org/fact-tank/2015/04/28/blacks-whites-police/.

Edwards, F., Lee, H., and Esposito, M. 2019. "Risk of Being Killed by Police Use of Force in the United States by Age, Race-ethnicity, and Sex." *Proceedings of the National Academy of the Sciences* 116 (34): 16793–16798.

Ekins, Emily. 2016. "Policing in America: Understanding Public Attitudes Toward Police. Results from a National Survey." Cato Institute, December 7, 2016. https://www.cato.org/survey-reports/policing-america.

French, L.A. 2018. *The History of Policing America: from Militias and Military to the Law Enforcement of Today*. Lanham, MD: Rowman & Littlefield.

Gallup "Confidence in Institutions." https://news.gallup.com/poll/1597/confidence-institutions.aspx.

Gill, Charlotte; Weisburd, David; Telep, Cody W.; Vitter, Zoe and Bennett, Trevor. 2014. "Community-Oriented Policing to Reduce Crime, Disorder, and Fear and Increase Satisfaction and Legitimacy Among Citizens: A Systematic Review." *Journal of Experimental Criminology* 10: 418–419.

Horton, Hayward Derrick. 1999. "Critical Demography: The Paradigm of the Future?." *Sociological Forum* 14 (3): 363.

Irby, Kate. 2018. "White and Far-Right Extremists Kill More Cops, But FBI Tracks Black Extremists More Closely, Many Worry." McClatchy DC, January 24, 2018. https://www.mcclatchydc.com/news/nation-world/national/article196423174.html.

Kindy, K. and Kelly, K. 2015, April 11. "Thousands Dead, Few Prosecuted." *The Washington Post*. https://www.washingtonpost.com/sf/investigative/2015/04/11/thousands-dead-few-prosecuted/.

Kurzman, Charles and David Schanzer. 2015. "Law Enforcement Assessment of the Violent Extremist Threat." Durham, NC: Triangle Center on Terrorism and Homeland Security, June 25, 2015, 4. https://sites.duke.edu/tcths/files/2013/06/Kurzman_Schanzer_Law_Enforcement_Assessment_of_the_Violent_Extremist_Threat_final.pdf.

Mapping Police Violence. 2015. "2015 Violence Report" and "2015 Unarmed Victims." https://mappingpoliceviolence.org/.

Muhammad, Ashahed M. 2016. "Organizing and Mobilizing for Justice: a Critical Time for America as Saviors' Day Draws Near and Justice or Else! Local Organizing Committees Work Hard Nationwide." *The Final Call*, February 9, 2016.

Muhammad, Eric Ture. 2017. "Rebuilding the Hood: 10,000 Fearless Opens 'Your Supermarket'." *The Final Call*, October 10, 2017.

Muhammad, Richard B.; Muhammad, Eric Ture and Muhammad, Kenetta. 2016. "'God is in The Bluff': Rebuilding a Forgotten, Neglected Neighborhood in Atlanta." *The Final Call*, April 19, 2016.

Obasogie, O.K. and Newman, Z. 2017. "Police Violence, Use of Force Policies, and Public Health." *American Journal of Law and Medicine* 43 (2–3): 279–295.

Perry Mark J. 2015. "Is There Really a 'War on Cops'? The Data Show that 2015 Will Likely Be One of the Safest Years in History for Police." *AEIdeas* (blog), American Enterprise Institute, September 9, 2015. https://www.aei.org/carpe-diem/is-there-really-a-war-on-cops-the-data-show-that-2015-will-likely-be-one-of-the-safest-years-in-history-for-police.

Pew Research Center. 2017. *Behind the Badge* (6. "Police Views, Public Views"), January 11, 2017. https://www.pewsocialtrends.org/2017/01/11/police-views-public-views/.

Potter, G. 2013, June 25. "The History of Policing in the United States, Part 1." *Police Studies Online*, Eastern Kentucky University. https://plsonline.eku.edu/insidelook/history-policing-united-states-part-1.

Primus, Kiplyn. 2017. "The Local Take: The 10,000 Fearless Bring God to The Bluff," WCLK. https://www.wclk.com/post/local-take-10000-fearless-bring-god-bluff.

Rasmussen Reports. 2015. "58% Think There's a War on Police in America Today." *Rasmussen Reports,* September 2, 2015.

Reichel, P.L. 1988. "Southern Slave Patrols as Transitional Police Types." *American Journal of Police* 7 (2): 51–78.

Sauter, Michael B. and Charles Stockdale. 2019. "25 Most Dangerous Jobs in America." 24/7 Wall St., January 2, 2019. https://247wallst.com/special-report/2019/01/02/25-most-dangerous-jobs-in-america-2/.

Speri, Alice. 2019. "Fear of a Black Homeland: The Strange Tale of the FBI's Fictional 'Black Identity Extremism' Movement." *The Intercept,* March 23, 2019. https://theintercept.com/2019/03/23/black-identity-extremism-fbi-domestic-terrorism/.

Stinson, P.M. 2017. "Charging a Police Officer in Fatal Shooting Case is Rare, and a Conviction is Even Rarer." *Criminal Justice Faculty Publications* 80. https://scholarworks.bgsu.edu/crim_just_pub/80.

U.S. Department of Justice. 2018. "Crime in the United States." *Federal Bureau of Investigations 2018*, Table 1. https://ucr.fbi.gov/crime-in-the-u.s/2018/crime-in-the-u.s.-2018/topic-pages/tables/table-1.

U.S. Department of Justice. 2016a. "2015 Law Enforcement Officers Killed and Assaulted, Washington, DC." Washington, DC: *Federal Bureau of Investigation, 2016.* https://ucr.fbi.gov/leoka/2015/resource-pages/leoka-2015-press-relelase.pdf.

U.S. Department of Justice. 2016b. "Black Identity Extremists Likely Motivated to Target Law Enforcement Officers." Washington, DC: *Federal Bureau of Investigation, 2016.* https://ucr.fbi.gov/leoka/2015/resource-pages/leoka-2015-press-relelase.pdf.

U.S. Department of Justice. 2015. "Race and Hispanic Origin of Victims and Offenders, 2012–2015." *Bureau of Justice Statistics.* https://www.bjs.gov/content/pub/pdf/rhovo1215.pdf.

U.S. Department of Justice. 2014. "Community Policing Defined." *Community Oriented Policing Services, 2014*, 1. https://www.nationalpublicsafetypartnership.org/clearinghouse/Content/ResourceDocuments/Community%20Policing%20Defined.pdf.

U.S. Department of Labor. 2018. "National Census of Fatal Occupational Injuries in 2017." *Bureau of Justice Statistics,* December 2018. https://www.bls.gov/news.release/pdf/cfoi.pdf.

Walker, Samuel and Katz, Charles M. 2002. *The Police in America: an Introduction.* 4th ed. New York, NY: McGraw Hill.

Walker, Samuel and Katz, Charles M. 2018. *The Police in America: An Introduction.* 9th ed. New York: McGraw Hill Education, 325–326.

Waxman, O.B. 2017, May 18. "How the U.S. Got Its Police Force." *Time.* https://time.com/4779112/police-history-origins/.

Williams, Keith L. 2003. "Peel's Principles and their Acceptance by American Police: Ending 175 Years of Reinvention." *The Police Journal* 76 (2): 97.

YouGov. "Trust in Law Enforcement." 2015. April 22, 2015. http://cdn.yougov.com/cumulus_uploads/document/p4203c8nf5/tabs_HP_trust_law_enforcement_20150420.pdf.

Zimmerman, Mark A. 2000. "Empowerment Theory." In *Handbook of Community Psychology*, edited by Julian Rappaport and Edward Seidman, 43. New York: Kluwer Academic/Plenum Publishers.

CHAPTER 5

African Americans' Response to Discrimination: Does Region Matter?

Jas M. Sullivan

Discrimination involves actions, behaviors, or policies that unfairly treat individuals. Today, discrimination is mostly concealed and difficult to identify (Feagin, 1991), and often done unconsciously (Nier and Gartner, 2012; Essed, 1991). Furthermore, discrimination often manifests in different forms. One form is microaggressions or everyday discrimination, which include unfair treatment and insults that are subtle and often unconscious in nature (Essed, 2002; Delapp and Williams, 2015; Sue, 2010). Research has shown that African American men experience more discrimination than African American women (Sellers and Shelton, 2003; Krieger and Sidney, 1996; Banks et al., 2006). In one study, "77% of African American women and 84% of African American men experienced racial discrimination in one of the seven situations"—that is, at school, getting a job, at work, getting housing, getting medical care, on the street or in a public setting, and from the police or in the courts (Krieger and Sidney, 1996, 1372).

Evidence of discrimination can be seen in many areas of American society. Both African American men and women were "equally likely to report discrimination in four of the seven situations—at school, at work, getting housing, and getting medical care" (Krieger and Sidney 1996, 1372). Nowhere is this more prevalent than in employment and housing (Karlsen and Nazroo, 2002). Through field experiments, Pager and Western (2012) explored discrimination in hiring practices. Their study found that white applicants were more likely to be contacted after the interview compared to similarly situated African American and Latino candidates. In another study, Pager and Western (2012) found that while employers in New York City contended that they did not make employment decisions without regard of race, they, at the same time, held stereotypical views of minorities. Specifically, many managers stereotyped African American men as "not having a strong work ethic, being intimidating, and being prone to criminal behavior."

Benedick, Jackson and Reinoso (1994) found a significant relationship between applicant race and job offers. They found that white candidates were significantly more likely to be offered a job compared to African American candidates, even though their education and experience was nearly identical. Going even further, they found that employers were more likely to give positive comments to white candidates for jobs than to African Americans. For example, 50 percent of white candidates received at least one positive comment, such as they were the right person for the job, compared to 18 percent of African American candidates who received at least one positive comment. Moreover, white candidates were (10 percent) less likely to receive negative comments (i.e., "this is not the type of job that you would prefer") compared to African American candidates (23 percent).

Discrimination can also take place within the criminal justice system. An area that has received recent attention is discrimination in policing. For example, Neir and Gartner (2012) found that police officers are more likely to use deadly force on African Americans and Latino men compared to white men. Studies also have shown that police officers were more likely to use lethal force against unarmed African American suspects. Peruche and Plant (2009) wanted to determine if police officers' explicit racial attitudes and racial bias towards African Americans influenced their decision to use deadly force. They found a significant relationship between negative attitudes towards African Americans and the likelihood of using deadly force against unarmed African American suspects in a simulated encounter. Police officers who believed that African Americans were more prone to criminal behavior were more likely use deadly force against unarmed African American suspects.

Discrimination is also evidenced in health care and education. For example, Green et al. (2007) explored if implicit bias among physicians influenced treatment recommendations for coronary issues for African American patients. The findings show that physicians with high levels of implicit bias were less likely to recommend the proper treatment to African Americans described as uncooperative. Further, the study revealed that doctors with greater levels of implicit bias towards African Americans were more likely to describe the patients as less willing to cooperate. Subsequent studies have indicated that doctors with higher levels of implicit bias were less likely to prescribe or assess proper treatment for African American patients (Penner et al., 2012). Likewise, in education, many African American students believe that low grades and negative assessments from teachers are due to racial bias (Chavous et al., 2008). Additionally, Fisher et al. (2000) found that minority students were more likely to believe that they were dissuaded from registering for advanced classes due to their race.

Prior research has shown that discrimination has a devastating impact on physical and mental health (Williams and Mohammed, 2009; Williams, 2012;

Pascoe and Smart Richman, 2009; Utsey, et al. 2002; Williams and Williams-Morris, 2000; Pascoe and Richman, 2009; Pieterse et al. 2012; Borrell et al. 2006; Paradies, 2006). Exposure to discrimination on physical health includes substance abuse (Curtis-Boles and Jenkins-Monroe, 2001; Terrell et al., 2006; and Gibbons et al., 2004); premature biological aging (Sullivan et al., 2019); hypertension (Matthews et al., 2005; Tomfohr et al., 2010; Beatty and Matthews, 2009; Goosby et al., 2015; and Krieger and Sidney, 1996); cardiovascular disease (Udo and Grilo, 2017; Krieger et al., 2013; Chae et al., 2010); and mortality (Barnes et al., 2005). For example, Chea et al. (2010) found that discrimination and negative beliefs about one's own group are risk factors for cardiovascular disease among African American men. Sullivan et al. (2019) found that among African American and white women, discrimination was associated with biological aging, measured by telomere length. Krieger and Sidney (1996) explored whether experiences with discrimination and responses to unfair treatment affect blood pressure. Their findings suggest that those who experience discrimination and the manner one responds to discrimination impacts systolic blood pressure.

Mental effects of discrimination have been equally shown to be damaging (Schulz et al., 2006; Waloszek et al., 2016; Matthews et al., 2013; Almeida et al., 2009; Clark et al. 1999; Watkins et al., 2011). Specifically, research has shown that experiences with discrimination increase symptoms of depression (Gibbons et al., 2004) and lower self-esteem (Williams et al., 1992; Watkins et al., 2010). For example, Hammond (2012) found that there was a significant, positive relationship between discrimination and depressive symptoms African American men. However, this relationship was "stronger among African American men with high restrictive emotionality, which was limited to men older than 30 years of age" (232). In another study of African American men, Matthews et al. (2013) found that discrimination and masculine self-reliance were positively correlated with symptoms of depression. Watkins et al. (2011) explored the role of racial discrimination and mastery (i.e., "an individual's perception of their ability to control their environment") on susceptibility to depression (271). Their research found a significant, positive relationship between discrimination and depressive symptoms among men 35 to 54; however, mastery was a "protective against depressive symptoms for all men" (269). Lastly, English et al. (2014) found a positive relationship between racial discrimination and depressive symptoms one year later. Their study focused specifically on African American adolescents from 7 through 10 grades. Furthermore, "the link between experienced racial discrimination at grade 7 and depressive symptoms at grade 8 was stronger for females than for males" (1190).

The ways one deals with psychosocial stressors (i.e., discrimination) have received scant attention. Research on coping is an understudied area, as shown in a meta-analysis study by Pascoe and Smart Richman (2009). They found that out of 134 articles on discrimination, only 9 studies explored the topic of coping. Recently, however, research on coping has gained some traction, mostly focused on identifying whether it mitigates physical and mental health issues (Logan et al., 2017; Carter et al., 2017; Lazarus and Flokman, 1984; Benner et al., 2018). Research findings have shown that the way one copes with psychosocial stressors affects health outcomes—e.g., blood pressure (James et al., 1983; Subramanyam et al., 2013), hypertension (Dressler et al., 1998; Nordby et al., 1995; Somova et al., 1995), cardiovascular reactivity (Wiist and Flack, 1992; Light et al., 1995; Wigg et al., 1996; Wright et al., 1996; Merritt et al., 2004), physical activity (Bild et al., 1993; Bonham et al., 2004), cholesterol (Wiist and Flack, 1992), depressive symptoms (Neighbors et al., 2007; Matthews et al., 2013; Bronder et al., 2014; Hudson et al., 2016), and tobacco use behavior (Fernander et al., 2005).

Prior research on racial discrimination explored its presence, health effects, and coping mechanisms. While brunt of this work is in the area of presence and health effects, we know much less about the ways one mitigates a stressor such as discrimination. Consequently, the purpose of this research is to explore reactions to experiences with discrimination. More specifically, this chapter asks the following question: Do African Americans in the non-South react to discrimination differently than African Americans in the South? Unlike previous research, the uniqueness of this study is on identifying regional differences in the reactions to discrimination. Based on prior research on the impact of Southern culture on attitudes and political predisposition (Maxwell and Shields, 2011 and Jordan, 2006), the preliminary hypothesis is that region will structure reactions to discrimination.

1 Data and Methods

1.1 *Sample*

Sample participants are from the National Study of American Life (NSAL), part of the National Institute of Mental Health Collaborative Psychiatric Epidemiology Survey (CPES), conducted by the *Program for Research on Black Americans* at the University of Michigan. The NSAL, a nationally representative sample of African Americans, was conducted between 2001 and 2003. All respondents were aged 18 and over. In the first phase, data were collected in face-to-face interviews using a computer-assisted program. After that, the second phase of the study involved completing a self-administrated questionnaire referred to as the NSAL Adult Re-Interview (RIW). Only African American respondents who completed both phases were included in the analysis—a total of 2,137 respondents.

1.1.1 Dependent Variables

Reactions to Discrimination: The NSAL asks African American respondents their reactions to experiences of discrimination. The exact wording of the question is as follows: How did you respond to this/these experience(s) of discrimination? Please tell me if you did each of the following things: The three reactions examined as dependent variables are as follows: (1) tried to do something about it; (2) got mad; and (3) prayed about it. Each item is coded using a four-point ordinal scale: from strongly disagree to strongly agree. Each of the three questions will be considered a dependent variable in the analysis.

1.1.2 Independent Variables

The primary independent variable is region. *Region* was coded as non-South and South. The other independent variables were selected based on *a priori* theory; these include gender, age, education, income, frequency of church attendance, living in a rural setting, and day-to-day discrimination. Age was coded as continuous. Respondents were simply asked to indicate their age at the time of the survey. *Education* was coded into three categories of school completion: 0–11years, 12 years, 13–15 years, and greater than or equal to 16 years. *Income* was coded as: less than $9,999; $10, 000–$14,999; $15,000–$24,999; $25, 000–$49,999; and $50, 000 or more. *Frequency of religious attendance* was coded as: less than once a year, few times a year, a few times a month, at least once a week, and nearly every day. *Rural setting* is accounted for because there is a higher share of African Americans living in rural areas in the South than in the non-South. NSAL does not have a measure of whether the respondent currently lives in a rural area, but the data include the county in which respondents live. Respondents were coded as living in a rural area or nonrural area based on the percent of individuals in the county who are designated as living in a rural area according to the U.S. Census.

Day-to-Day Discrimination measures respondents' experiences with "routine" and relatively minor day-to-day interpersonal experiences of unfair treatment (Hunte et al., 2012, 112). It is often referred to as "microaggressions" (Essed, 1991; Solorzano, 2000; Sue et al., 2007), and involves "character assaults" (Kessler et al., 1999, 212). Nine questions were used to capture the frequency of experiencing unfair treatment: being treated with less courtesy than others; being treated with less respect than others; receiving poorer restaurant service than others; being treated as if you are not as smart as others; others being afraid of you; being perceived as dishonest by others; people acting like they are better than me; being called names and insulted by others; and feeling threatened or harassed. Responses categories ranged from "never" (score =1) to "almost every day" (score = 6). Responses were summed and ranged from a low of 9 to a high of 54. Higher scores indicate higher frequencies of day-to-day discrimination.

1.2 Analytical Strategy and Model Selection

Since the outcome variables are binary (two response options ranging from no to yes), I estimated models for each of the three reactions to discrimination with logistic regression. For each type of reaction to discrimination, three separate models were analyzed—i.e., prayed about it, got mad, and did something about it. Presented in the models (See Table 5.3) are odds ratio estimates, 95% confidence intervals, and p-values. Finally, we included the standard demographic controls. Sample weights were created and used to account for non-response variations.

2 Results

2.1 Descriptive Characteristics

Table 5.1 presents demographic characteristics forNthe Study sample,Lin which 58% of the sample were women, while 41 percent were men. Further, 24% had less than a high school education, 23% had a household income of 50,000 or more, and 50% lived in the South. Mean day-to-day discrimination was 20.4, while mean age was 43. When asked about frequency of religious attendance, the majority of the respondents fell in the following the categories: a few times a year (21%), a few times a month (25%) and at least once a week (36%).

Table 5.2 presents the responses for African Americans' reactions to discrimination. FiNding indicate that 62% reported they prayed about it, in reacting to discrimination, while 37% said no. Further, 43% got mad about discrimination, while 56% said they did not get mad when confronting discrimination. In terms of doing something about it, as a reaction to discrimination, 30% indicated they tried to do something, while 69% did not do anything. Chi-squared and t-tests were analyzed to compare differences between non-Southern and Southern respondents in response to demographic and discrimination questions. Responses show that for reactions to discrimination, there was a Significant Lifference between non-Southern and Southern groups. There was also a

TABLE 5.1 Demographic characteristics, 2001–2003 National Survey of American Life (N=2,137)

	Total sample	Non-South	South	p-value*
N	2137	884	1198	
Day-to-day discrimination, wt. mean (SD)	20.43 (8.16)	20.97 (7.51)	19.89 (8.73)	0.13
Age, wt. mean (SD)	43.73 (15.05)	43.80 (14.01)	41.79 (15.88)	0.06
Gender, n (wt. %)				
Male	678 (41.06)	307 (42.54)	371 (39.58)	0.18
Female	1404 (58.94)	577 (57.46)	827 (60.42)	
Education, n (wt. %)				
0–11 years	530 (24.00)	197 (20.42)	333 (27.57)	5.08
12 years	784 (36.42)	307 (33.38)	477 (39.45)	
13–15 years	475 (24.90)	219 (27.28)	256 (22.54)	
Greater than or equal to 16 years	293 (14.67)	161 (18.92)	132 (10.43)	
Income, n (wt. %)				
Less than $9,999	404 (16.05)	174 (15.50)	230 (16.60)	0.03
$10,000–$14,999	248 (10.43)	102 (9.66)	146 (11.20)	
$15,000–$24,999	438 (19.27)	162 (17.11)	276 (21.43)	
$25,000–$49,999	618 (30.91)	256 (29.88)	362 (31.94)	
$50,000 or more	374 (23.33)	190 (27.85)	184 (18.83)	
Frequency of religious attendance, n (wt. %)				
Less than once a year	189 (11.6)	115 (15.64)	74 (7.20)	0.00
Few times a year	400 (21.42)	197 (24.87)	203 (18.07)	
A few times a month	506 (25.79)	196 (23.75)	310 (27.78)	
At least once a week	722 (36.20)	265 (31.96)	457 (40.32)	
Nearly every day	117 (5.22)	36 (3.79)	81 (6.61)	
Rural setting, n (wt. %)				

TABLE 5.1 Demographic characteristics, 2001–2003 National Survey of American Life (N=2,137) (cont.)

	Total sample	Non-South	South	p-value*
Rural	810 (35.98)	199 (20.94)	611 (51.13)	0.00
Urban	1247 (64.02)	678 (79.06)	569 (48.87)	

SOURCE: NATIONAL SURVEY OF AMERICAN LIFE (NSAL).
*p-value is chi-square for categorical variables and t-test for continuous variables.

TABLE 5.2 Reactions to discrimination, 2001–2003 National Survey of American Life (N=2,137)

	N (Weighted %)			
	Total	Non-South	South	p-value
Prayed about it				0.00
Yes	1030	415 (56.52)	615 (53.75)	
No	545	269 (43.48)	276 (41.11)	
Total	1575	684	891	
Got mad				0.00
Yes	684	339 (48.98)	345 (42.10)	
No	891	345 (45.78)	546 (54.22)	
Total	1575	684	891	
Tried to do something about it				0.00
Yes	458	251 (34.99)	207 (40.55)	
No	1118	434 (65.01)	684 (75.12)	
Total	1576	685	891	

SOURCE: NATIONAL SURVEY OF AMERICAN LIFE (NSAL).

significant difference between non-Southern and Southern groups on demographic questions, specifically, income and religious attendance.

2.2 *Prayed about It*

There was a statistically significant association between region and "praying" as a reaction to discrimination. See Table 5.3, (Model 1). Specifically, those from

TABLE 5.3 Odds ratios for reactions to discrimination by region and demographic characteristics, 2001–2003 National Survey of American Life

	Prayed about it		Got mad		Tried to do something about it	
	OR (95% CI)	p	OR (95% CI)	p	OR (95% CI)	p
Region		0.02		0.01		0.02
South vs. Non-South	1.30 (1.04, 1.63)		0.70 (0.53, 0.92)		0.68 (0.49, 0.95)	
Frequency of religious attendance		0.00		0.43		0.10
Few times a year vs. Less than once a year	1.62 (1.08, 2.43)		1.09 (0.67, 1.77)		1.14 (0.71, 1.82)	
A few times a month vs. Less than once a year	2.45 (1.59, 3.77)		0.89 (0.60, 1.33)		1.29 (0.82, 2.02)	
At least once a week vs. Less than once a year	4.19 (2.64, 6.67)		0.84 (0.53, 1.32)		1.80 (1.10, 2.94)	
Nearly every day vs. Less than once a year	6.64 (3.46, 12.71)		0.65 (0.35, 1.20)		1.91 (0.92, 3.97)	
Rural setting		0.52		0.68		0.03
Nonrural vs. Rural	1.08 (0.85, 1.37)		0.95 (0.72, 1.23)		1.42 (1.03, 1.97)	
Sex		0.02		0.00		0.04
Female vs. Male	1.47 (1.05, 2.06)		2.17 (1.65, 2.85)		1.32 (1.00, 1.73)	
Age	1.01 (1.00, 1.02)	0.14	1.00 (0.99, 1.01)	0.81	1.00 (0.99, 1.01)	0.93
Education		0.11		0.57		0.07

TABLE 5.3 Odds ratios for reactions to discrimination by region and demographic characteristics, 2001–2003 National Survey of American Life (*cont.*)

	Prayed about it		Got mad		Tried to do something about it	
	OR (95% CI)	p	OR (95% CI)	p	OR (95% CI)	p
12 years vs. 0–11	1.17 (0.76, 1.82)		0.84 (0.59, 1.18)		0.99 (0.69, 1.43)	
13–15 vs. 0–11	0.92 (0.61, 1.39)		1.07 (0.69, 1.67)		1.66 (1.07, 2.59)	
≥16 vs. 0–11	0.67 (0.41, 1.11)		0.96 (0.57, 1.61)		1.23 (0.76, 1.99)	
Income		0.00		0.03		0.67
10,000–14,000 vs. ≤ 9,999	1.21 (0.64, 2.27)		1.15 (0.75, 1.76)		1.56 (0.85, 2.86)	
15,000–24,000 vs. ≤ 9,999	1.43 (0.88, 2.32)		1.47 (0.99, 2.18)		1.27 (0.77, 2.07)	
25,000–49,000 vs ≤ 9,999	0.88 (0.49, 1.58)		1.50 (1.02, 2.21)		1.14 (0.72, 1.82)	
50,000 or more vs ≤ 9,999	0.59 (0.36, 0.95)		1.89 (1.29, 2.76)		1.11 (0.71, 1.75)	
Day-to-day discrimination	1.03 (1.01, 1.05)	0.01	1.05 (1.03, 1.07)	0.00	1.04 (1.02, 1.06)	0.00

SOURCE: NATIONAL SURVEY OF AMERICAN LIFE (NSAL).

the South (vs. non-South) were 30% (OR: 1.30; 95% CI: 1.03, 1.63) more likely to pray about it. Compared to those with less income (<9,999), African Americans whose income was $50,000 or more were 41% less likely (OR: 0.59; 95% CI: 0.36, 0.95) to pray as a reaction to discrimination. More frequency of religious attendance (OR: 6.64; 95% CI: 3.46, 12.71), females (OR: 1.47; 95% CI: 1.05, 2.06), and those experiencing greater day-to-day discrimination (OR: 1.03; 95% CI: 1.01, 1.05) were more likely to pray about it.

2.3 Got Mad

In Table 5.3 (Model 2), there was a statistically significant association between region and "getting mad" as a reaction to discrimination. Specifically, those from the South (vs. non-South) were 31% (OR: 0.69; 95% CI: 0.52, 0.96) less likely to get mad. Compared to those with less income (<9,999), African Americans whose income was between 25,000 to 49,999 and 50,000 and over were 50% and 88% more likely (OR: 1.50; 95% CI: 1.02, 2.21 and OR: 1.88; 95% CI: 1.29, 2.75) to get mad as a reaction to discrimination. Females (OR: 2.17; 95% CI: 1.65, 2.06), and those experiencing greater day-to-day discrimination (OR: 1.04; 95% CI: 1.03, 1.06) were more likely to get mad. In other words, females (vs. males) were 117% more likely to get mad, and those experiencing greater frequency of discrimination were 4% more likely to get mad as a reaction to discrimination.

2.4 Do Something about It

In Table 5.3 (Model 3), there was a statistically significant association between region and "trying to do something" as a reaction to discrimination. Specifically, those from the South (vs. non-South) were 32% (OR: 0.6; 95% CI: 0.52, 0.96) less likely to try to do something. Compared to those who live in rural areas, African Americans who reside in nonrural areas were 42% more likely (OR: 1.42; 95% CI: 1.02, 1.96) to try to do something as a reaction to discrimination. Females (OR: 1.31; 95% CI: 1.00, 1.73), and those experiencing greater day-to-day discrimination (OR: 1.04; 95% CI: 1.02, 1.05) were more likely to try to do something. In other words, females (vs. males) were 31% more likely to try to do something, and those experiencing greater frequency of discrimination were 4% more likely to try to do something as a reaction to discrimination.

3 Discussion

The findings in this chapter show that there is a differing reaction among African Americans in the non-South and African Americans in the South, in dealing with discrimination. Specifically, African Americans in the Non-SSuth weLe more likely to "try to do something" and "got mad," while African Americans in the South, when experiencing discrimination, were more likely to "pray about it." From prior research, there is some evidence that region plays a crucial role in structuring attitudes and behavior; however, most of this research has primarily focused on the effect of Southern culture on whites' predispositions and racial attitudes (Maxwell and Shields, 2011; Barth and Noel 1972; Simpson and Yinger 1972). For example, research indicates that white Southerners have had more conservative attitudes than other areas of the United States (Weakliem and Biggert, 1999; Edgell and Tranby, 2007). Specifically, Southerners show higher levels of racial intolerance and resistance to racial integration (Reed 1983; Taylor et al., 1978; Campbell 1971; Miller 1981) and support for certain roles for men and women in many facets of life (Campbell and McCammon, 2005; Odem, 1995; McCammon et al., 2007). While there this considerable debate as to whether differences in these sentiments (and others) have narrowed among Northerners and Southerners (Campbell and Marsden, 2012), there is no denying that region has an enormous impact on shaping white's attitudes and behaviors.

However, the role of region in shaping African Americans' attitudes and behaviors are much murkier. More recently, there has been some research on African Americans and regional influence. For example, Sullivan et al. (2017) explored the effects of Southern culture on the attitudes and political predisposition of Southern African Americans. Specifically, they look at whether African Americans in the non-South have a more positive opinion of the core American values than African Americans who reside outside the South. These values include national pride (i.e., proud to be American), work ethic (i.e., you only need to work hard to succeed), and authoritarianism (i.e., obedience and respect for are most important virtues children should learn). The findings show that African Americans in the South report "higher support for American values than their non-Southern counterparts, in national pride and authoritarianism, but not on work ethic" (Sullivan et al., 2017, 10), which is similar to white Southerners. The question then to ask is the following: Why would African Americans in the South hold such strong support for American values more than non-Southerners, despite a history of severe discrimination and oppression?

There are several possible arguments. The first is that region serves as a powerful socialization agent. Specifically, African Americans may have learned these values for reasons of survival, "in order to protect and build upon gains made in the Civil Rights movement" (10). Similarly, why would African Americans in the South more willing to "pray," than to "do something about it" when experiencing discrimination? The explanation is the same, as the one above—for survival reasons. Maybe "doing something about it" and "getting mad" could potentially reverse the hard-fought gains or more importantly, make future gains more difficult.

Another possible explanation of the findings is that African Americans in the South experience instances of discrimination so frequently that "getting mad" or "doing something about it" won't positively change the situation. Or, it could be that it's just an added physical or psychological burden, energy best spent on other areas of life. Both overt and covert forms of discrimination have always been part of the fabric of the South. While slavery and Jim Crow laws have shaped the South, so have racial stereotypes. Winthrop Jordan (2006) so pointedly wrote the following:

There is evidence in the 17th and 18th centuries of virtually all the imputations that can be found today. Expressions of these beliefs have appeared in such disparate media as jokes; informal and formal speech; symbols—human, bestial, and otherwise; locker-room walls; the Congressional Record; and somber scientific treatises. Such stereotypes and their primary animating energies include the well-hung male and the hot and easy female (sexual aggression), shiftlessness (imposed social role), dark fingernail moons in light-skinned individuals (inherency, the taint of ancestry or "blood"), affinity with apes (sexuality, historical happenstance, and supposed physiognomic attributes), peculiar musicality (cultural reality) (149).

While circumstances have changed over centuries and decades, dramatic inequalities and negative African American stereotypes and discrimination endure. Jordan (2006) writes, "Racial attitudes in the South have been peculiar, not for their existence or their content, but for their virulence, saliency, pervasiveness, and the predisposition of white people" (151). How did African Americans in the South respond to this bombardment of stereotypes and acts of discrimination? According to Jordan (2006): "The reaction of blacks to this barrage has shown great variability and ambivalence. For many years, blacks could not openly or safely express their attitudes. Undoubtedly many blacks acquiesced to or embraced the value whites placed..." (149). Consequently, it is not surprising that region could play a part in African Americans' reactions to experiences with discrimination, in that, for African Americans in the South, discrimination (whether explicit or implicit) is so pervasive in the South that it may prove a waste of time and energy confronting each occurrence. It is possible that African Americans at a young age, in the South, are socialized by parents, peers, and society on ways to deal with discrimination. Maybe dealing with it overtly is not one of them.

We know much more about the way region (especially the South) has shaped white attitudes. Jordan (2006) writes, "As the controlling group, whites have formalized and institutionalized their attitudes through literature, scientific dogma, laws, institutions, the economy, and enforced interracial etiquette" (150). However, for the better part of American history, research on African American attitudes was inadequate. According to Jordan (2006), "Black attitudes are especially difficult to assess because American society has discouraged their open expression to whites and even to other blacks, as well as self-acknowledgment" (150). Today, there is an abundance of research in every field of study on African American attitudes and behaviors; however, there is limited amount of research that, specifically, explores the role of region in shaping African Americans' attitude and beliefs.

It is essential that future research control for region, since region is in many ways a powerful socializing agent. For example, a more robust analysis should explore the ways region affects coping, not just reaction to discrimination, as I have done in this chapter. Questions could focus on whether African Americans in the South more likely to use "problem-focused coping" vs. "emotion focused coping" than non-South African Americans. Along these lines, how does region interact with the amount of discrimination experienced in effecting coping strategies? Another line of research could explore whether region and discrimination more broadly affect health behavior. As this exploratory research shows, region plays an important role in affecting African Americans' reaction to discrimination; however, much more research is needed.

Bibliography

Almeida, J.; Johnson, R.M.; Corliss, H.L.; Molnar, B.E.; and Azrael, D. 2009. Emotional distress among LGBT youth: The influence of perceived discrimination based on sexual orientation. *Journal of Youth and Adolescence*, 38, 1001–1014.

Banks, K.H.; Kohn-Wood, L.P.; and Spencer, M. 2006. An examination of the African American experience of everyday discrimination and symptoms of psychological distress. *Community Mental Health Journal*, 42, 555–570.

Barnes, L.L.; de Leon, C.F.M.; Lewis, T.T.; Bienias, J.L.; Wilson, R.S.; and Evans, D.A. 2008. Perceived discrimination and mortality in a population-based study of older adults. *American Journal of Public Health*, 98, 1241–1247.

Barth, E. and Noel, D. 1972. Conceptual frameworks for the analysis of race relations: An evaluation, *Social Forces*, 50, 333–348.

Beatty, D.L. and Matthews, K.A. 2009. Unfair treatment and trait anger in relation to nighttime ambulatory blood pressure in African American and white adolescents. *Psychosomatic Medicine*, 71, 813–820.

Bendick Jr, M.; Jackson, C.; and Reinoso, V. 1994. Measuring employment discrimination through controlled experiments. *The Review of Black Political Economy*, 23, 25–48.

Benner, A.D.; Wang, Y.; Shen, Y.; Boyle, A.E.; Polk, R.; and Cheng, Y.P. 2018. Racial/ethnic discrimination and well-being during adolescence: A meta-analytic review. *American Psychologist*, 73, 855–883.

Bild, D.E.; Jacobs, D.R.; Sidney, S.; Haskell, W.L.; Andersen, N.; and Overman, A. 1993. Physical activity in young black and white women the CARDIA Study. *Annals of Epidemiology*, 3, 636–644.

Bonham, V.L.; Sellers, S.L.; and Neighbors, H.W. 2004. John Henryism and self-reported physical health among high–socioeconomic status African American men. *American Journal of Public Health*, 94, 737–738.

Borrell, L.N.; Kiefe, C.I.; Williams, D.R.; Diez-Roux, A.V.; and Gordon-Larsen, P. 2006. Self-reported health, perceived racial discrimination, and skin color in African Americans in the CARDIA study. *Social Science & Medicine*, 63, 1415–1427.

Bronder, E.C.; Speight, S.L.; Witherspoon, K.M.; and Thomas, A.J. 2014. John Henryism, depression, and perceived social support in black women. *Journal of Black Psychology*, 40, 115–137.

Campbell, A. 1971. White attitudes toward black people. Institute for Social Research: University of Michigan.

Campbell, K.E. and Marsden, P.V. 2012. Gender role attitudes since 1972: Are southerners distinctive? In P.V. Marsden (ed.) *Social Trends in American Life: Findings from the General Social Survey since 1972*. Princeton: Princeton University Press.

Campbell, K.E. and McCammon, H. 2005. Elizabeth Blackwell's heirs: women as physicians in the United States, 1880–1920. *Work and Occupations*, 32, 290–318.

Carter, R.T.; Lau, M.Y.; Johnson, V.; and Kirkinis, K. 2017. Racial discrimination and health outcomes among racial/ethnic minorities: A meta-analytic review. *Journal of Multicultural Counseling and Development*, 45, 232–259.

Chae, D.H.; Lincoln, K.D.; Adler, N.E.; and Syme, S.L. 2010. Do experiences of racial discrimination predict cardiovascular disease among African American men? The moderating role of internalized negative racial group attitudes. *Social Science & Medicine*, 71, 1182–1188.

Chavous, T.M.; Rivas-Drake, D.; Smalls, C.; Griffin, T.; and Cogburn, C. 2008. Gender matters, too: The influences of school racial discrimination and racial identity on academic engagement outcomes among African American adolescents. *Developmental Psychology*, 44, 637–654.

Clark, R.; Anderson, N.B.; Clark, V.R.; and Williams, D.R. 1999. Racism as a stressor for African Americans. A biopsychosocial model. *American Psychologist*, 54, 805–816.

Condran, J.G. 1979. Changes in white attitudes toward blacks, 1969–1977. *Public Opinion Quarterly*, 43, 463–476.

Curtis-Boles, H., and Jenkins-Monroe, V. 2000. Substance abuse in African American women. *Journal of Black Psychology*, 26, 450–469.

Delapp, R. and Williams, M.T. 2015. *The Behavior Therapist*, April edition, 101–105.

Dressler, W.W.; Bandon, J.R.; and Naggers, Y.H. 1998. John Henryism, gender, and arterial blood pressure in an African American community. *Psychosomatic Medicine*, 60, 620–624.

Edgell, P. and Tranby, E. 2007. Religious influences on understandings of racial inequality in the United States. *Social Problems*, 54, 263–88.

English, D.; Lambert, S.F.; and Ialongo, N.S. 2014. Longitudinal associations between experienced racial discrimination and depressive symptoms in African American adolescents. *Developmental Psychology*, 50, 1190–1196.

Essed, P. 1991. *Understanding Everyday Racism*. Newbury Park, CA: Sage.

Essed, P. 2002. Everyday racism. In D.T. Goldberg and J. Solomos (Eds.), *A Companion to Racial and Ethnic Studies*, 202–217. Malden, MA: Blackwell.

Feagin, J.R. 1991. The continuing significance of race: Anti-black discrimination in public places. *American Sociological Review*, 56, 101–116.

Fernander, A.F.; Patten, C.A.; Schroeder, D.R.; Stevens, S.R.; Eiermann, K.M.; and Hurt, R.D. 2005. Exploring the association of John Henry active coping and education on smoking behavior and nicotine dependence among blacks in the USA. *Social Science & Medicine*, 60, 491–500.

Fisher, C.B.; Wallace, S.A.; and Fenton, R.E. 2000. Discrimination distress during adolescence. *Journal of Youth and Adolescence*, 29, 679–695.

Gibbons, F.; Gerrard, M.; Cleveland, M.J.; Wills, T.A.; and Brody, G. 2004. Perceived discrimination and substance use in African American parents and their children: A panel study. *Journal of Personality and Social Psychology*, 86, 517–529.

Goosby, B.J.; Malone, S.; Richardson, E.A.; Cheadle, J.E.; and Williams, D.T. 2015. Perceived discrimination and markers of cardiovascular risk among low-income African American youth. *American Journal of Human Biology*, 27, 546–552.

Green, A.R.; Carney, D.; Pallin, D.; Ngo, L.; Raymond, K.; Iezzoni, L.; and Banaji, M.R. 2007. Implicit bias among physicians and its prediction of thrombolysis decisions for black and white patients. *Journal of General Internal Medicine*, 22, 1231–1238.

James, S.A.; Hartnett, S.A.; and Alsek, W.D. 1983. John Henryism and blood pressure differences among black men. *Journal of Behavioral Medicine*, 6, 259–278.

Jordan, W. 2006. Racial Attitudes. In C.R. Wilson (ed.) *New Encyclopedia of Southern Culture*. Chapel Hill: University of North Carolina Press.

Karlsen, S. and Nazroo, J. 2002. Relation between racial discrimination, social class, and health among ethnic minority groups. *American Journal of Public Health*, 92, 624–631.

Krieger, N.; Waterman, P.D.; Kosheleva, A.; Chen, J.T., Smith, K.W., Carney, D.R., Bennett, G.G.; Williams, D.R.; Thornhill, G.; and Freeman, E.R. 2013. Racial discrimination and cardiovascular disease risk: My body my story. Study of 1005 US-born black and white community health center participants (US). *PloS One*, 8.

Krieger, N. and Sidney, S. 1996. Racial discrimination and blood pressure: The CARDIA study of young black and white adults. *American Journal of Public Health*, 86, 1370–1378.

Lazarus, R.S. and Folkman, S. 1984. *Stress, Appraisal, and Coping*. New York, NY: Springer.

Light, K.C.; Brownley, K.A.; Turner, J.R.; Hinderliter, A.L.; Girdler, S.S.; Sherwood, A.; and Anderson, N.B. 1995. Job status and high-effort coping influence work blood pressure in women and blacks. *Hypertension*, 25, 554–559.

Logan, J.G.; Barksdale, D.J.; James, S.A.; and Chien, L.C. 2017. John Henryism active coping, acculturation, and psychological health in Korean immigrants. *Journal of Transcultural Nursing*, 28, 168–178.

Matthews, D.D.; Hammond, W.P.; Nuru-Jeter, A.; Cole-Lewis, Y.; and Melvin, T. 2013. Racial discrimination and depressive symptoms among African-American men: The mediating and moderating roles of masculine self-reliance and John Henryism. *Psychology of Men & Masculinities*, 14, 35.

Matthews, D.D.; Powell, W.A.; Nuru-Jeter, A.; Cole-Lewis, Y.; and Melvin, T. 2013. Racial discrimination and depressive symptoms among African-American men. *Psychology of Men & Masculinities*, 14, 35–46.

Matthews, K.A.; Salomon, K.; Kenyon, K.; and Zhou, F. 2005. Unfair treatment, discrimination, and ambulatory blood pressure in black and white adolescents. *Health Psychology*, 24, 258–265.

Maxwell, A. and Shields, T. (Eds.) 2011. *Unlocking V.O. Key, Jr.: Southern Politics for the Twenty-first Century*. Fayetteville, AR: University of Arkansas Press.

McCammon, H.J.; Muse, C,; Newman, H.; and Terrell, T.M. 2007. Movement framing and discursive opportunity structures: The political successes of the U.S. women's jury movements. *American Sociological Review*, 72, 725–49.

Merritt, M.M.; Bennett, G.G.; Williams, R.B.; Sollers, J.J.; and Thayer, J.F. 2004. Low educational attainment, John Henryism, and cardiovascular reactivity to and recovery from personally relevant stress. *Psychosomatic Medicine*, 66, 49–55.

Neighbors, H.W.; Njai, R.; and Jackson, J.S. 2007. Race, ethnicity, John Henryism, and depressive symptoms: The national survey of American life adult re-interview. *Research in Human Development*, 4, 71–87.

Nier, J.A. and Gaertner, S.L. 2012. The challenge of detecting contemporary forms of discrimination. *Journal of Social Issues*, 68, 207–220.

Nordby, G.; Ekeberg, Ø.; Knardahl, S.; and Os, I. 1995. A double-blind study of psychosocial factors in 40-year-old women with essential hypertension. *Psychotherapy and Psychosomatics*, 63, 142–150.

Odem, M.E. 1995. *Delinquent Daughters: Protecting and Policing Adolescent Female Sexuality in the United States, 1885–1920*. Chapel Hill: University of North Carolina Press.

Paradies, Y. 2006. A systematic review of empirical research on self-reported racism and health. *International Journal of Epidemiology*, 35, 888–901.

Pascoe, E.A. and Smart Richman, L. 2009. Perceived discrimination and health: A meta-analytic review. *Psychological Bulletin*, 135, 531–554.

Penner, L.A.; Eggly, S.; Griggs, J.; Underwood III, W.; Orom, H.; and Albrecht, T.L. 2012. Life-threatening disparities: the treatment of black and white cancer patients. *Journal of Social Issues*, 68, 328–357.

Peruche, M. and Plant, E.A. 2006. The correlates of law enforcement officers' automatic and controlled race-based responses to criminal suspects. *Basic and Applied Social Psychology*, 28, 193–199.

Pieterse, A.L.; Todd, N.R.; Neville, H.A.; and Carter, R.T. 2012. Perceived racism and mental health among black American adults: A meta-analytic review. *Journal of Counseling Psychology*, 59, 1–9.

Reed, J. 1983. *Southerners: The Social Psychology of Sectionalism*. Chapel Hill: University of North Carolina Press.

Schulz, A.; Williams, D.; Israel, B.A.; Becker, A.; Parker, E.A.; James, S.A.; and Jackson, J.S. 2000. Unfair treatment, neighborhood effects, and mental health in the Detroit metropolitan area. *Journal of Health and Social Behavior*, 41, 314–342.

Sellers, R.M. and Shelton, J.N. 2003. The role of racial identity in perceived racial discrimination. *Journal of Personality and Social Psychology*, 84, 1079–1092.

Simpson, G.E. and Yinger, J.M. 1972. *Racial and Cultural Minorities: An Analysis of Prejudice and discrimination*. New York: Harper & Row.

Somova, L.I.; Diarra, K.; and Jacobs, T.Q. 1995. Psychophysiological study of hypertension in black, Indian and white African students. *Stress and Health*, 11, 105–111.

Subramanyam, M.A.; James, S.; Diez-Roux, A.; Hickson, D.; Sarpong, D.; Sims, M.; Taylor, H.; and Wyatt, S. 2013. Socioeconomic status, John Henryism and blood pressure among African-Americans in the Jackson Heart Study. *Social Science & Medicine*, 93, 139–146.

Sue, D.W. 2010. *Microaggressions in Everyday Life: Race, Gender, and Sexual Orientation*. Hoboken: John Wiley & Sons.

Sullivan, S.; Hammadah, M.; Al Mheid, I.; Shah, A.; Sun, Y.V.; Kutner, M.; Ward, L.; Blackburn, E.; Zhao, J.; Lin, J.; and Bremner, J.D. 2019. An investigation of racial/ethnic and sex differences in the association between experiences of everyday discrimination and leukocyte telomere length among patients with coronary artery disease. *Psychoneuroendocrinology*, 106, 122–128.

Taylor, D.G.; Sheatsley, P.B.; and Greeley, A.M. 1978. Attitudes toward racial integration. *Scientific American*, 238, 42–49.

Terrell, F.; Miller, A.R.; Foster, K.; and Watkins, C.E. 2006. Racial discrimination induced anger and alcohol use among black adolescents. *Adolescence*, 41, 485–492.

Tomfohr, L.; Cooper, D.C.; Mills, P.J.; Nelesen, R.A.; and Dimsdale, J.E. 2010. Everyday discrimination and nocturnal blood pressure dipping in black and white Americans. *Psychosomatic Medicine*, 72, 266–272.

Udo, T. and Grilo, C.M. 2017. Cardiovascular disease and perceived weight, racial, and gender discrimination in US adults. *Journal of Psychosomatic Research*, 100, 83–88.

Utsey, S.O.; Payne, Y.A.; Jackson, E.S.; and Jones, A.M. 2002. Race-related stress, quality of life indicators, and life satisfaction among elderly African Americans. *Cultural Diversity & Ethnic Minority Psychology*, 8, 224–233.

Waloszek, J.M.; Woods, M.J.; Byrne, M.L.; Nicholas, C.L.; Bei, B.; Murray, G.; Raniti, M.; Allen, N.B.; and Trinder, J. 2016. Nocturnal indicators of increased cardiovascular risk in depressed adolescent girls. *Journal of Sleep Research*, 25, 216–224.

Watkins, D.C.; Hudson, D.L.; Caldwell, C.H.; Siefert, K.; and Jackson, J.S. 2011. Discrimination, mastery, and depressive symptoms among African American men. *Research on Social Work Practice*, 21, 269–277.

Watkins, D.C.; Hudson, D.L.; Howard Caldwell, C.; Siefert, K.; and Jackson, J.S. 2010. Discrimination, mastery, and depressive symptoms among African American men. *Research on Social Work Practice*, 21, 269–277.

Weakliem, D.L. and Biggert, R. 1999. "Region and political opinion in the contemporary United States." *Social Forces*, 77, 863–86.

Wigg, S.; Wright, E.; Breach, P.; and Wilson, J.D. 1996. Is it diabetes mellitus or Munchausen's syndrome? *Australian and New Zealand Journal of Medicine*, 26, 841.

Wiist, W.H. and Flack, J.M. 1992. A Test of the John Henryism hypothesis: Cholesterol and blood pressure. *Journal of Behavioral Medicine*, 15, 15–29.

Williams, D.R.; Takeuchi, D.; and Adair, R. 1992. Socioeconomic status and psychiatric disorder and African Americans and Whites. *Social Forces*, 71, 179–194.

Williams, D.R. and Mohammed, S.A. 2009. Discrimination and racial disparities in health: Evidence and needed research. *Journal of Behavioral Medicine*, 32, 20–47.

Williams, D.R. 2012. Miles to go before we sleep: Racial inequities in health. *Journal of Health and Social Behavior*, 53, 279–295.

Williams, D.R. and Williams-Morris, R. 2000. Racism and mental health: The African American experience. *Ethnicity & Health*, 5, 243–268.

Wright, L.B.; Treiber, F.A.; Davis, H.; and Strong, W.B. 1996. Relationship of John Henryism to cardiovascular functioning at rest and during stress in youth. *Annals of Behavioral Medicine*, 18, 146–150.

PART 3

Africana Demography and Bridging Racial Gaps

∴

CHAPTER 6

Rethinking Black Families in Poverty: Postcolonial Critiques and Critical Race Possibilities

Deadric Williams

Black families are persistently more likely to live in poverty compared to white families. I define Black families here as Black families with children. For example, Black families are more likely to be low-income (61%), poor (34%), and live in deep poverty (17%) compared to white families (Koball and Jiang, 2018). Although one study points to declining trends in poverty across racialized groups (Iceland, 2019), the racial poverty gap remains. Given that poverty represents the lack of resources relative to need (Brady, 2019), there are far-reaching implication for Black families and children. For instance, low-income Black children tend to face several adverse outcomes (McLoyd, 1990). Even more, poverty is associated with lower relationship quality between intimate partners (Williams, Simon, and Cardwell, 2019). Thus, the overrepresentation of Black families in poverty has important implications for racial stratification across several indicators of well-being.

Since the emergence of the Moynihan Report (Moynihan, 1965) connecting Black family formations (e.g., nonmartial births) with poverty, family structure remains a dominant and persistent explanation for understanding Black families in poverty gap. Conventional sociology and demography continue to link family formations with economic advancement—albeit in universal and race-neutral ways (e.g., Brown, 2010; McLanahan and Percheski, 2008). Nevertheless, conventional approaches linking family formations and economic inequality has implications for understanding Black families. For example, Black families are disproportionately experience nonmarital births (Martinez, Daniels, and Chandra, 2012), and unmarried families are more likely to be poor (Koball and Jiang, 2018). As such, family structure remains an over-deterministic "cause" of Black families in poverty.

Despite the popularity of family structure as one of the leading explanations of Black families in poverty, recent studies show that family structure does not fully account for racial inequality in poverty (Thiede, Kim, and Slack, 2017). Thus, there exist a need to rethink the ways scholars theoretically approach understanding the disproportionate amount of Black families in poverty. Thus, in this chapter, I present a theoretical perspective for understanding

Black families in poverty that centers race and racism. The theoretical perspective offered in this chapter builds on a recent debate between Iceland (2019) and Williams (2019) on racial inequality in poverty. For instance, Iceland (2019) found that although the racial gap in poverty declined over time, a substantial gap persists and family structure does not fully explain racial inequality in poverty.

In a response to Iceland, Williams (2019) challenges Iceland's failure to fully account for the poverty gap, especially between Black and white Americans, by suggesting that the manuscript follows an epistemology that (a) treats race as an ahistorical characteristics of the population, (b) use social capital variables as race-neutral explanations, and (c) employ analyses that leads to analytic bifurcation, whereby racial groups are conceptualized as discrete essences with white Americans as the standard against which people of color are measured.

In addition, the theoretical postulate presented here takes up Martin's (2020) call for the need for Africana Demography that incorporates *Black sociology*'s "ideological commitment ... to the release of Black people from race-related social oppression" (Watson, 1976: 116) and *critical demography's* call to center racism in the study of racial inequality that moves beyond mere descriptions to predictions (Horton, 1999). Taken together, the chapter encompasses Wright and Calhoun's (2016) five essential principles of Black sociology whereby research is

(1)　led by a Black American,
(2)　interdisciplinary,
(3)　Black Americans centered,
(4)　generalizable to other oppressed populations, and
(5)　social and public policy orientated.

Thus, the goal of this chapter is to present a more holistic approach to the study of poverty among Black Americans.

This chapter is organized in the following ways. First, I present the early arguments on low-income Black families with a specific emphasis on cultural and structural arguments. Second, I provide a brief overview of scholarship by mostly Black scholars who have presented a more nuanced understanding of Black family life, but their research has been largely ignored. Third, I critique conventional family sociology in the context of postcolonial sociology to underscore why scholarship continue to view family structure as a feasible mechanism to poverty among Black families although research does not validate its use. Last, I offer a critical approach to the study of Black families in poverty by drawing on Critical Race Theory (CRT) to underscore the processes and mechanisms that leads to the overrepresentation of Black families in poverty.

1   Black Families, Family Structure, and Economic Inequality

Family structure has been an explanation for addressing the disproportionate amount of Black families living in poverty since the 1960s. For example, Daniel P. Moynihan's (1965) report (dubbed as the Moynihan Report) provided early conceptions of the family structure and poverty nexus for Black families. Although the Moynihan Report presented a range of arguments that highlighted both structure conditions (e.g., American racism, Black male joblessness) and cultural arguments (e.g., tangle of pathology, matriarchy thesis) among Black families, the latter was adopted by scholars, policymakers, and lay person alike compared to the former (e.g., Gans, 2011; Steinberg, 2015). For many Moynihan sympathizers, the directionality was clear: unmarried births lead to poverty (e.g., Haskins, 2009). Many scholars refer to this line of reasoning as the cultural deficit model (Steinberg, 2015).

As a counter to broad cultural arguments about poverty among Black families, some scholars shifted the emphasis on structural explanations. For instance, William Julius Wilson's (1987, 1996) notion of the "marriageable male hypothesis" placed the emphasis on (1) economic restructuring that left many Black men unemployed or underemployed and (2) the disproportionate amount of incarcerated Black men, especially in low-income, predominately-Black, and urban neighborhoods. Unlike the cultural deficit model, which places the directionality from family structure to poverty, Wilson's structural argument places the point of emphasis on the changing economic conditions. These economic changes affect family formations, and subsequently economic inequality.

Given these two explanations for understanding inequality among Black families, poverty scholarship employs indicators from both perspectives—although scholars do not make explicit culture versus structure arguments. Many scholars examine the extent to which family structure (e.g., cultural argument) and employment (e.g., structural argument) explain the Black-White poverty gap. For example, Baker (2015) examines the relative impact of family structure and work on child poverty. Baker found that the effect of marriage on child poverty has declined over time whereas work has increased in magnitude on decreasing child poverty. Theide, Kim, and Slack (2017) build on Baker's study by explicitly examining the Black-White poverty gap and found that unemployment explains much of the Black-White poverty gap than marriage. These findings are consistent with other studies on racial inequality in poverty (e.g., Iceland, 2019).

The failure of family structure to fully account for racial inequality in poverty calls into question that family formations is a "cause" of the disproportionate number of Black families in poverty. Conventional sociology and demography tend to position cultural and structural theoretical arguments against one another regarding Black family life (Raley and Sweeney, 2009; Raley, Sweeney, and Wondra, 2015). Although the goal of both perspectives is to understand racial inequality in economic outcomes, the point of emphasis differs. For instance, cultural perspectives tend to focus on behavioral explanations (e.g., family formations) in racial inequality in poverty whereas structural explanations tend to focus on demographic/economic changes (e.g., male/female ratio; Black male joblessness, etc.) that creates differences in family formations, which, in turn, leads to racial inequality in poverty. Herein lies the problem: both cultural and structural perspectives are concerned with behavior (e.g., family formations) (Brady, 2019), and consequently, both perspectives offer family structure as a cause of poverty and ignore systematic racism (Williams, 2019). In the end, this line of research undermines the adaptive capacity of Black families in response to deep-seated racism.

2 The Nuance of Black Families: the Missing Links in Conventional Research

Despite Black scholars' contribution to family sociology, conventional sociology and demography still position family structure as a universal and race-neutral form of human capital that has benefits for all families (Williams, 2019). While the Moynihan Report (1965) was generally viewed as a cultural argument to understanding Black families in poverty (Gans, 2011), cultural explanation to understand Black poverty remains a pertinent explanation (Darity, 2011). What is missing from conventional research on family structure and racial inequality in poverty are important nuances that considers racialized processes that are germane to understanding racial variations in family formations and economic inequality. Several Black scholars have offered a more nuanced understanding of Black family life by highlighting racial variations in family formations is a consequence—not a cause—of racial inequality.

I briefly discus scholarship on Black families across three important historical periods: slavery era, Emancipation era, and post-Civil Rights era. My intention here is not to present a racial progress narrative (Seamster and Ray, 2019); rather, my goal is to demonstrate how Black scholars contextualized Black families to consider the racialized processes and mechanisms that facilitated racial variations in family formations. Recognizing racialized processes challenge conventional sociology and demography's use of family structure as a race-neutral inequality reducing mechanism.

During the slavery era, divergent patterns of family experiences emerged between European women and enslaved Black women. European women migrated with men and children that proved to be advantageous to colonial efforts (Glenn 2015) whereas enslaved Africans faced restriction to marital relationships via discriminatory laws (Lenhardt, 2014). DuBois (1908) and Frazier (1939) wrote about the extent to which American chattel slavery affected Black families, and the diversity of conditions Black families had to operate under oppressive conditions.

The Reconstruction era presented a challenge for the stability of racial subornation and oppression. Given that individuals racialized as Black were viewed as inherently sub-human with chattel slavery as a legitimate plight, emancipation lead to new ways of racial subordination (e.g., black codes, Jim Crow laws, etc.). This led to white supremacy and patriarchy working together to maintain domination of Black bodies, especially Black women. For example, federal and state laws linked marriage to citizenship, established penalties for violating marriage, shifted the state's responsibility to provide aid for formerly enslaved persons to a national narrative of personal responsibility, and formalized men, including black men, as head of households (Franke 1999; Hill 2006; Hunter 2017; Lenhardt 2014). Marriage was a similar state-sanctioned and oppressive institution akin to slavery for black women (Lenhardt 2014).

As a response to systemic racial oppression, Black women developed alternative and adaptive strategies for family life that included a diverse set of family forms (e.g., marriage, cohabitation, "sweethearts"; Billingsley 1994; Frankel 1999; Hill 2006). Many Black women resisted the idea of the benefits of marriage because they saw no economic and gender privileges associated with the traditional marriage contract (Franke 1999; Hill 2006; Lenhardt 2014). Bloome and Mueller's (2015) empirical study on tenancy and African American marriage supports this idea by showing that many freedwomen resented their subordinate status in tenant marriages, which lead to union dissolution among freedpeople.

Many adaptive practices were carried forward into the 20th century. During the post-Civil Rights era, however, the state interpreted these adaptive strategies (e.g., nonmarital childbearing) as deficiencies and thus out-of-wedlock childbirths became a central explanation for racial inequality in poverty. Discriminatory tactics and racist and gendered stereotypes (e.g., welfare queen) shape social policies and public opinion (Neubeck and Cazenae 2002; Saito 2009). Most sociological research mirrored the social milieu of the day by adopting "blaming the victim" or deficiency narratives.

Black scholars pushed against deficiency narrative by providing critical assessments of sociological studies on Black families and highlighting the ethnocentrism embedded in sociological thought. For example, Billingsley (1970) and Staples (1971) explicitly critiqued how American social science disvalued Black family life. Moreover, post-Civil Rights era scholarship on Black families began to focus on the adaptive strategies via kinship networks (Stack, 1975), the strengths of Black families (Hill, 2003), and broader sociohistorical context of Black family life (Bryant et al., 2010). Collectively, these scholars provide a level of nuance that is absent from mainstream scholarship.

3 Family Structure and Economic Inequality: Postcolonial Critiques

Conventional sociology and demography continue to neglect the work of Black scholars on the nuances of Black family life. Consequently, mainstream sociology and demography remain committed to treating family structure as a plausible generic mechanism for explaining racial inequality in poverty. In this section, I argue that many studies follow an epistemology that obscures race and racism in the US and thus consequently ignores the voices of many Black scholars. To illustrate this, I rely on postcolonial sociology to challenge conventional and mainstream approaches to racial inequality in poverty. Postcolonial critiques build on first wave postcolonial scholars (e.g., W.E.B. Du Bois, Franz Fanon; Go, 2018; Weiner, 2018) who "documented Eurocentric colonial regimes' capitalist designs subjugating and extracting labor and profit from indigenous and kidnapped and enslaved African populations beginning in the late 15th century through settler colonialism" (Weiner, 2018:3).

Thus, postcolonial sociology is a way of thinking that recognizes empire and colonialism matter (Go 2018) in the creation and maintenance of racial inequality in the US. Hence, a postcolonial critique of sociology recognizes that sociology, as an academic discipline, follows an imperial episteme that (1) *represses colonial/imperial hist*ory, (2) favors *Eurocentric universalism*, and (3) engages in *analytic bifurcations* whereby racialized groups are dichotomized into essentialized distinctions. I offer this critique to family structure and economic inequality research.

First, previous research limits our understanding of race by repressing colonial/imperial history. This approach has important implications on how readers understand what race means, and how results and conclusions are interpreted. Repressing colonial history makes invisible the historical inequalities making race possible (Go, 2018). Specifically, inequality is the reason race arose as a historical category. Race did not produce inequality; inequality produced race (Fields and Fields, 2014; Williams, 2019). Ignoring this reality undermines the social construction of race, which obscures inherent relational aspects of racialized groups. Repressing colonial/imperial history mask the link between racism, family formations, and racial inequality and render invisible the work of Black scholars. This has implications for how scholars discuss racial trends in family formations and poverty.

Second, scholarship favors Eurocentric universalism when attempting to explain the racial gap in poverty. Eurocentric universalism refers to scholars employing explanations about the social world centering European experiences as universal templates (Go, 2013). Understanding Eurocentric universalism in the context of research on racial inequality in poverty is informative here. For example, previous research tends to conceptualize family structure, particularly marriage, as a generic form of social capital. Although this line of research is valuable, many studies ignore the role marriage played (and continues to play) in facilitating European colonial domination. As such, studies ignore the racialized processes that lead to racial variations in family formations. Ignoring these racialized processes reinforce European universalisms, which, inevitably mask structural racism. Scholars continue to put forth family structure as a plausible explanation by ignoring the scholarship that highlight the processes and mechanisms that undergird racial variations in family formations across important historical eras.

Last, previous research relies on analytic bifurcation that treats racialized groups as distinct, separate essences. Scholars employ analytic bifurcation due to the repression in colonial history. As such, analysts proceed with analytical techniques to "explain away" or attenuate racial variations in poverty. This approach limits our understanding of racial inequality in two ways. First, given the lack of conceptualizing and historicizing race (as discussed above), race comparisons reproduce racialized readings of reality (Bonilla-Silva and Baiocchi 2001) whereby interpretations of "racial differences" can be attributed to cultural or behavioral differences.

Second, this approach facilitates a racial progress narrative, which implies that things are "getting better" between racialized groups. This statement reflects a linear logic of time, which befuddles how racial inequality is reproduced by new mechanisms (Seamster and Ray 2018). For example, in a review article on racial variations in family formations, Raley, Sweeney, Wandra (2015) mentions that marriage rates continued to decline for Black families, even as racial discrimination was declining. Raley and colleagues' conception of the decline in racial discrimination represents their view of the unemployment rate of Black men. These scholars, however, do not consider the disproportionate amount of Black men incarcerated, which has an important impact on the unemployment rate of Black men (Western and Pettit, 2005). Thus, presenting the unemployment rate for Black men without taking into consideration mass incarceration (i.e., the new Jim Crow; Alexander, 2012) presents a false sense of racial progress.

Thus, given the racialized processes that shape racial variations in family formations, there is a need for scholars to abandon family structure as a generic mechanism for the persistence of poverty among Black families. My central critique is that family formations have no theoretical nor analytical purchase as an explanation for the overrepresentation of Black families in poverty. In what follows, I present an alternative theoretical framework to explicitly center race and racism in understanding the disproportionately number of Black families in poverty.

4 Critical Race Theory: New Theoretical Possibilities

Critical Race Theory (CRT) provides an alternative to conventional approaches to understanding the Black families in poverty. Unlike conventional sociology and demography perspectives, which focus on individualist (or cultural) explanations such as family structure, CRT centers race and racism. CRT has roots in legal scholarship with concerns about understanding the maintenance of racial inequality in the post-Civil Rights era (Delgado and Stefancic, 2017). Given the utility of CRT in addressing racial inequality, scholars are beginning to encourage sociologists to employ CRT as a theoretical postulate across sub-fields (Christian, Seamster, and Ray, 2019). I take-up this call and employ CRT to understanding the disproportionate amount of Black families in poverty in the United States.

Several tenants help to guide CRT. For this chapter, I focus on two tenants: (1) the social construction of race thesis and (2) the permanence of racism in shaping racial inequality (Delgado and Stefancic, 2017). In doing so, I present a Critical Race Theory of poverty among Black families in the US by offering historically sensitive and flexible ways to contextualize socially constructed racialized, hierarchal relationships. My point of departure is that race is relational (Emirbayer 1997), and thus racial inequality should be understood in hierarchal and relational terms. I view each tenant as a tool to help scholars depart from epistemologies grounded in Eurocentric understandings of the world and refrain from treating race as ontologically real through its use as a non-hierarchal or nominal concept (e.g., Sen and Wasow 2016).

In Figure 6.1, I provide a conceptual model that incorporates CRT tenants. First, the model begins with the direct path from racism to superordinate and subordinate groups to highlight directionality whereby racism was the reason race arose as a historical category (Fields and Fields, 2012). Given the socially constructed nature of race, racialized groups exist in hierarchal and relational

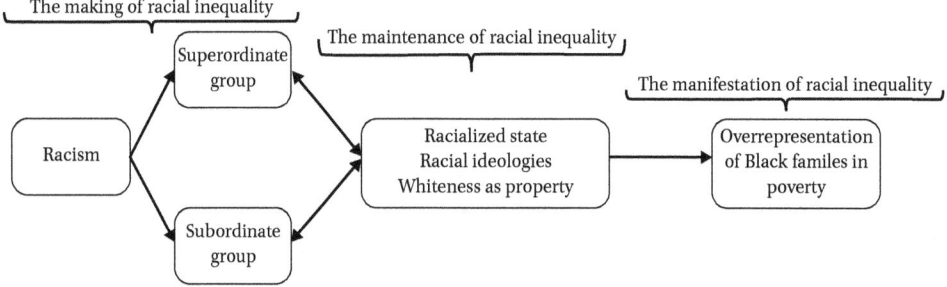

FIGURE 6.1 Conceptual model indicating a critical race theory of the overrepresentation of Black families in poverty

terms. Thus, rather than naming racial groups (e.g., Black, White, etc.), the model emphasizes the relational aspect the groups such superordinate (i.e., Whites) and subordinate (e.g., Blacks). This part of the model illustrates the making of racial inequality.

Second, the model provides a bidirectional association between the superordinate and subordinate groups and specific mechanisms that influence the Black-White poverty gap (e.g., the racialized state, racial ideologies, and whiteness as property). The bidirectionality of the association indicates that the hierarchical nature of the groups unequally impacts each mechanism, and in turn, the mechanisms reinforce the hierarchal character of racialized groups. This section of the model illustrates the maintenance of the racial inequality. Last, the model shows a path from the mechanisms to the Black-White poverty gap. This part of the model highlights the manifestation of racial inequality whereby the disproportionate number of Black families in poverty is the direct result of racialized social system that advantages whites while simultaneously disadvantages Black Americans. I elaborate below.

4.1   *The Social Construction of Race*

Many sociologists and demographers contend that race is socially constructed. Yet, in racial inequality in poverty research, the constructionist view of race is assumed rather than demonstrated (Benjamin 2014). From this approach, the reader must assume what race is, and how race is being conceptualized. This has important implications for drawing conclusions about racial inequality in poverty. Two broad racial conceptualizations dominate our understanding of race—the constructionists view and the essentialist view (Morning, 2011; Roth et al., 2020). The essentialist approach views race as biological whereas the constructionist approach to race views racial groups as a social invention to justify European domination and oppression (Feagin, 2013).

Given that constructionist versus essentialist view of race is far from resolved (Morning, 2011) scholars must be intentional and upfront with their conceptualization of race to limit misinterpretations (Williams, 2019). Conceptualizing race as a social construction provides a more historically sensitive and accurate understanding of racialized groups and racial inequities. Moreover, a constructionist view of race provides a way of seeing the world in its own right. For instance, if race is a social construction, then an elaboration on why, and for what purpose, race was constructed is warranted. From this view, racism is the reason race arose as historical categories (Fields and Fields, 2014).

The social construction of race is concerned with the *making of the racial hierarchy and racial inequality*. To elaborate on the making of the racial hierarchy and racial inequality, I rely on Glenn's (2015) notion of "settler colonialism as an ongoing structure" to capture the material conditions (e.g., land and labor) necessary in the construction of racialized groups. Glenn (2016) posits that settler colonialism must be understood in the context of land acquisition by colonialists via Indigenous genocide and the enslavement of Africans. The process of land acquisition not only leads to the unequal distribution of resources but also sets in motion a socially constructed racial hierarchy between racialized groups.

Indeed, scholars who frame race in the context of settler colonialism points out how the racialization process—given meaning to otherwise meaningless categories (e.g., phenotypical features; Bonilla-Silva 1997)—was contingent upon the colonial relationship with Europeans (Wolfe 2006). For instance, Wolfe (2006) argues:

> ...we cannot simply say that settler colonialism or genocide have been targeted at particular races, since a race cannot be taken as given. It is made in the targeting. Black people were racialized as slaves; slavery constituted their blackness. Correspondingly, Indigenous North Americans were not killed, driven away, romanticized, assimilated, fenced in, bred White, and otherwise eliminated as the original owners of the land but as Indians (388).

Thus, Glenn's (2015) "settler colonialism as ongoing structure" is useful as it helps to recover what Go (2018) contends, colonial racialization has continuities into the present. Settler colonialism is not an event; rather, it represents a process, and thus can help catalog continuity and change in power relations and material conditions across racialized groups.

4.2 The Permanence of Racism

The second CRT tenant is the permanence of racism. This tenant recognizes that "racism is ordinary, not aberrational" (Delgado and Stefanic 2017, 8). The permanence of racism can be seen across several indicators of well-being, including health (Phelan and Link, 2015), wealth and homeownership (Oliver and Shapiro, 2006), and mortality (Hummer, 1996). This tenant is concerned with the *maintenance of the racial hierarchy and racial inequality* and is sensitive to stability (e.g., persistent racial gaps in poverty) and change (e.g., shift from overt racism to covert racism). Thus, the permanence of racism can help understand why racial inequality persists in the post-Civil Rights era.

For this chapter, I elaborate on maintenance of the disproportionate number of Black families in poverty by relying on three mechanisms: (1) the racialized state, (2) racial ideologies, and (3) whiteness as property. My argument is that these mechanisms work to maintain the overwhelming amount of Black families in poverty by offering race-neutral explanations of racial inequality while simultaneously masking racism. These three mechanisms are not necessarily mutually exclusive; however, for the sake of clarity, I elaborate on each mechanism separately.

Frist, the US is a *racialized state* (Bracey, 2015). Like other scholars (Omi and Winant, 2014), I conceptualize the state as the "constellation of institutions, policies, the conditions and rules which support and justify them, and the embedded social relations" (83). The state is an essential and important institution as it is responsible for the distribution of economic resources for historically and contemporarily oppressed populations (Brady, 2009). As such, the state plays a vital role in the creation and maintenance of racial inequality.

The state maintains racial inequality in poverty by offering generic, race-neutral policies to address rather than explicitly focusing on structural racism. For instance, the state promoted marriage as an explanation for understanding poverty that included both welfare reform and healthy marriage initiatives (Johnson, 2012; Parolin, 2019). Given that Black families disproportionately live in poverty (Koball and Jiang, 2018), these policies had far-reaching implications for Black families and children (Johnson, 2012). My contention is that the focus on marriage as a way to ameliorate poverty obscures the role of systemic racism in the maintenance of racial inequality in poverty.

Despite the state's negligence in addressing structural racism, a burgeoning line of research is beginning to address the direct link between the state and poverty in the US. For example, Brady (2009) critiques conventional approaches to poverty research that highlight individualistic explanations and puts forth Institutionalized Power Relations Theory to highlight the inherent unequal relationships between actors. Empirical research shows the utility of this theoretical perspective in understanding the association between the state's welfare generosity and poverty (Brady, 2009), including the Black-White gap in poverty (Parolin, 2019). Although Institutionalized Power Relations Theory provide useful insights for the racial inequality in poverty research, the perspective is intended to capture a broad, international account for the unequal distribution of poverty in wealthy nations and thus does not explicitly theorize race and racism at the state level.

Thus, to be more explicit about the overrepresentation of Black families in poverty, I use Bracey's (2015) Critical Race Theory (CRT) of the State. From this perspective, the point of emphasis is "the state is a tool created, maintained, and used by whites to advance their collective racial interest" (558). Thus, for Bracey, white racial interests are naturalized as state interests. Although previous research has not examined CRT of the State in the context of racial inequality in poverty, CRT guide a few empirical studies on race and poverty more broadly (Brown, 2013; Constance-Huggins, 2011; Soss, Fording, and Schram, 2008). In addition, the state, via slavery, has been linked to the contemporary forms of racial inequality in poverty (O'Connell, 2012). Thus, the state has a racialized history of overt expressions of racial domination and continues to subjugate Black families through covert ways. Thus, future research should be mindful of the state as a racial apparatus that maintains racial inequality in poverty.

Second, I rely on *racial ideologies* to help understand the overrepresentation of Black families in poverty. Racial ideologies provide cognitive and cultural schemas in explaining racial inequality to maintain (e.g., superordinate group) or challenge (e.g., subordinate group) the racial status quo (Doane 2017). To understand racial ideologies, I rely on Doane's (2017) definition, which sees ideologies as "collections of beliefs and understandings about race and the role of race in social interaction—ideas that are anchored in existing social (material) relations" (p. 976). What is particularly useful here is that racial ideologies do not cause racism; rather, racial ideologies emerge to explain and justify the existing racial order (Bonilla-Silva 2006). For instance, given settler colonialist created a socially constructed racial hierarchy, racial ideologies thus preserve and maintain the racial status quo (Bonilla-Silva 2006; Doane 2017).

Colorblind racism (or color evasiveness) is a specific type of racial ideology (Doane, 2017; Bonilla-Silva, 2017). From a colorblind racism perspective, the persistence of racial inequality is not due to racism; rather, the point of emphasis in on meritocracy and individualism (Bonilla-Silva, 2017; Doane 2017). Laws and policies, social practices, and everyday discourse via racial ideologies continue to minimize the role of racism in maintaining the racial hierarchy (Feagin, 2013).

From a racial ideology perspective, I contend that the belief that marriage works as a racial inequality reducing mechanism functions as a racial ideology. That is, marriage provides a cognitive frame for explaining *why* Black Americans are disproportionately poor. Proposing marriage as a racial inequality reducing mechanism ignores structural inequalities, obscure the adaptive strategies families of color respond to persistent inequality, and places the responsibility of racial inequality on Black families. From this perspective, one could argue that the Moynihan Report (discussed above) and the reports' sympathizers are employing a racial ideology.

What is particularly important about racial ideologies is that Black Americans may hold similar views as white Americans (Bonilla-Silva, 2017). For example, although whites and Black Americans have divergent views on structural racism, whites (55%) and Blacks (57%) have convergent views that family instability is "the reason that many Blacks are not getting ahead" (Paker, Horowitz, and Mahl, 2016). Views of marriage as a mechanism to reduce economic inequality among Black Americans are reinforced through media, politicians, and religious institutions (Johnson and Loscocco, 2015).

There are important implications for future research in understanding the belief that family life is a contributor to racial inequality. For example, marriage can be viewed as a form of "cultural racism" whereby family life serves as a cultural explanation for racial inequality (Bonilla-Silva, 2017). Thus, one could argue racial ideologies are the cognitive and schematic conditions whereby the state uses to execute policies. Data collection efforts via repeated cross-sections (e.g., General Social Survey; Pew Research Center) could begin asking questions over time about the link between family life and racial inequality. This could help us understand trends in public opinion between and within racialized groups. For example, analyses could be performed to assess age-period-cohort effects and patterns. Moreover, scholars could begin to conceptualize the idea that family life as a reason for Black inequality as "cultural racism" and perform analyses to examine differences and similarities across racialized groups. The ability for scholars to juxtapose structural racism and cultural racism can help inform our understanding of what, and why, policies get put forth to ameliorate inequality over others.

Last, *whiteness as property* serves as mechanism that contributes to the disproportionate number of Black families in poverty. Whiteness as property is a key tenant of CRT. Harris (1993) put forth whiteness as property to capture the material (and psychological) benefits of being racialized as white in the United States. The central argument is "white" as a racial identity merge with property to construct notions of freedom and personal sovereignty in relation to Black subordination via slavery, black codes, and Jim Crow laws (Harris).

Thus, whiteness as property presents a *relational* approach to racial inequality in poverty. A relational perspective views White advantage and Black disadvantage as mutually constitutive. To point bluntly, white Americans are less likely to be poor relative to people of color because, as Seamster and Ray (2018) insists, "...whites' well-being is the manifestation of a hierarchal system. Whites are doing better because the structural relations of race benefit, reward, and empower them" (333). Moreover, "whiteness has been constructed and defended as a rigidly exclusive category precisely because it is not a descriptor of national origin but a marker of entitlement to colonial power, privilege and property" (Saito, 2015, p.62).

Thus, given that the state operates as a tool for white interests (Bracey, 2015), and colorblind racism serves as a cognitive schema to justify race-neutral explanations of inequality that reproduces the racial status quo (Bonilla-Silva, 2017), white racial identity embodies the benefits of these tools and schemas while simultaneously encoding Black racial identity as a perpetual subordinate status. Thus, individuals who identify as "white" have lived experiences that differ from individuals racialized as "Black" due to the differential material (and psychological) conditions between racialized groups.

To understand the extent to which whiteness as property is a mechanism that leads to the overrepresentation of Black families in poverty, I focus on two property functions of whiteness as property: (1) whiteness as the right to exclude and (2) whiteness as the right to use and enjoyment (Harris, 1993). First, whiteness as a right to exclude supports a substantial line of research on racial residential segregation (Massey and Denton, 1993). Racial segregation is not only about the physical separation between racialized groups but also access to valued economic, social, and psychological resources (Phelan and Link, 2015). For instance, Black Americans, compared to white Americans, are more likely live in deep and concentrated poverty (Jargowsky, 2015; Koball and Jiang, 2018). The sorting of individuals into geographic spaces via systemic racist policies (e.g., red lining; restrictive covenants), discriminatory practices (e.g., denied bank loans, stirring from real-estate agents), and racist attitudes (e.g., white flight) fundamentally shaped racial and economic segregation (Massey and Denton 1993).

Second, another property function of whiteness is the right to use and enjoyment. That is, whiteness can be deployed and experience as a resource (Harris, 1993). To illustrate this property function, Ray (2019) argues that "whiteness is a credential" whereby white racial identity affords "white" individuals "access to organizational resources, legitimizing work hierarchies, and expanding white agency" (41). Given the relational nature of racialized groups, whiteness as a credential must be understood in relation with "Blackness" as a negative credential (Ray, 2019). Although Ray focuses on racialized organizations, understanding racialized credentialing in understanding families in poverty is noteworthy.

For instance, the lived experiences of individuals racialized as white are not only taken-for-granted but also are assumed that, if adopted by those racialized as Black, would lead to greater economic equality. Geronimus (2003), in an essay on culture, identity, privilege and teenage childbearing, discusses the implications of white as property. Geronimus contends that European Americans tend to

(1) take for granted the broad and ubiquitous range of resources that help support their nuclear families,
(2) use their resources to discredit or censor alternative family forms, and
(3) perpetuate and rationalize their family forms via the public "damning" of African American family patterns through the racialized state and racial ideologies.

Consequently, African American alternative family forms are interpreted as "causes" of racial inequality rather than an adaptation to racial inequality.

Moreover, understanding white racial identity as a credential and Blackness as a negative credential gives credence to the unequal returns in marriage across racialized groups. What is important here is that white racial identity as a credential works in tandem with other human capital resources (e.g., marriage, education, etc.) to create racial inequities among similarly situated Black Americans. For example, Black Americans who are married are more likely to be poor compared to married white Americans (U.S. Census Bureau, 2018). Moreover, research on wealth demonstrates that white Americans in single-parent families have more wealth than Black families in two-parent families (Traud et al., 2017), and discriminatory penalties increase for higher educated Black men (Tomaskovic-Devey, Thomas, and Johnson, 2005), reinforcing the logic of whiteness as credential and blackness as a negative credential.

5   Conclusion and Discussion

The overrepresentation of Black families in poverty is the manifestation of a racialized social system (Bonilla-Silva, 1997). American racism produced socially constructed, hierarchical groups. The racialized state, racial ideologies, and whiteness as property serves as important mechanisms that produces (and reproduces) racial inequality in poverty. Despite interest in race and poverty, there lacks a theoretical postulate that addresses *why* Black families are disproportionate represented in poverty. Conventional approaches to racial inequality in poverty focus largely individualist explanations such as family structure (e.g., Parolin, 2019). Yet, despite the popularity of family structure, racial variations in family formations fail to explain racial inequality in poverty (Parolin, 2019; Thiede, Kim, and Slack, 2017). Even more, family structure explanations tend to obscure the sociohistorical context of race and racism in the US.

The current chapter challenges conventional theoretical perspectives addressing the overrepresentation of Black families in poverty by presenting a critical race perspective to poor Black families. Scholarship among Black scholars have long placed Black families in a larger racialized context and have consistently argued that variation in family formations among Black families represent as an outcome, rather than a cause, of racial inequality (e.g., Billingsley, 1994; Hill, 2006; Lenhardt, 2014). I build on the previous work of Black scholars by employing Critical Race Theory as a theoretical postulate for understanding the overrepresentation of Black families in poverty—with an emphasis on the racialized state, racial ideologies, and whiteness as property. Thus, taking a CRT approach to understanding the overrepresentation of Black families presents an explanation of how, and in what ways, poverty is maintained between racialized groups. I frame this perspective in the context of Africana Demography (Martin, 2020) to combine both Black sociology (Watson, 1976) and critical demography (Horton, 1999) to present a more holistic approach for understanding poor Black families.

A CRT approach to Black families in poverty has important research and policy implications. For instance, racism should be the default explanation of the overrepresentation of Black families in poverty. Scholars who study racial inequality in poverty should move away from asking what mechanisms account for the racial gap in poverty towards asking *maintains* the racial gap in poverty? The former question suggests that some race-neutral human capital variable could explain racial inequality in poverty. The latter question, however, focuses on the mechanisms that perpetuate the overrepresentation of Black families in poverty. Thus, by focusing on what maintains racial inequality in poverty begins with the assumption that white racial interests (e.g., whiteness) are not anomalous but foundational to the making and maintenance of racial inequality in the U.S.

Research programs that place race and racism as the point of departure should be mindful of the ways that "race" is conceptualized and analyzed in quantitative studies. For instance, many research surveys tend to ask questions about a respondent's race and ethnicity. The decision to mark "white" or "Black" represents a person's experience in the world. As such, there is a profound need for researchers to be upfront with the conceptualization of race. Research on racial inequality tends to treat race as an ahistorical demographic characteristic of the population (i.e., nominal variable), and thus ignore the racist processes and mechanisms that made race possible in the first place (Williams, 2019). My argument is that the point of emphasis should be on racial stratification instead of treating race as an ahistorical demographic characteristic.

Using CRT to understand the overrepresentation of Black families in poverty has important policy implications. These implications involve scholars, policy makers, and layperson moving away from marriage to ameliorate racial inequality toward structural-based solutions. Although policy efforts to reduce poverty focused on marriage, empirical studies do not support the connection between family structure and racial inequality in poverty (e.g., Thiede, Kiim, and Slack, 2017). As such, scholars (Lenhardt, 2014; Letiecq, 2019) and family advocacy groups (Fremstad, Glynn, and Williams, 2019) are beginning to leverage the idea of family justice to incorporate a more inclusive understanding of families. The general idea is re-think how family formations outside of marriage are perceived in the U.S. and recognize divergent family formations across racialized groups reflect adaptive strategies within a larger context of structural racism.

Rather than thinking about marriage as a remedy to poverty, there has been a push towards more structural approaches to tackling racial inequality. For example, Paul, Darity, Hamiliton, and Zaw (2018) call for a federal job guarantee to create a path out of poverty via ending unemployment. Given that unemployment is closely linked to poverty (e.g., Thiede, Kiim, and Slack, 2017), this program proposes a permanent job guarantee to supply full time employment for any American citizen over eighteen with nonpoverty wages plus benefits. Family policy and economic policies recommendations are usually mentioned in isolation of one another. I argue however, that they should be mentioned in tandem for a more holistic and bold approach to ameliorating poverty for Black families and other oppressed groups in the U.S.

In conclusion, Africana Demography is a much-needed intervention to the study of Black families in poverty. Africana Demography points to the need for ending racial oppression and dominations of Black people by centering racism as a key mechanism of racial inequality (Martin, 2020). Centering racism as a theoretical point of departure and arguing for family policies to be more inclusive to all family forms, scholars can begin to not only highlight the power of white supremacy but also begin to limit its power by creating a more inclusive and fair society.

Bibliography

Alexander, Michelle. 2012. *The New Jim Crow: Mass Incarceration in the Age of Colorblindness.* New York, NY: The New Press.

Baker, Regina S. 2015. "The Changing Association among Marriage, Work, and Child Poverty in the United States, 1974–2010." *Journal of Marriage and Family* 77 (5): 1166–1178.

Benjamin, Ruha. 2014. *Conjuring Difference, Concealing Inequality: A Brief Tour of Racecraft.* New York: Springer.

Billingsley, Andrew. 1970. "Black Families and White Social Science." *Journal of Social Issues* 26 (3): 127–142.

Billingsley, Andrew. 1994. *Climbing Jacob's Ladder: The Enduring Legacies of African-American Families.* New York: Simon and Schuster.

Bonilla-Silva, Eduardo. 1997. "Rethinking Racism: Toward a Structural Interpretation." *American Sociological Review* 62 (3): 465–480.

Bonilla-Silva, Eduardo. 2017. *Racism without Racists: Color-Blind Racism and the Persistence of Racial Inequality in America.* Lanham, MD: Rowman & Littlefield.

Bonilla-Silva, Eduardo, and Gianpaolo Baiocchi. 2001. "Anything but Racism: How Sociologists Limit the Significance of Racism." *Race and Society* 4 (2): 117–131.

Bracey, Glenn E. 2015. "Toward a Critical Race Theory of State." *Critical Sociology* 41 (3): 553–572.

Brady, David. 2009. *Rich Democracies, Poor People: How Politics Explain Poverty.* Oxford: Oxford University Press.

Brady, David. 2019. "Theories of the Causes of Poverty." *Annual Review of Sociology* 45: 155–175.

Brown, Hana E. 2013. "Racialized Conflict and Policy Spillover Effects: The Role of Race in the Contemporary US Welfare State." *American Journal of Sociology* 119 (2): 394–443.

Brown, Susan L. 2010. "Marriage and Child Well-Being: Research and Policy Perspectives." *Journal of Marriage and Family* 72 (5): 1059–1077.

Bryant, Chalandra M., K.A.S. Wickrama, John Bolland, Barlynda M. Bryant, Carolyn E. Cutrona, and Christine E. Stanik. 2010. "Race Matters, Even in Marriage: Identifying Factors Linked to Marital Outcomes for African Americans." *Journal of Family Theory & Review* 2 (3): 157–174.

Christian, Michelle, Louise Seamster, and Victor Ray. 2019. "Critical Race Theory and Empirical Sociology." *American Behavioral Scientist* July 7, 2019. https://doi.org/DOI: 10.1177/0002764219859646.

Constance-Huggins, Monique. 2011. "A Review of the Racial Biases of Social Welfare Policies." *Journal of Human Behavior in the Social Environment* 21 (8): 871–887.

Darity, William. 2011. "Revisiting the Debate on Race and Culture: The New (Incorrect) Harvard/Washington Consensus." *Du Bois Review: Social Science Research on Race* 8 (2): 467–476.

Delgado, Richard, and Jean Stefancic. 2017. *Critical Race Theory: An Introduction*. NYU Press.

Doane, Ashley. 2017. "Beyond Color-Blindness:(Re) Theorizing Racial Ideology." *Sociological Perspectives* 60 (5): 975–991.

Du Bois, W.E.B. 1908. *The Negro American Family*. Atlanta, GA: Atlanta University Publications.

Emirbayer, Mustafa. 1997. "Manifesto for a Relational Sociology." *American Journal of Sociology* 103 (2): 281–317.

Feagin, Joe. 2013. *Systemic Racism: A Theory of Oppression*. New York: Routledge.

Fields, Karen E., and Barbara Jeanne Fields. 2014. *Racecraft: The Soul of Inequality in American Life*. London; New York: Verso Trade.

Fording, Richard, Joe Soss, and Sanford F. Schram. 2008. "Distributing Discipline: Race, Politics, and Punishment at the Frontlines of Welfare Reform." *University of Kentucky Center for Poverty Research Discussion Paper Series* 69. https://uknowledge.uky.edu/ukcpr_papers/69.

Franke, Katherine M. 1999. "Becoming a Citizen: Reconstruction Era Regulation of African American Marriages." *Yale JL & Human* 11 (2): 251.

Franklin, Frazier E. 1939. *The Negro Family in the United States*. Chicago: University of Chicago Press.

Fremstad, Shawn, Sarah Glynn, and Angelo Williams. 2019. "The Case against Marriage Fundamentalism: Embracing Family Justice for All." Washington, DC. familystoryproject.org.

Gans, Herbert J. 2011. "The Moynihan Report and Its Aftermaths: A Critical Analysis." *Du Bois Review: Social Science Research on Race* 8 (2): 315–327.

Geronimus, Arline T. 2003. "Damned If You Do: Culture, Identity, Privilege, and Teenage Childbearing in the United States." *Social Science & Medicine* 57 (5): 881–893.

Glenn, Evelyn Nakano. 2015. "Settler Colonialism as Structure: A Framework for Comparative Studies of US Race and Gender Formation." *Sociology of Race and Ethnicity* 1 (1): 52–72.

Go, Julian. 2013. "For a Postcolonial Sociology." *Theory and Society* 42 (1): 25–55.

Go, Julian. 2018. "Postcolonial Possibilities for the Sociology of Race." *Sociology of Race and Ethnicity* 4 (4): 439–451.

Harris, Cheryl I. 1993. "Whiteness as Property." *Harvard Law Review* 106 (8), 1707–1791.

Haskins, Ron. 2009. "Moynihan Was Right: Now What?" *The Annals of the American Academy of Political and Social Science* 621 (1): 281–314.

Hill, Robert Bernard. 2003. *The Strengths of Black Families*. University Press of America.

Hill, Shirley A. 2006. "Marriage among African American Women: A Gender Perspective." *Journal of Comparative Family Studies* 37 (3), 421–440.

Horton, Hayward Derrick. 1998. "Toward a Critical Demography of Race and Ethnicity: Introduction of the 'R' Word." Sociology Faculty Scholarship. 1. https://scholarsarchive.library.albany.edu/sociology_fac_scholar/1.

Hummer, Robert A. 1996. "Black-White Differences in Health and Mortality: A Review and Conceptual Model." *The Sociological Quarterly* 37 (1): 105–125.

Hunter, Tera. 2017. *Bound in Wedlock: Slave and Free Black Marriage in the Nineteenth Century*. Cambridge, MA: Belknap Press of Harvard Univ. Press.

Jargowsky, Paul. 2015. "The Architecture of Segregation." *The Century Foundation* 7.

Johnson, Kecia R., and Karyn Loscocco. 2015. "Black Marriage through the Prism of Gender, Race, and Class." *Journal of Black Studies* 46 (2): 142–171.

Johnson, Matthew D. 2012. "Healthy Marriage Initiatives: On the Need for Empiricism in Policy Implementation." *American Psychologist* 67 (4): 296–308.

Koball, Heather, and Yang Jiang. 2018. "Basic Facts about Low-Income Children: Children under 9 Years, 2016." New York: National Center for Children in Poverty, Columbia University Mailman School of Public Health.

Lenhardt, Robin A. 2014. "Marriage as Black Citizenship." *Hastings LJ* 66: 1317.

Letiecq, Bethany L. 2019. "Surfacing Family Privilege and Supremacy in Family Science: Toward Justice for All." *Journal of Family Theory & Review* 11 (3): 398–411.

Martin, Lori. 2019. "Africana Demography: Lessons from Founders E. Franklin Frazier, W.E.B. Du Bois, and the Atlanta School of Sociology." *Issues in Race and Society* 8: 5–28.

Martinez, Gladys, Kimberly Daniels, and Anjani Chandra. 2012. "Fertility of Men and Women Aged 15–44 Years in the United States: National Survey of Family Growth." *National Health Statistics Reports*, 1–28.

Massey, D.S., and N.A. Denton. 1993. *American Apartheid: Segregation and the Making of the Underclass*. Harvard University Press.

McLanahan, Sara, and Christine Percheski. 2008. "Family Structure and the Reproduction of Inequalities." *Annu. Rev. Sociol* 34: 257–276.

McLoyd, Vonnie C. 1990. "The Impact of Economic Hardship on Black Families and Children: Psychological Distress, Parenting, and Socioemotional Development." *Child Development* 61 (2): 311–46.

Morning, Ann. 2011. *The Nature of Race: How Scientists Think and Teach about Human Difference*. Univ of California Press.

O'Connell, Heather A. 2012. "The Impact of Slavery on Racial Inequality in Poverty in the Contemporary US South." *Social Forces* 90 (3): 713–734.

Oliver, Melvin L., and Thomas M. Shapiro. 2006. *Black Wealth, White Wealth: A New Perspective on Racial Inequality*. Taylor & Francis.

Omi, Michael, and Howard Winant. 2014. *Racial Formation in the United States*. New York: Routledge.

Parker, Kim, Juliana Horowitz, and Brian Mahl. 2016. *On Views of Race and Inequality, Blacks and Whites Are Worlds Apart: About Four-in-Ten Blacks Are Doubtful That the US Will Ever Achieve Racial Equality*. Pew Research Center.

Parolin, Zachary. 2019. "Temporary Assistance for Needy Families and the Black–White Child Poverty Gap in the United States." *Socio-Economic Review*, mwz025, https://doi.org/10.1093/ser/mwz025.

Paul, Mark, William Darity, Darrick Hamilton, and Khaing Zaw. 2018. "A Path to Ending Poverty by Way of Ending Unemployment: A Federal Job Guarantee." *RSF: The Russell Sage Foundation Journal of the Social Sciences* 4 (3): 44–63.

Phelan, Jo C., and Bruce G. Link. 2015. "Is Racism a Fundamental Cause of Inequalities in Health?" *Annual Review of Sociology* 41: 311–330.

Raley, R. Kelly, and Megan M. Sweeney. 2009. "Explaining Race and Ethnic Variation in Marriage: Directions for Future Research." *Race and Social Problems* 1 (3): 132–142.

Raley, R. Kelly, Megan M. Sweeney, and Danielle Wondra. 2015. "The Growing Racial and Ethnic Divide in US Marriage Patterns." *The Future of Children/Center for the Future of Children, the David and Lucile Packard Foundation* 25 (2): 89.

Reichman, Nancy E., Julien O. Teitler, Irwin Garfinkel, and Sara S. McLanahan. 2001. "Fragile Families: Sample and Design." *Children and Youth Services Review* 23 (4/5): 303–26.

Roth, Wendy D., Şule Yaylacı, Kaitlyn Jaffe, and Lindsey Richardson. 2020. "Do Genetic Ancestry Tests Increase Racial Essentialism? Findings from a Randomized Controlled Trial." *PloS One* 15 (1): e0227399.

Seamster, Louise, and Victor Ray. 2018. "Against Teleology in the Study of Race: Toward the Abolition of the Progress Paradigm." *Sociological Theory* 36 (4): 315–342.

Sen, Maya, and Omar Wasow. 2016. "Race as a Bundle of Sticks: Designs That Estimate Effects of Seemingly Immutable Characteristics." *Annual Review of Political Science* 19: 499–522.

Stack, Carol B. 1975. *All Our Kin: Strategies for Survival in a Black Community*. Basic Books.

Staples, Robert. 1971. "Towards a Sociology of the Black Family: A Theoretical and Methodological Assessment." *Journal of Marriage and the Family* 33 (1): 119–138.

Steinberg, S. 2015. "The Moynihan Report at Fifty: The Long Reach of Intellectual Racism." *Boston Review*, June 24, 2015.

Thiede, Brian C., Hyojung Kim, and Tim Slack. 2017. "Marriage, Work, and Racial Inequalities in Poverty: Evidence from the United States." *Journal of Marriage and Family* 79 (5): 1241–1257.

Tomaskovic-Devey, Donald, Melvin Thomas, and Kecia Johnson. 2005. "Race and the Accumulation of Human Capital across the Career: A Theoretical Model and Fixed-Effects Application." *American Journal of Sociology* 111 (1): 58–89.

Traub, Amy, Laura Sullivan, Tatjana Meschede, and Tom Shapiro. 2017. "The Asset Value of Whiteness: Understanding the Racial Wealth Gap." *Demos* (February 6, 2017), http://Www.Demos.Org/Publication/Asset-Valuewhiteness-Understanding-Racial-Wealth-Gap.

US Census Bureau. 2017. "Historical Poverty Tables: People and Families—1959–2016."

Watson, Wilbur H. 1976. "The Idea of Black Sociology: Its Cultural and Political Significance." *The American Sociologist* 11 (2): 115–123.

Weiner, Melissa F. 2018. "Decolonial Sociology: WEB Du Bois's Foundational Theoretical and Methodological Contributions." *Sociology Compass* 12 (8): e12601.

Western, Bruce, and Becky Pettit. 2005. "Black-White Wage Inequality, Employment Rates, and Incarceration." *American Journal of Sociology* 111 (2): 553–578.

Williams, Deadric T. 2019. "A Call to Focus on Racial Domination and Oppression: A Response to 'Racial and Ethnic Inequality in Poverty and Affluence, 1959–2015'." *Population Research and Policy Review* 38 (5): 655–663.

Williams, Deadric T., Laura Simon, and Marissa Cardwell. 2019. "Black Intimacies Matter: The Role of Family Status, Gender, and Cumulative Risk on Relationship Quality Among Black Parents." *Journal of African American Studies* 23 (1–2): 1–17.

Wilson, W.J. 1987. *The Truly Disadvantaged: The Inner City, the Underclass, and Public Policy*. Chicago: University of Chicago Press.

Wilson, William Julius. 1996. *When Work Disappears: The New World of the Urban Poor*. New York: Alfred A. Knopf.

Wolfe, Patrick. 2006. "Settler Colonialism and the Elimination of the Native." *Journal of Genocide Research* 8 (4): 387–409.

CHAPTER 7

Embodying a Hybrid Habitus: Identity Construction and Social Mobility among Working-class Black Women

Tifanie Pulley and Arthur Whaley

In the fields of sociology and demography, approaches to class analysis concerning the African American community remain a perpetually understudied area. For one, mainstream demographers use factors like one's family values and socioeconomic status (SES); one's level of educational attainment; and even one's occupational classification for techniques of measurement in class difference. They tend to ignore demographic behavior in its social and cultural context. With that being the case, one of the most popular views used to frame class in the lives of African Americans is presented in the works of sociologist William Julius Wilson whose research on race and class in *Declining Significance of Race* (1978) and *The Truly Disadvantaged* (1987). Critical to his analyses when comparing the contemporary situation of African Americans to their situation of the past, for the last 30 years, include the recent mobility patterns of blacks. Wilson (1978) writes

> The recent mobility patterns of blacks lend support to the view that economic class is clearly more important than race in predetermining job placement and occupational mobility. In the economic realm, then, the black experience has moved historically from economic racial oppression experienced by *virtually* all blacks to economic subordination for the black underclass. And as we begin the last quarter of the twentieth century, a deepening economic schism seems to be developing in the black community, with the black poor falling further and further behind middle- and upper-income blacks. (152)

The recent mobility patterns to which Wilson is referring are based on educational criteria, which is a significant factor in determining life chances among blacks and accounting for a more stratified class. For example, blacks that were less skilled and uneducated were relegated to low-wage sector occupations, while talented and educated blacks were experiencing unprecedented job opportunities in the growing government and corporate sectors (Wilson, 1978). Wilson attributes much of this success to affirmative action programs, which he explains, were due in part to the efforts of "the more educated blacks" (Wilson, 1978, 142). On the other hand, his exclusive focus on the "truly disadvantaged" established how African Americans are locked out of the labor market, ignoring a substantial number of African Americans who are in the labor market as working-class and poor.

Conversely, many scholars (Martin, Horton, & Booker, 2015; Arena, 2011; Diamond, 2009; Omari & Cole, 2003) have challenged Wilson's (1978) position in terms of race, arguing that much of the emphasis is placed on the Black middle-class and the disadvantaged (Horton, 2000; Collins, 2000), which omits the relevance of working-class Blacks. Even less is known of how they engage in social mobility to higher classes. How people behave within their class status is very much part of the African American experience. As part of Africana Demography we use this study to explore the meaning of social class and upward mobility in the lives of working-class Black women, paying particular attention to how these women construct and negotiate their identities and their habitus as academicians. A critical question is how do Black women professors acquire the habitus for their occupational role as academicians, which is usually inconsistent with the experiences of their working-class background?

There is a dearth of research on working-class Black women in general, and even less on their upward social mobility (Martin, Booker, Horton, 2015; Marsh, Darity, Cohen, Lynne & Salters, 2007; Lacy, 2004). At the same time, African American women earn 63 percent of what white men earn (National Women's Law Center, 2014). This income gap is even larger among African American women who have a high school degree or less, with the pay wage gap at 62 cents for every dollar white men earn (NWLC, 2014; Bureau of Labor Statistics-Black Labor Force, 2012). Black middle-class women's earnings amount to 85% of white women (Butler-Sweet, 2017). This stands in contrast to Black men's earnings, which only represent 64% of that of white men (Sweet, 2017; Attewell, P., Lavin, D., Domina, T., & Levey, T., 2004). But the income and educational attainment of middle-class Black women when compared to Black men and white women masks the plight of working-class Blacks, specifically what it means when social scripts complicate their ascribed and achieved status. Study participants are in a social setting that is unfamiliar and incompatible with their working-class histories, which calls attention to the concept of habitus (i.e., a set of class-based practices, values, and standards).

1 Habitus

Pierre Bourdieu (1984) developed the concept of habitus to analyze social stratification in French society. For Bourdieu, individuals who are located within different strata of the social structure have different life experiences and therefore develop distinct ways of thinking, feeling, and acting. The habitus is comprised mostly of subconscious individual judgments about tastes, norms, and behaviors that determine boundaries, the "rules of the game" that uncover how well individuals cross class boundaries—especially in terms of social mobility. However, Bourdieu's conceptualization of habitus as fixed, immutable, and dichotomous is unable to account for the experiences of individuals whose upward mobility requires the acquisition of new social scripts.

According to Schneider and Lang (2014), Bourdieu's habitus cannot adequately explain the hybridity and multiplicity of experiences associated with social mobility. They argue that individual habitus does not necessarily involve an 'either-or' acquisition of habitus, but individuals that move upward often switch between 'habitual' codes and languages as part of navigating from one social environment to another. As a result, they propose 'habitus diversification' as a more promising concept. Lofton and Davis (2015) recognized that Bourdieu's concept of habitus helped to explain individuals' cultural socialization, but they criticized its limited role in understanding the experiences of African Americans in the United States. Therefore, these scholars expand Bourdieu's notion of habitus to account for the socialization experiences of African Americans, "which connects systemic inequalities to their own cultural practices, logics, and actions" (Lofton & Davis, 2015, 215). Application of Bourdieu's notion of habitus to mainstream ideologies of U.S. sociology does not fully address the African American experience (Dancy, 2014; Young, 2004a). While Bourdieu's analysis recognized the social origins of family as an important part of perpetuating and reinforcing life chances, the process by which the influence of race and gender play to limit women from reaching their desired potential because of individual and institutional discrimination are hidden. As part of the distinct journey of African Americans in U.S. society, an ideological framework of "Black habitus" needs to be developed which also addresses the negative experiences of being Black America.

2   Theoretical Framework

In order to investigate the experiences of working-class Black women as professors in the academy and the ways in which they negotiate the challenges of social mobility, this study combines critical race theory and intersectionality with the theoretical contributions of Pierre Bourdieu. While Pierre Bourdieu's (1984) habitus constitutes a set of acquired dispositions in terms of family upbringing, with respect to critical theories, an important factor affecting life chances is race. Using his theoretical contributions as conceptual scaffolding,

I aim to understand how race shapes habitus, such that race constitutes conditions for sharing a similar habitus. As a result, Dubois' *double consciousness* (1903) helps to frame the unique experiences of Black working-class women in the academy in conjunction with intersectionality theory. Taken together, the role of habitus alone does not explain how Black women move from the working to the middle-class, nor does it explain how moving from one class to another impacts how they see themselves and how others see them.

2.1   Double Consciousness

W.E.B DuBois (1903) described "double consciousness" as "...a peculiar sensation ... an American, a Negro ... two unreconciled strivings" (16–17). Put simply, according to DuBois (1903), African Americans must contend with the dilemma of living in two separate worlds divided by the "color line." The use of double consciousness refers to the divergent realities that incorporate race and gender in the development of the self and identity formation created by the duality of working-class biographies and achievement of faculty status in higher education settings among Black women. At the same time, understanding how working-class Black women make meaning of social class and mobility is complex.

That is to say, racial analysis related to the upward mobility of Black Americans does address the complexity of experiences at the intersection of gender, class, and race (Martin, Horton & Booker, 2015; Cole & Omari, 2003). This is akin to Bourdieu's (1990) habitus as a conceptual framework of class-based mediating forces overlooking the role that race plays for African Americans (Lofton & Davis, 2015). For this reason, DuBois' framework makes a useful contribution to understanding the habitus of African Americans-"which connects systemic inequalities to their own cultural practices, logics, and actions" (Lofton & Davis, 2015, 215). Combining the various frameworks allows for a better understanding of the intersection of race, gender, and class in Black women's identities. This integrated approach helps to explore the struggles that Black women must confront during social mobility within higher education institutions which promote an unfamiliar cultural heritage.

2.2   Intersectionality

Intersectionality, a component of critical race theory, was applied to better understand what ties working-class Black women to the academic profession as faculty members. Critical race frameworks challenge dominant liberal ideals such as colorblindness and meritocracy (Crenshaw, Gotanda, Peller, & Thomas, 1995). As Flores (2000) suggests, "the task for critical race scholars is to uncover and explore the various ways in which racial thinking operates" (437).

Intersectionality has emerged in feminist theory as an important dimension to critical race analysis when addressing power relations defined by race, class, gender, sexuality, and other axes of domination. A key to understanding the historical and contemporary dilemmas of class mobility and educational attainment of Black working-class women involves recognizing race, class, and gender as interlocking systems of oppression, while contextualizing social relations in terms of dominance and resistance. The privileges associated with faculty status, as the professoriate is one of the most prestigious (and segregated) occupations in the United States, pose major challenges for working-class, Black women.

Unlike working-class occupations with relatively little power or authority, academic positions in higher education are marked by increased autonomy, greater prestige and higher salaries. Therefore, it is important to understand the influence of race/ethnicity, class and gender on African American women's identity change and survival strategies in psychological and behavioral responses to social and cultural demands in the academy. How academic settings, particularly institutions of higher education, are linked to social class status is equally important where the intersections of race, with gender and class largely determine economic and occupational patterns that result in the black woman deemed virtually "invisible"(Collins, 2000; Crenshaw, 1991, 1995).

3   Methodology

The aim of this study is to advance knowledge of identity change amongst Black women from working-class backgrounds and the relationship to their life chances and educational attainment. The intersection of race, gender, and class as a guide, the research questions and analysis involved qualitative interviews to investigate the ways that these women think, feel, and experience becoming members of a highly privileged educational group. Drawing upon in-depth interviews with Black women possessing doctorate degrees who self-identified as having a working-class family of origin, this study explores competing perspectives on the relative influence of habitus in upward mobility. By taking into account the intersectionality of race, class, and gender, study participants' stories revealed the challenges of negotiating social identity in exchange for economic opportunity. In other words, a new identity is constructed that accommodates the social expectations of academia without nullifying lower-class origins. Using an intersectional lens, the following research questions were addressed:

(1) How do Black women from working-class backgrounds experience the 'new social milieu' of academia?
(2) How do Black women from working-class backgrounds, who achieve faculty status, balance their obligations to their family of origin and the demands of academic institutions?

Data generation and analysis was informed by a grounded theory approach with a loosely structured interview process that allowed concepts and themes to emerge from the conversations with participants. The data collection strategies were fluid throughout the course of the research project and interview questions were altered as core ideas developed. It was an excellent way of obtaining interview data by permitting the interviewee to be an active participant in constructing their own stories. All procedures in this research project were approved by the Louisiana State University's Institutional Review Board (IRB).

4 Participants and Procedures

4.1 *Participants*

The sample consisted of 20 self-identified working-class Black women with doctoral degrees. All of the Black women were first-generation with doctorate degrees and employed by institutions of higher education in the role of professor or administrator. Participants ranged in age from 26 to 65, with a mean age of 43. Annual income for these women ranged from $40,000 to over $100,000 per year, with a mean annual salary of $72,500. The distribution by job type was six administrators, five assistant professors, four full professors, three associate professors, and two faculty administrators. Their various disciplines included education, social sciences, engineering, and technology. Some participants held dual appointments in a second department at their university. Of the 20 participants, the majority (N=13) held positions at Research 1 institutions and the remaining works at schools with lower Carnegie classifications. Ten of the women were married, one divorced, one widowed, and eight unmarried. Eleven participants had children while the remaining nine had none.

4.2 *Procedures*

Recruitment Phase. The recruitment phase began by using purposive sampling selecting individuals or cases that provide the information needed to address the research question. Participants were initially recruited using a compilation of over 36 listservs for organizations that target Black faculty and administrators across disciplines (i.e. Sociology, African American Studies, Higher Education,

Business, Law, Women's and Gender Studies, Education Policy), associations for women and minorities (i.e. Sisters of the Academy (SOTA), Women of Color in the Academy Project (WOCAP), Womanist Talk; The Feminist Wire; American Association of University Women (AAUW), Sociologists for Women in Society), and mentoring associations for people of color. Participants were also recruited at professional meetings, such as the Association for Black Sociologists (ABS), National Association for Multicultural Education (NAME), and Society for the Study of Social Problems (SSSP) where the study was advertised resulting in the recruitment of five participants. By agreeing to participate in this project, participants were asked to sign an informed consent form. This means individuals agreed to be interviewed about their experiences, or to withdraw from the study at any time.

After the initial contact, participants were e-mailed additional information in a packet that included a demographic sheet, consent form, and sample interview questions. Potential participants were asked to indicate their interests in the research project. Most of the women initially contacted were from middle- to upper-class backgrounds. However, these middle- and upper-class Black women became a resource for finding those who met the criteria. Recruitment took place through a variety of phases from March 2014-September 2015. By the end of September 2014, ten participants were recruited. Recruited participant were also asked if they had a friend or acquaintance that fit the criteria and might be willing to participate in the research. Seven others were recruited using the "Call for Participants" via listservs, and the final three were follow-ups. That is, initial contacts based on a referral with no confirmation were followed up with a request for participation in the study. The follow-up strategy led to three more individuals agreeing to participate. Recruitment was completed in March 2015.

Interview Phase. The interviewing of participants began in March 2014. The questions used in the initial interviews are presented below in Table 7.1. Interviews took place in an offices or conference room on the university campus where participants worked. The majority (N=15) were teleconference interviews. For those that were conducted via telephone, a free conference call number through FreeConferenceCall.com—a free live conferencing facility. Five face-to-face interviews were conducted with women who worked at the same institution as the primary author. The interviews lasted between 45–90 minutes and were audio-taped. As part of a telephone conferencing protocol, participants were first notified via e-mail and given an agreed upon date and time, dial-in number and Meeting ID. All the telephone conferencing interviews used the same dial-in-number and entered the same Meeting ID, followed by the # key. As the host, the interviewer had to enter a PIN to connect

TABLE 7.1 Sample questions

Part(s)	Category	Question(s)
Part I: Initial open-ended questions	General	Talk to me about what it means to be a Black woman in the academy from a working-class background? How, if at all, has your view of the academy changed since you've obtained your Ph.D. as opposed to before?
Part II: Intermediate questions	Personal experience	What, if anything, did you know about the academy prior to completing your doctorate program?
	Perceptions of performance, race, class, and gender	Talk to me about your professional peer relationships with your colleagues, for example, how would you describe your social and interpersonal relations with them?
	Work/life balance	What helps you to manage your space in the academy and at home? What problems might you encounter in view of your family roles?
Part III: Ending questions	Lessons	Is there anything else you think I should know to understand women of color from working-class backgrounds navigating the academy better?

SOURCE: AUTHOR GENERATED.

with the caller through the call center. All participants were informed during the conference call when the recording started and ended. Each participant was informed of her right to refuse to answer any question she felt was too personal, inappropriate, or uncomfortable. Participants were also informed of their right to terminate the interview at any time if so desired. None of the participants refused to answer any questions or opted to terminate the interview at any time.

The interview protocol developed for the study was guided by Holstein and Gubrium's (1995) *Active Interviewing* strategies. This research method is utilized in examining the relational effects of race, class, and gender to identify multiple sources of oppression. In this approach, the participant is not a passive vessel of knowledge, but instead "...consults repertoires of experience and orientations, linking fragments into patterns, and offering theoretically coherent descriptions, accounts, and explorations" making her somewhat of a researcher in her own right, (Holstein and Gubrium, 1995, 29). Following each interview, brief memos detailing the major themes that surfaced during the interview were recorded. Five of the interviews were transcribed by the primary author, and the services of a professional transcriptionist were used for the other fifteen recorded interviews. There were notable differences in the level of intimacy between in-person and telephone interviews, specifically in terms of participant's actions and understanding within the setting. For example, some participants cried, paused, and folded their hands during the in-person interviews. By contrast, it was hard to detect if this was the case during telephone interviews. These observations are addressed during data analysis.

5 Data Analysis

Self-reflexivity. The primary author is a working-class, Black woman with a doctorate in Sociology. Her subjective experiences serve as a starting point to help understand the multiple layers of both identity and socialization in transition to educational privilege. The desire to understand her experience as a Black woman from a working-class background in the academy reflects "the need to reconcile subjectivity and objectivity in producing scholarship" (Collins, 2000, p. ix). It is what Collins (2000) calls the power of self-definition, which refers to ideologies, epistemologies, and paradigms shaped within a community of Black women scholars whose knowledge claims represent their interests from their standpoint. As a result, the stories of these participants provide insights into the lived experiences of Black women academicians from working-class backgrounds which can be lessons to students from similar backgrounds, including the primary author, how to navigate the competing demands of their dual existence.

Data Coding. The initial stage of analysis included the open-coding of all data for relevant themes and patterns, followed by the second stage of more focused coding. An Excel spreadsheet was created, organized by date, description, code (for open/ focused), and notes. The brief notes taken immediately after the interview captured broad categories and themes that emerged. Entire narratives were pasted into the spreadsheet and examined for each case line by line. More focused coding followed by breaking the data down into subcategories for the categories of themes and ideas. Gradually, participants' narratives reflected a tension in identity negotiation between their working-class background and current life circumstances. Axial coding provided the framework for revealing the covert connections between social class and upward mobility in relation to educational attainment.

While in the midst of data collection, theoretical sampling was performed to refine the concepts and codes. An example of a theory-driven code (Charmaz, 2014) is the concept of *double consciousness*, which DuBois defines as an internal conflict within African Americans stemming from a view of the self as a Black person and seeing oneself through the eyes of (White) American society. Subsequently, more abstract codes and *a hybridity of habitus* emerged. This involved the complexities of Black working-class women negotiating the habitus of African Americans. Class, for example, is modes of dress and foods that people eat, which are visible signs of culture and social class status (e.g. achieved status). Whereas, race and gender are "ascribed statuses" making for a cultural experience different from participants' socialization in terms of the physical, social, and psychology elements of their working-class background, thus, developing a new habitus as they are becoming socially mobile.

During the data analytic process, several particular themes were revisited (i.e. "ascribed versus achieved status") via theoretical sampling with the women that were previously interviewed. These strategies provided further insight to how these women managed to reconcile the competing demands of their working-class origins and academic accomplishments.

Narrative Themes. The analysis begins with a discussion of the economic realities associated with upward social mobility of Black working-class women in the academy. They come from families and communities with limited economic resources and their transition to middle-class status has major implications for their original lifestyles. Participants reflect upon their new higher-class status relative to their working-class backgrounds in terms of aesthetic differences of a lifestyle far more disparate from their previous social standing. Then, participants reported on how they stayed grounded as part of maintaining a habitus rooted in their family of origin. Finally, they talked about 'playing the game' –as they construct a hybrid habitus- as part of balancing their faculty status and a habitus grounded in their family of origin, which involved keeping their personal life secret and apart from their professional responsibilities.

6 Results

6.1 Economic Realities: a Consciousness for Striving

When asked what it means to be a Black woman in the academy from a working-class background, participants often constructed a narrative that began with the economic challenges of their working-class history. For example, Abigail, a 33 year-old, unmarried, assistant professor responded, "So, I'm not well traveled. Before people classed me, before I got this Ph.D., like my family went on vacation every summer within the U.S., you know, California, Chicago, New York. I've never been off the Continental Americas." Dana, a 58-year-old associate professor of economics, shared a similar working-class experience stating, "We had no running water, we had no car. So, I was in college when we got running water. I was in high school when we got a car." Abigail and Dana construct working-class identities based on different access to and disposability of economic resources, for example, traveling outside of the U.S. and living in a home without running water. An important issue concerning Dana and Abigail in their working-class biography is the strong relationship between education and class habitus. This involves explaining the lack of economic resources in their upbringing, and the *dispositional aspects* of achieving upward social mobility primarily based on their educational attainment. Seen in this way, my participants' habitus not only make class distinctions more visible as faculty, but they also have to find their way into the field of academia with individuals whose habitus they are not familiar.

7 Making Distinctions: a Taste of Academia

It is not just the higher salaries and occupational prestige of college professors that separate them from working-class families; it is also lifestyle—i.e., values, tastes and preferences, availability of resources, and (elite) social circles. As such, 'a taste of academia' reflects the middle-to upper-class lifestyles members of the academy enjoy in comparison to individuals from the working-class. Ellen's narrative, a 31-year-old staff psychologist at a university, revealed these lifestyle differences:

> He ran in certain circles and he was the president of an HBCU. He ran in certain college circles in general, particularly in black college circles, and there were certain items of clothing that people wore that I didn't expect. I wore a cute little purple dress that I got from Ross ... But then I got to the event and like his staff was there and other people were there you know

> ... the big donors to the university were there, and these people were wearing St. Johns suits and Ann Taylor suits, and they were carrying Louis Vuitton and you know like the shoes were like Tory Burch, and I didn't learn about what a Tory Burch was until I had a Ph.D.

Ellen's narrative demonstrates how an individual's dress and aesthetic influence social expectations. Arguably, her fashion and style—e.g., the dress from Ross' symbolizes working-class practices and social scripts pertaining to social class differences. Ellen clearly felt like an outsider by wearing a dress from Ross, when she noticed other people wearing St. Johns and Ann Taylor suits. It is evident that fashion and dress can make a statement about middle-class status to the upwardly mobile, but they are also reminders of social class differences.

In another case, Linda, a 39-year-old, married mother of two, and associate professor of sociology illustrated in her comments how "figurines" represented social class differences in taste. She stated:

> Okay, so, we start talking and these are some older women, too, and so they start talking about these All God's Children figurines and how they have so many of them and this collection of them and how much each of the pieces cost, and I'm like, "Who's buying all these figurines," but they portray all these figures of black history and there might be a Harriet Tubman one or of a little girl, and they come with these certificates of authenticity, and I was just lost in the discussion about how much each of the figurines cost ... The other story was about how one of them was in an accident or something and the appraiser came and she got a check for over a $1,000. I'm just standing there like, "For some figurines?"

In both the cases of Ellen and Linda, it is apparent that Black women from working-class backgrounds become exposed to the habitus of the higher social classes through encounters with other Blacks from middle-class and upper middle-class families. And when this happens, they don't necessarily see themselves as equals. These experiences underscore the material constraints in the early lives of these Black working-class families, as well as the extent to which social class diversity exist within the African American community.

The stories of the women who were interviewed also revealed how *the* habitus of Whites and Blacks were divided along racial lines. An excellent example was the case of Abigail, who explained:

> I think White people treat Black people like we all "niggers," regardless, like nigger you ... and I know that's really crass, but eventually it will come

> out of White people that you just Black. White people understand Black people as similar. At a very basic level they understand all of us as just being Black, but they will kind of understand that I may be a little bit different Black because I have a Ph.D ... but it's almost like I have to remind them ... they have to remind themselves.

Central to Abigail's narrative in explaining the social mobility process with respect to habitus is *the* habitus of African Americans—"which connects systemic inequalities to their own cultural practices, logics and action" (Lofton & Davis, 2015, 215). At the same time, Bonilla-Silva (2004) observed, "Whites, as members of the dominant racial group will be oblivious to the racial components of their own socialization and how that may affect their perceptions of Blacks" (29). This is evidenced in Vanessa's narrative, a 46- year-old assistant professor of psychology as she drew upon the habitus of African Americans:

> This is status quo but, again, just to give you a sense of how things haven't changed. A couple years ago, I'm in the departmental office again, White faculty member, female, comes to me; I think I was making copies, and she said what are you? You want to tell her you're a human ... Meanwhile though, mind you, I got nappy hair, but I'm very, very light. So, again, what are you ... she made up something after that, and was like, I thought you were Greek. I've gone natural to push against being racially ambiguous— it's the hardest thing to deal with in the world, in my opinion.

Taken together, Abigail and Vanessa's narratives prioritize race, which involves cultural practices engendered by the same habitus (disposition) (Lofton & Davis, 2015; Schneider & Lang, 2014). By this, I'm referring to how the Black population tends to be viewed as a homogenous group by White America, which is a cultural consequence of the enslavement of Africans.

8   Staying Grounded

Participants' upward social mobility and transition to higher social strata associated with their faculty status impacted the family as a whole through preserved familial and communal ties. All participants except one emphasized that communal relationships and mutual support systems were constructed as mechanisms for survival and put in place long before earning a Ph.D. When asked about adapting to new ways of thinking and acting in the academy, Emily, a 53 -year-old married mother of two and full professor of history explained:

> ...regardless of where I go, I know where my roots are and I don't look down on people who aren't where I am because I can see in my own family just how different kinds of opportunities and stuff results in different types of outcomes. And so, you know, there are people in my family who've been in jail, people who are single moms, people on welfare, I have other relatives who are successful, you know. And so I can be more realistic...I look at my job as a job that pays the bills.

Emily makes the point that she understands that opportunities can lead to different life outcomes. She witnessed this in her family of origin where relatives had a range of life outcomes from the stereotypically poor outcomes (e.g., welfare, jail. single parenthood) to successful careers. These experiences have taught her humility about her own success in the academy. In others, she views her career as a job that allow her to "pay the bills," but it does not make her better than people of her working-class background.

> Julie, a 45- year old, assistant professor in public health shares a similar story:
> So I don't necessarily want to live in like a one-room shack like my grandparents did.... So trying to find those places where I feel comfortable being myself but I'm also, you know, being able to take advantage of a higher income and live in a place where I could invite my colleagues over. But, in the academy, sort of intellectual space is not how I grew up. You know what I mean? When I'm in that place, I tap into the part of myself that grew up with the hopes that one day somebody would go to college and that sort of pride in me ... it helps me to be grounded in where I came from and to always remember that.

The majority of participants talked about the importance of being grounded and rooted in their families of origin. However, they also spoke about the challenges of balancing academic and working-class worlds. To this end, creating spaces where the subjects could maintain their family and friend ties often involved 'sabbaticals' to get out, to get time away, while navigating the tenure process. Others reported attending church and using prayer to maintain a strong spiritual center in order to keep their social advancement in perspective. Although several participants expressed firm commitment to their faith in staying grounded, this was not the case for others.

8.1 *'Playing the Game' of Keeping the Personal Hidden*

Participants spoke about the importance of maintaining a division between the personal hidden habitus, grounded in their family of origin, and their professional identity. Thus, these women engaged in 'playing the game', as they developed new interests, tastes, and lifestyles of mainstream academia. Study participants indicated that they must learn how to navigate two social worlds and to keep them separate. Aubrey has internalized quite well the "rules of the game," i.e. the habitus and strategies needed to be successful on the job. For example, when asked about transitioning to a higher social stratum in the academy, Aubrey, a 45 year-old unmarried, assistant professor of sociology and criminal *justice* responded:

> I could never admit that I actually listen to rap music. Like admit that I actually like rap music and that I actually listen. Like they just make assumptions that I listen to NPR and I watch the news every night. I don't do any of that. It's like I don't listen to NPR, I don't read the New York Times, I don't watch the news every night, I just don't. That's not how I was raised, I'm not really interested in watching the news, I don't really like NPR, I think it's dry and boring. I tried it, but there are just these assumptions that ... And they just talk to me as if that's what I do because, of course, I have to do that, I'm an intellectual, I'm a professor, I must do those things, and no. So I just pretend like I do those things even though I don't.

Aubrey keeps the two worlds are separate; however it's clear that her self-identification is rooted in her upbringing. Despite white middle-class teenagers being the biggest consumers of rap music, it is my contention that her preference for rap music, builds upon racial stereotypes of Black people from a low socioeconomic status. She also engages in practices adapting to her new habitus as an intellectual and professor. In this way, Aubrey represents both her working-class, poor, Black culture and intellectuals who listen to NPR in her social identity.

Leah, a 26 year-old married, chemist, revealed a similar experience about how she communicates with family and friends. She explained:

> There's an intro in a Roots album where they are in a disagreement with their record label. And the record label's very upset because they feel as though they were accosted by the band members. And one of the members in the band says nobody's mad at you, nobody's ... nobody's screaming and yelling at you, this is how we interact, this is how we are, we've been screaming.... Yes, so this is how we've been yelling and screaming at each other all our lives. Not to say that I'm screaming and yelling at my colleagues, but my reactions in moments of surprise or when my guard is down is something that I have to be very mindful of.... I had to learn those politics.

Eva, much like Aubrey, illustrates how she is able to navigate between two totally distinct cultures. In these cases, the patterns of acting and thinking like their middle-class colleagues involved a kind of watchfulness and chronic monitoring in their behavior, tastes, and language, while simultaneously managing the habitus of their upbringing.

This was the case with Deborah, a 46-year-old full professor in engineering, who explained how she was learning the norms of her highly privileged institution including the difference between red wines:

> Where I come from, there are norms that I just was unfamiliar with ... Like I still had ... I had to learn ... I had to learn the politics of navigating through a highly privileged institution ... very conservative, very white... at the same time I was learning what a white wine glass looks like, what's a Malbec and what's the difference between a Malbec and a Shiraz. I don't know. I just want a glass of red wine, you know ... So I ... I don't think that there's a place to be who you really are in the academy. I think that the people who are chameleons are the ones who are successful. So if you can learn how to blend, if you can learn how to hide that part of who you are, if you can learn how to act like them, talk like them, walk like them, dress like them, you'll be fine.

The narratives of Aubrey, Leah, Eva, and Dana indicates that each have learned to transcend class boundaries as they move in between the habitus of their working-class backgrounds and the new status of their middle-class academic positions. The majority of participants viewed life in the academy simply as a profession, and not an extension of the habitus associated with their family of origin. Participants situated the upward mobility associated with their profession in the context of struggles against institutionalized racism and racial oppression crossing boundaries that strain family ties. Black women academicians from working-class backgrounds must navigate a duality of living in two separate worlds. Factors like their family values, socioeconomic status (SES), and limited educational attainment serve as the foundation of their habitus and identity.

9 Conclusion

All of the Black female participants in this study grew up in working-class families with no relevant role models, so they had to adapt intuitively to the field of academia. The transition from a lower to higher social stratum is not accompanied by a 'how-to guide', at the same time, the habitus acquired from communities in which they grew up provided conditions for staying grounded. The skills and socio-cultural competencies needed to survive in their profession are found in their ability to develop a hybrid habitus in transition between the two worlds. Equally as important is the creation of a new model that reflects the socialization process in terms of identity construction. Even though Bourdieu's habitus accounts for class behavior in its social and cultural contexts, his model doesn't adequately address race (and gender), reinforcing much of the ingenuity of mainstream demographers who view the African American experience as monolithic, which results in a very narrow view of how working-class African Americans, particularly its women engage in social mobility. Another important point that needs to be in Africana Demography is the limitation of Critical Race Theory (CRT), which fails to adequately address class; therefore, it is our contention that a better approach requires a merging of these two theories with regards to race, gender, and class. These complimentary paradigms when put together constitutes a comprehensive understanding of class, race, and gender in the socialization process of African American women, especially its working-class, thus a 'hybrid habitus'. One of the biases assumed by mainstream sociologists and demographers alike is the inextricable link between the class status and life chances. The view that whatever class one is socialized into, one will not move out of that class. Black women from working-class backgrounds are now employed in middle-class positions in the academy, specifically as tenured or tenure-tracked professors, the one demographic that does not fit the American faculty profile, especially at traditionally white universities (Evans, 2007; Feagin, 2006; Guy-Sheftall & Cole, 2003; Hill-Collins, 2000), which challenges both Bourdieu's perspective and mainstream demography. Taken together, the role of habitus alone does not explain how Black women move from the working to the middle class, nor does it explain how moving from one class to another impacts how they see themselves and how others see them.

As a result, for Africana Demography, this research calls attention to how class differences move beyond economic means. We found that how these women negotiate social class practices, like purchasing a dress from Ross, knowing Malbec is a red wine, or collecting high-priced figurines (e.g. *All God's Children*) are based on aesthetic differences that cross class boundaries from their families of origin. On the other hand, in their roles as university faculty, working-class Black women problematize mainstream demographers indicators associated with class status. Seen in this way, working-class Black women offer a more comprehensive view of striving for and holding a good professional job that's critical to Africana Demography in terms of habitus. Habitus functioned as a skill, adaptive in nature, which means their ability to simultaneously adopt new patterns of acting and thinking in an unfamiliar environment resulted in a 'hybrid habitus'.

Bibliography

Anderson, E. 2012. "Race, Culture, and Educational Opportunity." *Theory and Research in Education*, 10 (2): 105–129.

Arena, J. 2011. "Bringing In the Black Working-class: The Black Urban Regime Strategy." *Science & Society*, 75 (2): 153–179. https://doiorg.libezp.lib.lsu.edu/10.1521/siso.2011.75.2.153.

Bell, D. 1992. *Faces at the Bottom of the Well: The Permanence of Racism*. New York: Basic Books.

Biernacki, P. and Waldorf, D. 1981. "Snowball Sampling: Problems and Techniques of Chain Referral Sampling." *Sociological Methods & Research*, 10: 141–163.

Bonilla-Silva, E. 2004. "Where is the Love? Why Whites Have Limited Interaction With Blacks." *The Journal of Intergroup Relations*, 31 (1): 24–38.

Bonilla-Silva, E. 2013. *Racism Without Racists: Color-Blind Racism and the Persistence of Racial Inequality in the United States*. Lanham, MD: Rowman and Littlefield.

Bourdieu, P., & Passeron, J.C. 1977. *Reproduction in Education, Society, & Culture*. Beverly Hills, CA: Sage Publications.

Bourdieu, P. 1977. *Outline of a Theory of Practice*. Cambridge, OK: Cambridge University Press.

Bourdieu, P. 1984. *Distinction: a Social Critique of the Judgement of Taste*. London: Routledge & Kegan Paul.

Bourdieu, P. 1990. *The Logic of Practice*. Cambridge, UK: Polity Press.

Bourdieu, P. 1993. *The Field of Cultural Production: Essays on Art and Literature* (ed.and introd. by R. Johnson), Cambridge: Cambridge University Press.

Charmaz, K. 2000. Grounded theory: Objectivist and constructivist methods. In N.K. Denzin and Y.S. Lincoln (Eds.) *Handbook of Qualitative Research*, 509–536. Thousand Oaks, CA: Sage.

Charmaz, K. 2002. Qualitative interviewing and grounded theory analysis. In J.F. Gubrium and J. Holstein (Eds.) *Handbook of Interview Research*, 675–694. Thousand Oaks, CA: Sage.

Cole, E.R. & Omari, S. 2003. Race, Class and the Dilemmas of Upward Mobility for African Americans. *Journal of Social Issues* 59 (4): 785–802.

Cole, J. & Guy-Sheftall, B. 2003. *Gender Talk: The Struggle for Women's Equality in African American Communities*. New York, NY: Ballantine Publishing.

Collins, P.H. 1986. Learning from the Outsider Within: The Sociological Significance of Black Feminist Thought. *Social Problems* 33 (6): 514–532.

Collins, P.H. 2000. *Black Feminist Thought: Knowledge, Consciousness, and the Politics of Empowerment*. (2nd ed.). New York: Routledge Classics.

Crawford, K., & Smith, D. 2007. Climbing the Ivory Tower: Recommendations for Mentoring African American Women in Higher Education. *Race, Gender & Class*, 14 (1): 253–265.

Crenshaw, K. 1991. "Mapping the Margins: Intersectionality, Identity Politics, and Violence against Women of Color." *Stanford Law Review* 43 (6): 1241–99.

Crenshaw, K. 1995. "Critical Race Theory: The Key Writings That Formed the Movement." In *Mapping the Margins: Intersectionality, Identity Politics, and Violence against Women of Color*, edited by K.Crenshaw, N. Gotanda, G. Peller, and K. Thomas, 357–383. New York: New Press.

Draut, T. 2018. "Understanding the Working-class." Demos—An Equal Say and Equal Chance for All-Policy and Research. https://www.demos.org/sites/default/files/publications/WorkingClass_Explainer_Final.pdf.

DuMonthier, A., Childers, C. & Mili, J. 2017.The Status of Black Women in the United States. A report in collaboration with the National Domestic Worker's Alliance and The Institute for Women's Policy Research.

Duncan, E., Holmes, K., Miller, K., & Holmes, B. 2011. The Impact of Popular Culture's Strong Black Woman (SBW) Image on Black Women Faculty at Historically Black Colleges and Universities (HBCU): A Multidisciplinary Analysis. *Journal of the Mid-Atlantic Popular/American Culture Association*, 20: 155–175.

Evans, S. 2007a. *Black Women in the Ivory Tower*. Gainesville, FL: University of Florida Press.

Evans, S. 2007b. Women of Color in Higher Education. *The NEA Higher Education Journal*, 15 (1): 131–138.

Evans-Winters, V., & Esposito, J. 2010. Other Peoples' Daughters: Critical Race Feminism and Black Girls' Education, *Educational Foundations*, Winter-Spring, 11–24.

Feagin, J. 2010. *The White Racial Frame: Centuries of Racial Framing and Counter-Framing*. New York, NY: Routledge.

Ferguson, S. 2015. Class Struggle in the Ivory Towers. *Philosophy of African American Studies*. (pp. 15–57). New York, NY: Palgrave Macmillan.

Finley, S., Gray, B., & Martin, L.L. 2018. "Affirming Our Values": African American Scholars, White Virtual Mobs, and the Complicity of White University Administrators. *AAUP Journal of Academic Freedom*, 9: 1–20.

Freeman, K & Brown II, M.C. 2005. *African Americans and College Choice: The Influence of Family and School*. Albany: State University of New York Press.

Frye, J. 2018. "A Commitment to Black Women's Equal Pay is Essential to the Nation's Economic Progress." Center for American Progress-Valuing Black Women's Work https://www.americanprogress.org/issues/women/news/2018/08/07/454508/valuingblack-womens-work/.

Glaser, B.G., & Strauss, A.L. 1967. *The Discovery of Grounded Theory: Strategies for Qualitative Research*. Hawthorne, NY: Aldine de Gruyter.

Goffman, Erving. 1963. *Stigma: Notes on the Management of Spoiled Identity*. Englewood Cliffs, NJ: Prentice-Hall.

Green, D., Pulley, T., Jackson, M., Martin, L., & Fasching-Varner, K. 2016. Mapping the Margins and Searching for Higher Ground: Examining the Marginalisation of Black Female Graduate Students at PWIs. *Gender and Education*, 30 (3): 295–309. https://doi.org/10.1080/09540253.2016.1225009.

Grzanka, P. (Ed.). 2014. *Intersectionality: A Foundations and Frontiers Reader*. Boulder, CO: Westview Press.

Gutiérrez, M.G. 2012. *Presumed Incompetent: The Intersections of Race and Class for Women in Academia*. Boulder, CO: University Press of Colorado.

Halle, D., & Weyher, L.F.L. 2005. New Developments in Class and Culture. In D. Jacobs & N. Hanrahan (Eds.), *The Blackwell Companion to the Sociology of Culture*, 207–219.

Harper, S. 2012. Race without Racism: How Higher Education Researchers Minimize Racist Institutional Norms. *The Review of Higher Education*, 36 (1): 9–29.

Harris-Perry, M.V. 2011. *Sister Citizen: Shame, Stereotypes, and Black Women in America*. New York: Mary Cady Tew Memorial Fund.

Holstein, J.A., & Gubrium, J.F. 1995. The Active Interview. *Qualitative Research Methods Series 37*. Thousand Oaks, CA: Sage.

Hooks, B. 1993. Keeping Close to Home: Class and Education. In M. Tokarczyk, & E. Fay, (Eds.), *Working-Class Women in the Academy: Laborers in the Knowledge Factory*, 99–111. Boston, MA: University of Massachusetts Press.

Hooks, B. 2000. *Where We Stand: Class Matters*. New York: Routledge.

Horton, H., Allen, B, Herring, C. & Thomas, M. 2000. Lost in the Storm: The Sociology of the Black Working-class, 1850 to 1990. *American Sociological Review*, 65: 128–137.

Jackson, L.J. 2005. *Real Black: Adventures in Racial Sincerity*. Chicago, IL: University of Chicago Press.

Johnson, O. 2014. Still Separate, Still Unequal: The Relation of Segregation in Neighborhoods and Schools to Education Inequality. *The Journal of Negro Education*, 83: 199–215.

Jones, J. 2017. "The racial wealth gap: How African Americans have been shortchanged out of the materials to build wealth." Economic Policy Institute- https://www.epi.org/blog/the-racial-wealth-gap-how-african-americans-have-been-shortchanged-out-of-the-materials-to-build-wealth/.

King, E.J. 1991. Dysconscious Racism: Ideology, Identity, and the Miseducation of Teachers. *The Journal of Negro Education*, 60: 133–146.

Lacy, K. 2004. Black Spaces, Black Places: Strategic Assimilation and Identity Construction in Middle –Class Suburbia. *Ethnic and Racial Studies*, 27 (6): 908–930.

Lacy, K. 2015. "Race, Privilege and the Growing Class Divide." *Ethnic and Racial Studies* 38 (8): 1246–1249.

Ladson-Billings, G., & Tate, W.F. 1995. "Toward a Critical Race Theory of Education." *Teachers College Record*, 97: 47–68.

Lee, E. & Maynard, T. 2017. "In Class, Sharing Class: Faculty Members from Low-Socioeconomic Status Backgrounds and Status Visibility." *Journal of Working-Class Studies*, 2 (2): 36–53.

Lofton, R. & Davis, J.E. 2015. "Toward a Black Habitus: African Americans Navigating Systemic Inequalities within Home, School, and Community." *Journal of Negro Education*, 84(3): 214–230.

Mann, S.A. 2012. *Doing Feminist Theory: From Modernity to Postmodernity*. Oxford: Oxford University Press.

Martin, L., Horton, H. & Booker, T. 2015. *Lessons from the Black Working-class: Foreshadowing America's Economic Health*. Santa Barbara, CA: Praeger.

Mazumder, B. 2014. "Black-White Differences in Intergenerational Economic Mobility in the United States." *Economic Perspectives*, 38: 1–18.

Mitchell, R., & Rosiek, J. 2006. "Professor as Embodied Racial Signifier: A Case Study of the Significance of Race in a University Classroom." *The Review of Education, Pedagogy, and Cultural Studies*, 28: 395–409.

Moore, M. 2017. "Women of Color in the Academy: Navigating Multiple Intersections and Multiple Hierarchies." *Social Problems*, 64: 200–205.

Moynihan, D.P. 1965. *The Negro Family: The Case for National Action*. Washington, DC: Office of Policy Planning and Research. Retrieved January 27, 2018 http://hdl.handle.net/2027/mdp.39015038910553.

National Science Foundation (NSF) and National Center for Science and Engineering Statistics (NCSES). 2016. Survey of Earned Doctorates – 2016 Doctorate Recipients from U.S. Universities. Retrieved from https://www.nsf.gov/statistics/2018/nsf18304/.

Niemann, Y. 2016. "The Social Ecology of Tokenism in Higher Education," *Peace Review*, 28 (4): 451–458, DOI: 10.1080/10402659.2016.1237098.

O'Connor, C. 2002. "Black Women Beating the Odds From One Generation to the Next: How Changing Dynamics of Constraint and Opportunity Affect the Process of Educational Resilience." *American Educational Research Journal*, 39 (4): 855–903.

Omi, M., & Winant, H. 1994. *Racial Formation in the United States: From the 1960s to the 1990s*. New York: Routledge.

Patrick, K. 2018. "The Proof is in the Numbers: Black Women are Still Unemployed." National Women's Law Center. https://nwlc.org/blog/the-proof-is-in-the-numbers-black-women-are-still-unemployed/.

Patton, L., Harper, S. 2003. "Mentoring Relationships among African American Women in Graduate and Professional Schools." *New Directions for Student Services*, 104: 67–78.

Rodgers-Rose, L. 1980. *The Black Woman*. Beverly Hills, CA: Sage.

Schneider, J., & Lang, C. 2014. "Social Mobility, Habitus and Identity Formation in the Turkish-German Second Generation." *New Diversities*, 16 (1): 89–105.

Shavers, M. & Moore, J. 2014. "The Double-Edged Sword: Coping and Resiliency Strategies of African American Women Enrolled in Doctoral Programs at Predominately White Institutions." *Frontiers*, 35 (3): 15–38.

Smith, D. 1987. *The Everyday World as Problematic: A Feminist Sociology*. Toronto: University of Toronto Press.

Strauss, A. & Corbin, J. 1998. *Basics of Qualitative Research: Techniques and Procedures for Developing Grounded Theory (2nd ed.)*. Newbury Park, CA: Sage.

Tea, M. (Ed.). 2004. *Without a Net: The Female Experience of Growing Up Working-class*. Seattle, WA: Seal Press.

Tokarczyk, M., & Fay, E. (Eds). 1993. *Working-Class Women in the Academy: Laborers in the Knowledge Factory*. Amherst, MA: University of Massachusetts Press.

Veblen, T. 1899. "Conspicuous Consumption." In *The Theory of the Leisure Class*. (Ch. 4) Project Gutenberg, http://www.gutenberg.org/files/833/833-h/833h.htm.

Welsch, K.A. 2005. *Those Winter Sundays: Female Academics and their Working-Class Parents*. Lanham, Md: University Press of America.

Wilson, W.J. 1978. *The Declining Significance of Race: Blacks and Changing American Institutions. 3rd ed.* Chicago, IL: University of Chicago Press.

Wilson, W.J. 1987. *The Truly Disadvantaged*. Chicago, IL: University of Chicago Press.

Wilson, W.J. 2011. "The Declining Significance of Race: Revisited & Revised." *Daedalus*, 104 (2): 55–69.

CHAPTER 8

A Black Theology of Liberation: the Black Church and a Living Wage

Weldon McWilliams

1   Introduction

Racism and capitalism are as endemic to the United States as anything else and these two aspects of American life that have been around since the nation was birthed. The Civil Rights Movement of the 1950's and 1960's brought the issue of racial inequality to the forefront of American politics for the first time since the Reconstruction Era after the nation's Civil War. Although many will concur that there was progress made during the Civil Rights Movement, there were many aspects of that social justice movement that still has yet to be addressed in a serious manner.

Toward the end of his life, Dr. Martin Luther King, Jr. acknowledged that there were "three evils" that that kept the United States from becoming the beloved community that he was prayerfully hoping it would still become. Those evils were Racism, Militarism, and Poverty. I would contend that at best, the needle of progress has moved very little if at all, and at worst, in the opposite direction of progress in post- civil rights America. At the time of this writing, America is prepared to spend more on its military in 2020 than at any other time in American history since World War II (Stein and Gregg 2019). In the age of Trump, overt racist rhetoric has reached a level inside American politics at a level not seen in my lifetime. The man who fan the flames of racism with the "birther" debate during Barack Obama's presidency, has now found himself at 1600 Pennsylvania Ave and even that has not stopped Donald Trump from his highly offensive rhetoric, which has seemed emboldened white nationalists to come from out of hiding. The poverty rate in 2017 in the United States was 12.3%, about 39.7 million people and this number did not change from 2016 into 2017.[2] It is safe to say that the fight for freedom is continuing and there is much more work that needs to be done. The three evils that were identified by Dr. King are still very prevalent in today's America and new methods and strategies may now need to be implemented to address the social issues that still confront Black folk today. There are limitations to the way most research seek to examine the racial economic equality that still exists in these United States. One limitation is that most research still do not seek out Black epistemology. Much of the research that is out there does not take into account how stark the differences are in the Black and white experience in America; so much so that where they look for solutions also probably differ. Although the wealth gap that exists between Black and White Americans is virtually unchanged since the 1960's, there is a prevalent perception that there has been significant racial progress in America. The only thing that has seen significant progress is the numerous efforts used to cover up and hide the reality of the stagnation of racial progress. As a result, there is an exaggeration of racial progress typically found in whites and an underestimation of past racial discrimination in blacks. This is revealed through the works of people like, Michael W. Kraus, Julian M. Rucker, and Jennifer A. Richeson, in their research study entitled, "Americans Misperceive Racial Economic Equality." When research like this becomes available there seems to be an automatic assumption that the institutions that need to lead this change are the same institutions that benefited from the racial inequalities in the first place. To address the issue of the need for a living wage, I make the case that the source for this call, the leading voice of this call must not come from the traditional institutions that typically are shaped by mainstream thought and theory, but it must come from a Black epistemological root. The effort to bring forth racial economic equality most come from sources of knowledge that go beyond the traditional mainstream white institutions. They themselves have benefitted from the societal inequality. In some cases, they have even help contribute and produce the inequality.

2   Addressing Economic Inequality in America

Answers to the myriad of problems that impact Black people in America, will not be found in solutions that simply attempt to have Black people mimic solutions that may have worked for White People. In this society race plays such a pivotal part in one's lived experiences and it should not be ignored. Colorblindness is not the cure for racism. Because of the role of race, the lived American experience is different for white folks than it is for Black folks. This must also be taken into account when academics, intellectuals and/or social scientist study the issue at hand and whenever they propose a solution. The solutions themselves should utilize the lived experience itself as a primary source. In other words, Black people need to be heard and the primary source when trying to solve problems that impact Black people differently of disproportionately. Black folk and Black Institutions have to be the primary sources for Black solutions.

In a nation that often times uses the terms of freedom and economic opportunity as promotional tools for others across the world, economic inequality in the United States has not become better but the gulf between the rich and the poor has grown and become progressively worse. According to a Washington Post article, there is nowhere in the country where one can work full time on minimum wage and rent a modest two-bedroom apartment, anywhere in the United States. "Not even in Arkansas, the state with the cheapest housing in the country. One would need to earn $13.84 an hour — about $29,000 a year — to afford a two-bedroom apartment there. The minimum wage in Arkansas is $8.50 an hour" (Jan. 2018). Downsizing to a one-bedroom apartment doesn't fair much better. According to the same Washington Post article, a one-bedroom apartment would only be available in 22 counties in the country, for workers who work fulltime at minimum wage (Jan. 2018).

What does this say about a nation that proclaims itself to be a land of opportunity? The question becomes, "Opportunity for who?" What does it say about policies of a nation where a full-time wage earner can't afford a one- or two-bedroom apt. What does it say about the society of a nation that refuses to give a sufficient wage to her workers? It conveys a bankruptcy of the soul. It conveys a lack of empathy and a lack of care. It also conveys a notion of privilege and notion of superiority. For those who love justice and fairness, there must be a willingness to fight against such an injustice that is the inability to earn a wage that would allow one to have a decent living despite the fact that they are working full time at their place of employment. The question is not whether or not it should be combated, but rather how should this be combated? Who is most qualified to combat it?

3 Look to the Black Church and Black Liberation Theology?

This phenomenon should be combatted by many folks on many sides. This evil is profound enough that its combatants will have to be many, and there has to be a strong willfulness to combat it. But this fight is not and should not be looked at as just a physical or policy issue but there is a spiritual aspect to this fight. There is a spiritual dimension that must be exposed and addressed and the fight to combat this must also acknowledge this. No other entity has done this in America like the Black Church. The Black Church has a long history of combatting American mainstream norms that have always promoted false senses of superiority and inferiority, from the time it existed as the "invisible institution" during enslavement all the way up to its leadership in the Freedom Movement of the 1950's and 60's. However, this fight cannot and should not be led by any Black church: it must be led by a Black church that is informed by a desire and a genuine belief to see justice come into fruition. It must be led by a Black Church that is informed by a faith that conveys the notion that the fight for racial justice and economic justice are indeed part of the work of Jesus Christ and supported by GOD. Is must be led by a Black Church whose theology is rooted in a Black Theology of Liberation.

Black Theology of Liberation (also known as Black Liberation Theology) as a conceptual framework has been around since the mid 1960's when urban rebellions were taking place in cities like Los Angeles, Detroit and Newark. While there was a large segment of the Black Church that condemned these rebellions (the word "riots" was used by the mainstream media), there was also a segment that refused to condemn those Black men and women who were active in the rebellions. On July 31, 1966, the National Council of Negro Churchmen placed an op-ed in the New York Times expressing their support for the call for Black Power. "We deplore the overt violence of riots, but we feel it is more important to focus on the real sources of these eruptions."[5] The sources of those rebellions were the covert ways in which racism operated and functioned in the nation's urban northern ghettos. Political and economic immobility was how racism functioned and according to the National Council of Negro Churchmen, that immobility had to be eliminated.

A Black Theology of Liberation is a theology that positions God on the side of the oppressed. "Black Theology…views theology as a participation in passion in behalf of the oppressed" (Cone 2004, 11; Snarr 2011) A Black Theology of Liberation does not promote a GOD that is neutral in the face of injustice. GOD is emphatically on the side of the oppressed and if we are doing God's work then we must also be on the side of the oppressed. In the fight for a fair a decent wage, those who are oppressed, those who are exploited are those who are in poverty and the working class. The faith community must get involved in this fight and the faith community must work on the side of the impoverished and working class in order to be on God's side.

A Black Theology of Liberation takes what James 1:22 says to heart when it tells the reader to "But be doers of the word, and not hearers only, deceiving yourselves." It is not enough to be able to quote, memorize, or even locate them in the Bible, but to truly be a Christian and a disciple of Jesus the Christ, you have to be actively engaged in seeking to liberate the marginalized, oppressed and exploited. The moral thing to do is not just to know what is right, but to actively stand up against and combat what is wrong. So, the fight for justice, the fight for equality and the fight for righteousness are all fights that Christians should be actively engaged in. A Theology of Black Liberation holds to the position that there is no contradiction in actively combating social injustices and being a Christian. As a matter of fact, it holds to the position that one cannot truly be a Christian unless they are actively fighting against the social ills of injustice. "Black theology is the theology of a community whose daily energies must be focused on physical survival in a hostile environment."[7] The fight for a living wage is a fight for the physical survival. It could even be posited as a fight for life or death. There are people who are fight for a living wage because even the wage of a full-time job is not enough to live comfortably in this society.

The faith community has always played a pivotal role in the "living wage" fight. When one examines the fight for freedom and justice in America, they would be hard pressed to try to find a movement that did not include participation of a progressive religious leaders. However, ever rise of the conservative movement in the late 1970's and 1980's and the rise of "Moral Majority," the conservative evangelical Christian movement has seemed to monopolize the perception of what Christian activism looks like. Those who adhere to the real liberative, revolutionary, progressive gospel of Jesus Christ cannot allow the conservative evangelical Christian movement to determine the definition of Christianity. The Progressive Christian and Progressive Christian organizations must reclaim what it means to be Christian. There must be a reclamation of the radical message that is the gospel of Jesus Christ. Perhaps this is something that is beginning to happen now. "…many religious organizers have sought to counter these more conservative religious activities with a new kind of organizing meant to bolster progressive religious organizations' presence in local, national, and international politics, particularly around poverty issues."[8] Black Liberation Theology is not just progressive but it's radical in its orientation. It is a theology that does not allow its advocates to waiver. It is explicitly clear that those who adhere to this theology must clearly place themselves on the side of the oppressed, because that is where GOD is. That is the side GOD is on, and it is the side that one must be on in order to do the work of GOD.

4   The Case for a Living Wage

There must also be a clear definition of what a "living wage" is. Is it the minimum wage? Does it come about by raising the minimum wage? I even contend that a living wage cannot be defined as just making enough money so that you just make it above the poverty line ($25,750 for a family of 4). According to the Global Living Wage Coalition, a living wage is defined as: "The remuneration received for a standard workweek by a worker in a particular place sufficient to afford a decent standard of living for the worker and her or his family. Elements of a decent standard of living include food, water, housing, education, health care, transportation, clothing, and other essential needs including provision for unexpected events" (Anker) But some may even contend that even this definition does not look at life in a holistic sense that should also include family time to enjoy one another. Does the living wage calculate time for recreation? Does it calculate for maternity/paternity leave? Does it calculate for a family vacation every few years? These are things that also improve the quality of life and contribute to the work that one produces. The living wage must be an amount that does not just simply lift a family out of poverty, but a number that truly allows a family to have the basic necessities of life and also allows one to live life. A living wage calculation should also include time for family to enjoy family. This may seem like a radical notion for some but having the ability and the time for self-care and time for family outings is something that has to be considered. To simply be enslaved to a job does not help create a productive individual for their place of employment or for their household. A living wage cannot simply be a wage that will allow an individual/family to just keep their head above water.

Although this may seem to be an economic issue, a Theology of Black Liberation does not ignore the role that race plays within the poverty line. Although whites outnumber all races when it comes to who is in poverty, Blacks are overrepresented in the count of those who are living in it. "Almost one quarter of all blacks, 21.2% of Latinos (compared to 9.2% of non-Latino whites) …fall below the official federal poverty threshold in the United States." (Ross 2003) Institutionalized racism permeates all aspects of American life and its impact on poverty in the United States is included in this. Racism can only exist and thrive in an environment where one race internalizes a false sense of superiority. One cannot fight against poverty without fighting against the racism that helps to justify its existence. A Theology of Black Liberation will make sure that the fight against poverty will also include the fight against the racist structure of the economic system that produces poverty while also critiquing the income inequality. To honestly eradicate poverty and establish a fair and decent wage for all, there must be a simultaneous fight to dismantle systems that create attitudes of superiority. Inequality can only exist where the prevailing thought is that it is justified. Racial and Income equality only exists because prevailing thought in America is that there are folks who are superior and there are others who are inferior.

Any economic system that produces vast inequalities between GOD's children must be viewed as suspect. Any economic system that produces vast gaps in creating, obtaining and sustaining opportunity for some and those same opportunities are not availability to all based on economic reasons, should at the very least be investigated to monitor how and why those gaps exist in the first place. One who adheres to a Theology of Black Liberation understands that the Capitalism for the masses of Black People has not brought about the level of black economic empowerment that many capitalists would like to have you believe. Black Liberation Theologians like everyone else can see clearly that capitalism does not empower everyone and produces a class of "Have" and a group of "Have Not's." As much as capitalism produces a wealthy/rich class, it also produces a poor class. Under the system of capitalism, both out comes are necessary. The motivation of capitalism is profit and as it functions in this society, in order for one to profit another must lose. For this reason, the Black Liberation Theologian is willing to critique and if necessary, criticize the functions of capitalism as it relates to Black folk in America, and the masses at large. In the United States, the richest 1 percent own 34 percent of the wealth and the richest 10 percent of the nation own 74 percent of the wealth (Hodgson 2016). These statistics show that capitalism is a deterrent to liberation. That is why one who subscribes to a Theology of Black Liberation knows that at best, capitalism needs to operate differently and at worst be completely eradicated and replaced with a more egalitarian economic model. Some inequality results from individual differences in talent or skill. But this cannot explain the huge gaps between rich and poor in many capitalist countries. Much of the inequality of wealth found within capitalist societies results from inequalities of inheritance. The process is cumulative: inequalities of wealth often lead to differences in education, economic power, and further inequalities in income (Hodgson 2016). Capitalism doesn't only produce inequalities, but it helps maintain it as well. In a racist society such as the United States, there is no question that Blacks in America experience the inequalities produced by capitalism at disproportionate levels. Wealth is passed down from generation to generation and inheritance is one of the best ways that wealth stays within a family. The history of America is a history of benefits, policies and laws that have systematically left blacks from being able to pass down generational wealth. "More than half of white families end up with more wealth than their parents, while only 23 percent of blacks are able to do the same." (Jones 2017) The median household of black families in 2017 was $33,969 compared to $183,050 for white families. But statistics show that even after an inheritance, the wealth gap only increases. Median family households for black families after an inheritance is $38,174 compared to $287,457 for white families. The inheritance increases the wealth gap by over $100,000 dollars for white families while only increasing a little more than $4,000 for black families. (Jones 2017) For decades and even centuries, there was no wealth for black folk to pass down to future generations and in those same years white families continued build upon wealth that they could pass down. The economic gap between black and white families has not only maintained itself, it has grown through inheritance. White families have always had more to pass down and inherit within their families.

Child poverty in this country is also at a level that should make all uncomfortable. According to the Children's Defense Fund's website, 1 in 6 children (about 11.9 million) are poor. 73% of those children are children of color, and 5 million of those children live in extreme poverty on less than $9 a day. Consideration for a Universal Basic Income should be taken for these aforementioned statistics as well. The federal government already has programs that seek to give financial relief to families with young children, such as the Earned Income Tax Credit (EITC) and the Child Tax Credit. "The $1,000 per child per year Child Tax Credit and a $4,000 per child per year tax exemption (often referred to as the child deduction) mostly go to families with incomes well above the poverty line, at a combined annual coast of $97 billion (Tax Policy Center)...Together, the EITC and the CTC lift more children out of poverty than any other federal program." (Shaefer et al. 2018, 23) Instead of giving out these credits to families with children one time during the year, why not disperse theme throughout the year. Why not take the $5,000 and split them into monthly, bi-weekly or even weekly payments? For families where parents cannot find stable work throughout the year, the number of programs available to them is very limited. The availability of accessible income is what is ultimately needed by America's extreme poor. The monies that are available through federal programs that only come around once a year are not able to address the ongoing and emergency needs that millions of families with children experience. "Thus, America's transition to a work-based social safety net, begun in the 1990's, remains incomplete because it has failed to ensure stable base-level source of cash income for all children" (Shaefer et al. 2018, 23). Children must be invested in. There must be means by which parents can invest in their children. Dare I say, because I do believe, that a parent's ability to invest in their child should not rest on that parent's income? Every child should be exposed to all the opportunities that exist out there for that child. Perhaps a Universal Basic Income (UBI) allows for a parent to get their child a tutor. Perhaps a UBI allows for a parent to place their child in a recreational sports league, or to take music lessons or so much more. Shouldn't we as a nation believe that?

5 Where Do We Go From Here?

The Black Liberation Theologian and advocates understand that benefits, laws, and policies like these helps contribute to the economic wealth gap. The

Theologian of Black Liberation knows that benefits, law, and policies that have been created by a power structure created to not only give a certain group a series of advantages, but to also keep a group of people in bondage. Any policy or law that is created to keep GOD's children in bondage is a policy that works against the will of GOD. The Black Liberation Theologian takes that position that Black folk need to seek liberation because they deserve liberation. The Black Liberation Theologian sees Jesus the Christ as one whose gospel was one that did just highlight a spiritual reality but also commentary on the social conditions of the world. The economic reality in this country is one of the many forms of that have kept Black Americans in bondage.

To be clear, a Universal Basic Income will not do the same thing that a living wage for all will do, but a UBI can be a very important first step and trying to address the rampant inequality that capitalism has produced in the United States. How quickly could UBI be implemented? What is the best way to implement it? Federalism allows for the possibility of a UBI being implemented without waiting on the Federal government to do it. A UBI could first be implemented in municipalities, so its impact could be studied and researched. Mayor Michael Tubbs of Stockton, California has done just that. The first mayor-led income initiative in the United States is called the Stockton Economic Empowerment Demonstration (SEED) and this pilot selected 125 adult residents of Stockton California "...where the annual median income was at or below the city's average of $46,033" (Holder 2019). Almost half-way through the initial pilot, preliminary data has been made available. According to the data "Unemployment rates in the county reach about 7.5 percent, higher than the state average of 4.3 percent. Stockton is ranked 18th for child poverty out all U.S. cities" (Holder 2019).

> About 43 percent of SEED recipients are currently working full or part-time, according to the researchers—11 percent are taking care of parents or children, 20 percent reported a disability, 8 percent had retired, 5 percent were students, and only 2 percent said they weren't actively looking for work.
>
> And the economic decisions they made during the first five months of the program were "really rational," said Stacia Martin-West, an assistant professor at the University of Tennessee College of Social Work and the co-principal investigator on the project. Each recipient was given a debit card that automatically loads with $500 each month, so the researchers can categorize spending.
>
> Of the money tracked, 40 percent went towards food. Sales and merchandise made up another quarter of the monthly spending, and about 12 percent was spent on utilities (Holder 2019).

Since the pilot is only half-way through, its success is still yet to be determined. There are still other questions that present themselves; for example, would the SEED payments place residents above certain economic ceilings may make them ineligible for other benefits they were previously afforded.

This is the type of radical, "outside of the box," thinking that will be required to really address the poverty that taints this nation. The lead on these poverty related issues may not come from the federal government, but rather from the innovative, radically open-minded grassroots organizers, local city leaders and the like. It will most likely come from someone who is not intimidated by the bureaucratic nature of politics, and the traditions of national politics. It is for these reasons that compel me to say that Black Liberation Theologians are best positioned to lead the radical, prophetic call for the eradication of poverty. Black Liberation Theologians have already had to challenge the traditional, mainstream thought of theology as it relates to the Christian faith. It was radical, prophetic thought that placed God on the side of the oppressed rather than a place of neutrality in this world. That was the work of Black Liberation Theology. It was radical, prophetic thought that voiced the impact that Race and Racism had on man and woman's interpretation of God in the United States. That was the work of Black Liberation Theology. Fighting for the ultimate eradication of poverty is something that just naturally aligns with Black Liberation Theology. It is a fight that ultimately places the theologian on the side of the Oppressed, where God is believed to be in solidarity with. Combating societal ills also makes "action" as a central part of the faith. Black Liberation Theology contends that one cannot be a bystander in the fight for righteousness, in which Freedom and Liberation are contained within. Black Liberation Theology as an academic enterprise finds its roots in the Civil Rights Movement. A movement where Black Americans had to actively participate in, in order for the movement to be successful in which the Black clergy was a significant portion represented within leadership. The most integral part of the Civil Rights Movement was that it was action oriented. It encouraged Black folk in the South to become active participants in the fight for their liberation. One's participation in the Civil Rights Movement was a liberative experience in itself. There is something liberative about actively participating in the fight for righteousness. There is something liberative about not only knowing you contribute to the solution, but your activity was part of the solution. The ability to actively combat the social ill, and no longer passively complain about that ill's existence may be the most important contribution left by the gains of the Civil Rights Movement, the ability to confront our fears. Black Liberation Theology is "...the result of an effort to interpret in language that spoke to Black people themselves of 'God's liberating presence in a society where Blacks are being economically exploited and politically marginalized because of their skin color" (Cone 2004, 6). Black Liberation Theology is "...meant to serve as a 'theological witness' that rejected racism and affirmed that the Black struggle for freedom was not only consistent with Christ's gospel but also that it was the proclamation of that gospel" (Hayes 1996, 71). Black Liberation Theology contends that the theological response to injustice is to confront it; to stand up to it. The theological response to Racism, Economic Equality, Political impotence is to stand up and confront it even combat it, head on. Injustice forces will not go away until there is a just force that is willing to go toe to toe with it. This may not always look pretty and it may not always fit nicely into the imaginations of those who imagine what a Christian response should look like, but that does not in any way negate that it is a theological response based on the notion that GOD is just and GOD is also fighting on the side of those who have been oppressed and dealt with unjustly.

The Black Liberation Theologian must articulate, or if necessary, create a theological response to poverty. Poverty must be presented and seen as something that is antithetical to the prophetic gospel of Jesus Christ. Poverty and the systems that help create it and sustain it must also be seen as anti-Christian. Working to combat the reality of poverty and working to combat all that seeks to sustain poverty must be seen as being aligned with being a Christian. There is a distinction made of those who choose to aid the less fortunate and those who decide not to, found in scripture and specifically in the Gospel.

> "Then these righteous ones will reply, 'Lord, when did we ever see you hungry and feed you? Or thirsty and give you something to drink? Or a stranger and show you hospitality? Or naked and give you clothing? When did we ever see you sick or in prison and visit you?'" "And the King will say, 'I tell you the truth, when you did it to one of the least of these my brothers and sisters, you were doing it to me!'" (Matt. 25:37–40).

And for those who will choose not to aid the less fortunate:

> "Then the King will turn to those on the left and say, 'Away with you, you cursed ones, into the eternal fire prepared for the devil and his demons. For I was hungry, and you didn't feed me. I was thirsty, and you didn't give me a drink. I was a stranger, and you didn't invite me into your home. I was naked, and you didn't give me clothing. I was sick and in prison, and you didn't visit me.'" "Then they will reply, 'Lord, when did we ever see you hungry or thirsty or a stranger or naked or sick or in prison, and not help you?'" "And he will answer, 'I tell you the truth, when you refused to

help the least of these my brothers and sisters, you were refusing to help me.'" "And they will go away into eternal punishment, but the righteous will go into eternal life." (Matt. 25:41–46).

There is a clear line of distinction made between the one who seeks to help and the one who seeks to ignore in the eyes of "the King." The Gospel is a lived experienced where one must be an actor and not simply a spectator.

For this and other reasons previously mentioned, the call for a national living wage should come from Theologians of Black Liberation. To bring about a living wage in this country will take a world view and precise action that is rooted in the notion that GOD is not pleased with the reality of God's children living in poverty. Theologians of Black Liberation see Jesus Christ as a liberator who sought to empower a people who were oppressed and exploited by a powerful Roman empire that ultimately cost him his life for the greater good. Doing the work of Christ, being a Christian, is doing the liberative work of setting the captives free from all things that keep them bound.

Bibliography

Anker, Richard. 2011. "What Is A Living Wage." Global Living Wage. https://www.global-livingwage.org/about/what-is-a-living-wage/.

Cone, James. 1984. *For My People: Black Theology and the Black Church*. Maryknoll: Orbis Press.

Cone, James. 2010. *A Theology of Black Liberation*. Maryknoll: Orbis Press.

Economic Policy Institute. 2017. https://www.epi.org/publication/receiving-an-inheritance-helps-white-families-more-than-black-families/.

Fontenot, Kayla, Jessica Semga and Melissa Kollar. 2018. "Income and Poverty in the United States: 2017." United States Census Bureau. September 12, 2018. https://www.census.gov/library/publications/2018/demo/p60-263.html.

Hayes, Diana L. 1996. *And Still We Rise: An Introduction To Black Liberation Theology*. New York and Mahwah, NJ: Paulist Press.

Hodson, Geoffery M. 2016. "How Capitalism Actually Generates More Inequality." Evonomics, August 11, 2016. https://evonomics.com/how-capitalism-actually-generates-more-inequality/.

Holder, Sarah. 2019. "In Stockton, Early Clues Emerge About Impact of Guaranteed Income." City Lab.com. October 3, 2019. https://www.citylab.com/equity/2019/10/stockton-universal-basic-income-pilot-economic-empowerment/599152/.

Jan, Tracy. 2018. "A Minimum Wage Worker Can't Afford a 2-Bedroom Apartment Anywhere in The U.S." *The Washington Post*, June 13, 2018. https://www.washingtonpost

.com/news/wonk/wp/2018/06/13/a-minimum-wage-worker-cant-afford-a-2-bedroom-apartment-anywhere-in-the-u-s/.

Jones, Janelle. 2017. "Receiving an Inheritance Helps White Families More than Black Families." Economic Policy Institute February 17, 2017. https://www.epi.org/publication/receiving-an-inheritance-helps-white-families-more-than-black-families/.

Matthew 25:37–40 (New Living Translation).

Matthew 25:41–46 (New Living Translation).

Ross, Rosetta E. 2003. *Witnessing and Testifying: Black Women, Religion, and Civil Rights.* Minneapolis: Fortress Press.

Shaefer, H. Luke, Sophie Collyer, Greg Duncan, Kathryn Edin, Irwin Garfinkel, David Harris, Timothy M. Smeeding, Jane Waldfogel, Chirstopher Wimer, Hirokazu Yoshikawa. 2018. "Universal Child Allowance: A Plan to Reduce Poverty and Income Instability Among Children in the United States." *The Russell Sage Foundation Journal of the Social Sciences* 4 (2): 23.

Snarr, C. Melissa. 2011. *All You That Labor: Religion and Ethics in the Living Wage Movement.* New York: NYU Press.

Stein, Jeff and Aaron Gregg. 2019. "U.S. Military Spending Set to Increase for Fifth Consecutive Year, Nearing Levels During Height of Iraq War." *The Washington Post*, April 18, 2019. https://www.washingtonpost.com/us-policy/2019/04/18/us-military-spending-set-increase-fifth-consecutive-year-nearing-levels-during-height-iraq-war/.

CHAPTER 9

Reducing the Achievement Gap of African Americans through a Mental Health Lens

David I. Rudder and Anthony Hill

1 Introduction

The racial achievement gap in education is one of the most difficult issues confronting African American males. Regardless of socio-economic status, African Americans are besieged with variables that undermine and impede their ability to be successful due to structural inequalities, implicit and unconscious bias, harsh disciplinary practices and racism by faculty and staff in America's institutions of learning. African American males are exposed to traumatic experiences at significantly higher rates than other demographic groups (Graham 2017, 105–118). These areas, if not addressed, will continue to have a detrimental impact on African American students despite attempts to help them be successful while on a college campus. Students may not be able to receive and benefit from academic content when they are struggling with the fact that they are being targeted as young men of color and may not feel welcome and safe while at institutions of higher learning.

It is important for educators and administrators on college campuses to not only accept diverse students but also support students beyond just academic support that may provide additional tutoring, writing, and study skills. There are additional interventions that are essential in supporting students emotionally, helping them persist in attaining their college degree, and working on retention efforts so that they are on track for graduation.

This requires a re-engineering of higher education to support and retain students of color with the importance of incorporating self-care strategies, time management skills, stressing the value and importance of a higher education degree, addressing their mental health and well-being, and promoting positive masculinity. Historically, most programs in institutions of higher education are initiatives focused on how African American students need to adapt to their new surroundings and getting students access to academic support systems on campus. We offered a more holistic approach through our emphasis on the social and mental well being of African American males, in addition to focusing on their academic success. The aim of this chapter is to improve the persistence and retention of diverse male students. We will also explore the extent to how this initiative can be replicated and improved. It is important for officials on college campuses to not only accept diverse students but also cultivate student support systems beyond just an academic support center that may provide additional tutoring, writing, and study skills.

2 Higher Education and Black Achievement

According to data from the U.S. Department of Education, National Center for Education Statistics, in 2016 the total college enrollment rate was higher for Asian young adults (58 percent) than for young adults who were White (42 percent), Hispanic (39 percent), Black (36 percent), Pacific Islander (21 percent), and American Indian/Alaska Native (19 percent). The gap between female and male enrollment was widest for Black students (62 vs. 38 percent). Additionally, in 2016 a greater percentage of post baccalaureate students were female than male across all racial/ethnic groups. The gap between female and male enrollment was widest for African American students (70 vs. 30 percent). The data above indicate that 7 out of 10 African American male students do not graduate in six years. It is clear that African American males are most vulnerable and interventions are needed to improve their college completion rates and their economic and career advancement.

Research contends there are numerous barriers to graduating from college for some African American students, which is evidenced by the low retention rates of black students. Among students enrolled in four-year public institutions, 45.9 percent of black students complete their degrees in six years—the lowest rate compared to other races and ethnicities (Bridges 2018). Black men have the lowest completion rate at 40 percent. The financial burden of attending college, lack of academic preparedness, and social isolation are the primary factors explaining poor performance and retention of African American students. Several researchers found that many differences in graduation rates disappeared when such pre-college student factors as high school grade-point average (GPA), gender and parental education were taken into account explained two-thirds of the differences between institutions' graduation rates (Engle and Tinto 2008). More importantly, this finding suggests that the graduation and retention challenges found within particular student populations are as much the result of student experiences before entering college as their experiences during college (Venezia et al. 2005).

Like the overall rate of educational attainment for the nation as a whole, the rate for Blacks has risen in recent years. Blacks who earned an associate degree or a bachelor's or higher degree have risen over the past 24 years while shares with a high school diploma or less have fallen (Rollen and Tossi 2018). The sharpest increase in attainment is at the level of bachelor's degree and higher. In 1992, about 16 percent of Blacks in the labor force had at least a 4-year degree compared to 29 percent by 2016. Historically, Black men have had a higher labor force participation rate than Black women but the gap has narrowed throughout the 1980s and 1990s. The men's rate is projected to decline at a faster rate than women from 2016 to 2026. It is critical that African American men continue to pursue and succeed in college in order to participate in the current economy.

3 The Safety of Black Males

Before entering college many African American males regardless of socioeconomic status are operating within an environment where their mere presence creates uneasiness, they are deemed hostile, there's little value for their life, or they are regarded as behavioral issues or morally corrupt individuals, which is detrimental to their academic success. As this generation grows up in times of the Black Lives Matter Movement, they have been made aware of the police violence on black men such as Eric Garner, Freddie Gray, Mike Brown, Alton Sterling, Philando Castile and countless others. In 2018, 992 people were fatally killed by police officers in America (Muyskens 2018). The majority of the fatal killings were perpetuated by white male law enforcement officers. African American males continue to be overrepresented in these tragic and violent interactions based on the percentage of the U.S. population. More and more of those incidents are being captured on mobile phone videos, shot mostly by bystanders and then broadcast widely on social media and cable news. Research on trauma has revealed that there are psychological effects of watching footage of police brutality and medical health experts contend there can be long-term implications — especially for those, who are the same race as the people being beaten and shot (Aronson 2002, 113–125). No matter where a black male may live or the economic status of his family he is inherently part of a stigmatized community due to this race. Subsequently, black men do not feel safe when they see themselves being victimized.

Adverse childhood experiences (ACEs) discuss the impact of social risk factors, mental health issues, child physical or sexual abuse, emotional neglect, substance abuse, incarceration, domestic violence, and risky adult behaviors.

Some stress in life is normal and necessary for development. However, when a child experiences ACEs, it becomes a form of toxic stress. The response to this toxic stress can be incredibly damaging and last a lifetime. A child who has experienced an adverse childhood experience is more likely to have learning and behavioral issues. These effects can negatively influence one's healthy development throughout the life cycle if the traumatic experiences are not addressed. Factors such as poverty, abuse, racism, neglect, bullying, witnessing crime, violence, and living in unsafe neighborhoods are detrimental to an individual's well-being. This sort of prolonged stress response can distort the development of the brain into the adult years. Witnessing and being exposed to these events, even if the home itself is a safe environment, causes a person to experience stress since their mind will react to these threats with survival instincts leading to potential traumatization. On a college campus, African American students may have experienced multiple traumas that may have affected their families for generations. It is essential for students to have a safe haven to process and address these harmful experiences while attending institutions of higher learning.

In addition, Blacks are often the subject of negative media attention. The media plays a critical role in shaping public perceptions and attitudes toward black males and their ability to be successful. Television viewers perceive the occupational roles and personality characteristics that African Americans portray on television as real or true to life. Bussell and Crandall (2002) noted that there were prominent media images of African American as being criminals or unemployed individuals. In accordance with these images, the viewers felt that the negative personality characteristics of African Americans that were shown on television were realistic images. The overall presentation of black males in the media is distorted in a variety of ways, relative to the real-world facts. Some black males themselves embrace these stereotypes, often as a form of resistance to the lack of power they feel they have to actually shape their lives; by confirming to hyper-masculine stereotypes (Topos Partnership and The Opportunity Agenda 2011). Subsequently, black males are also influenced by the media and consume those same images and stereotypes of themselves.

The mass incarceration crisis is another example that illustrates the fragility of the lives of African American men and underscores the deep-rooted conflict between persons of color and law enforcement officials. African American and Latino men are also disproportionately represented in our nation's criminal justice and penitentiary system (Alexander 2011) and are dropping out of school at alarming rates (Noguera 2008). The War on Drugs had decimated the lives of many in African Americans communities, particularly for men in low-income communities and limited their educational attainment for the last forty years.

This government intervention under the Nixon administration initially created the mass incarceration of Black and Latino men. Black Americans are nearly six times more likely to be incarcerated for drug-related offenses than their white counterparts, despite equal substance usage rates (NAACP 2018). It also added billions to law enforcement on the national and local level, produced more violence due to gang turf wars, eroded civil rights, and helped to promote the criminalization of behavior issues in the K-12 system that results in the school-to-prison pipeline (Wade and Ortiz 2017, 181–191).

According to United States Government Accountability Office, students in K-12 that experienced discipline actions that resulted in classroom removal are more likely to repeat a grade, drop out of school, and become involved in the juvenile justice system. Black students, boys, and students with disabilities were disproportionately disciplined (e.g., suspensions and expulsions) in K-12 public schools, according to GAO's analysis of Department of Education (Education) national civil rights data for school year 2013–14, the most recent available. These disparities were widespread and persisted regardless of the type of disciplinary action, level of school poverty, or type of public school attended. For example, Black students accounted for 15.5 percent of all public school students, but represented about 39 percent of students suspended from school—an overrepresentation of about 23 percentage points (United States Accountability Office 2018). A public school district in the state of Massachusetts has made changes to their code of conduct to combat zero tolerance policies. Due to the high rates of suspension for students of color, changes were made to no longer allow thirty day out of school suspensions. Interventions and processes were put into place to ensure suspensions were handled appropriately. This legislation was necessary, yet the problem still lies within school administrators who enforce the code of conduct. School administrators are finding loopholes such as not recording incidents and giving children days off instead of following the new procedure. There is also a rise in internal school suspensions for students of color which limit effective teaching and learning for students and increases their drop-out rate and transition them into the criminal justice system.

Many school administrators have abdicated their role in administering disciplinary measures to school resource officers (SRO) as a way to handle and manage student behavior. The criminalization of youth of color has led to disproportionate school discipline rates and unequal and punitive treatment of youth African American males (Wade and Ortiz 2017). The negative interaction with SROs and administrators in schools can be a source of trauma or re-traumatization for African American and diverse students attending public schools in the United States.

This issue not only impacts African American boys but also impacts African American girls as well. The National Women's Law Center 2017 Let Her Learn Survey ("Let Her Learn Survey") national data shows that Black girls are 5.5 times more likely and Native American girls are 3 times more likely to be suspended from school than white girls. "Black girls face high and disproportionate suspension rates across the country—and it's not because they are misbehaving more frequently than other girls but is often the result of deeply ingrained racist and sexist stereotypes that push black girls out of school" (Onyeka-Crawford, Patrick, & Chaudhry 2017) In addition to these barriers, girls of color are more likely to attend under-resourced schools that are not culturally competent or personalized to their needs or interests, which negatively affect their educational opportunities and future earnings.

The school-to-prison pipeline, the War on Drugs legislation and zero tolerance policies were created under the guise of keeping the public safe; however, legislators were not personally and professionally aware of their own biases. The Fair Sentencing Act and zero tolerance policies were created with implicit bias; targeting vulnerable populations punitively rather than understanding their needs and challenges (Barbadoro 2017). Subsequently, policymakers at the national and local levels of government initiated harsher sentencing laws and increased enforcement actions, especially for low-level drug offenses, which are disproportionately target African Americans for enforcement which yields in discriminatory practices across the justice system.

4 Structural Realities of Urban Areas

Students of color in our nation's urban centers fare poorly in education, employment, health, housing, high school graduation, and college attendance rates (Children's Defense Fund 2017). The social isolation and the coupling targeting punitively actions in the K-12 educational system spawn neighborhood behaviors that push blacks to have lower educational attainment or may lead to non-mainstream behaviors such as crime and drug abuse, violence, and other coping techniques or actions that result as barriers to educational attainment. Poor urban areas were a direct result of deliberate efforts that promoted the uneven development of suburban areas and the abandonment of central cities (Jackson 1985). Many inner-city neighborhoods have been destroyed because of Urban Renewal programs and other public policy programs that left cities disproportionately plagued by unemployment, underemployment, and labor force withdrawal among residents. Federal government housing acts took on various forms of discrimination in the form of redlining inner-city housing that contributed to cities being abandoned, while suburban areas were given substantial money for development (Jackson 1985). Blacks in the inner city are unable to take advantage of growing job opportunities in suburban locations due to the lack of transportation and job information access (Holzer 1997, 218–242).

There is a growing income gap due to the restructuring of the economy that is directly related to center city decline, especially the inner city. Globalization has also resulted in the decline of cities and their neighborhoods. This has reduced the number of businesses in the industrial and manufacturing sectors, resulting in the displacement of low-skilled workers that had access to jobs concentrated in cities (Beneria and Santiago 2001; Wilson 1996). In the 1950s and 1960s, the economy transformed from goods processing to basic services, and then from a basic service economy to one of information processing and administrative control in the 1970s and 1980s. International competition and corporate restructuring have combined with inappropriate public policy to severely disrupt the economies of cities formerly manufacturing-based (Goldsmith 1992, 104).

Not only have jobs been removed from cities to suburban areas, but they have been relocated also in countries with cheaper labor. The global economy and the expansion of foreign markets are factors that contribute to the decline of many urban neighborhoods. Communities that lack market-relevant advantages have limited prospects for effective development activity given their vulnerability to technological change and national conditions in the economy (Imbroscio 1997; Newman, Lyon, and Philip 1986; Shramm 1987; Weiwel, Tietz, and Giloth 1993). With a lack of economic growth within the cities, and the inability to retain businesses, inner-city workers are at a disadvantage due to limited job options and pay scale. This explains how cities would end up with poorly funded public education and become bountiful with illegal economy that provided an employment and supported the mass incarceration movement.

Scholars also contend that as blacks continue to be blocked out of the mainstream economy, and the vibrant ethnically controlled neighborhood economy no longer seems to exist, blacks are propelled to get involved in the "underground" economy(Anderson 1999; Fitzgerald and Patton 1994; Wilson 1996). The actions that take place in the "underground" economy may deal with drug selling and trafficking. Consequently, the lucrative illegal drug activity absorbs the unemployed black labor force. In order for African Americans males to not only survive but to thrive socially, physically, and economically, a college education has the chance to transform their lives. Protective factors in addressing these issues are supportive relationships on a college campus which provide African American students the opportunity to heal and promote growth, build resiliency, and for students to realize their worth in attaining academic and career success.

5 Men of Excellence—a Solution

Pedro Noguera states that "…education can serve as a means to empower and open doors of opportunity to those who have been disadvantaged by poverty, racism, and injustice" (2008, 120). School and social challenges and failure during one's childhood and adolescence inevitably leads to negative adult life experiences. Mentors can play an instrumental role in encouraging students to reach their academic potential and identifying, preventing, and helping children eliminate, overcome, or reduce the problems that are obstacles to successful academic, social, and cultural learning in higher education settings. It is essential that institutions of higher learning create pathways for African Americans to be successful academically, socially, and psychologically so that they can live productive, fulfilling lives and be positive contributors in society. By facilitating the Men of Excellence initiative, we agree with Dr. Noguera that, "education can transform lives by inspiring young people and exposing them to knowledge that makes it possible to dream, aspire, and imagine new possibilities for themselves and the world" (Noguera 2008, 120)

African American students may lack a sense of belonging and be more susceptible to psychological distress as they seek to integrate in institutions of higher learning. Due to inadequate education preparation at the pre-K-12 level, coupled with low high school graduation and low college attendance rates, African American male students need a nurturing environment, specialized support and interventions to meet their needs, and an environment that promotes wellness when they enter into institutions of higher learning. Underrepresented students (i.e., first generation college students, students from historically underrepresented racial/ethnic groups, and students from economically disadvantaged backgrounds) have to contend with a variety of other factors such as financial strain, culture shock, and discriminatory treatment. (Hurd et al. 2018, 1100–1112) These authors contend that the identification of assets and resources that foster mental wellness and academic achievement among this group can remedy disparities in higher education. Shawn Ginwright states that there is a need for radical healing which is "a process that builds the capacity of people to act upon their environment in ways that contribute to the well-being for the common good (Ginwright 2016, 8). This is particularly important in helping students acquire a sense of agency in changing maladaptive thought patterns and behaviors. Radical healing also instills young people with hope and builds their confidence that they have the power to construct positive personal, academic, and professional outcomes.

6   Men of Excellence (MOE): Moving from Theory to Practice

This section highlights the Men of Excellence (MOE), a student club at a predominantly white four-year private institution, whose club members are primarily men of color. The group focuses on leadership, peer support, mentoring, and community service. MOE was founded in 2017, the founding members wanted a safe space to meet, develop their leadership skills, and learn how to expand and cultivate the tools necessary to be successful inside and outside the classroom.

General body meetings were bi-weekly run from 90–120 minutes. There are meeting agendas, regular updates and time for open discussion at all meetings. The open discussion time provide students with the opportunity to bring up issues on campus or items in the "real world" that was deemed important. Eboard meetings are on alternate weeks and lasted one hour with the four eboard positions of President, Vice President, Secretary and Treasurer. Much of this time focused on principles on:

1) creating a safe space in the group;
2) tools to promote dialogue and active listening;
3) strategies to increase student engagement, and
4) learning how to run an effective meetings.

Through the MOE meetings, it is our aim to build coping, positive interpersonal and socio-emotional skills and help students overcome previous traumatic experiences. The weekly group meetings, activities, and programs serve as a safe haven allowing MOE members to express their emotions in a safe environment. Because these are often done in group settings, it gives the young men the opportunity to build social skills, especially when a positive role model as the club advisor is modeling appropriate behavior.

Two faculty members, served as club advisors, explored students' previous K-12 schooling experiences, their home life, issues in their community, and discuss their experiences on campus and perceived inequities at the institution. One of our primary aims was giving these young men a sense of agency and voice through the development of meaningful or transformational relationships with their peers, faculty and staff. We also discussed current political, social and sporting events that students found relevant and challenged them to reflect on the impact of their structural realities and also pay it forward to members of the community by engaging in community service activities to help mentor high school youth, volunteer to help individuals impacted by homelessness, and engage in other forms of community service.

A central theme in all MOE meetings is the opportunity for students to explore the significance of their education and a forum to discuss their academic and social challenges on campus in a safe space. For instance, we provide opportunities to produce alternative narratives to counter negative peer pressures and to promote academic success. A considerable amount of time is spent on helping students to heal from challenging home environments and dysfunctional public school experiences settings. We are able to do this by fostering and engaging in transformational relationships through unconditional positive regard, support, mentoring, guidance and teaching healthy forms of masculinity. The safe space created consistency, structure and helped young men to feel free to reach out to us with a sense of hope in completing their studies at a predominantly white institution. Much of our approaches were rooted in work on radical healing (Ginwright 2018); we had students engaged in working through or begin the process of addressing their personal traumas in order to prepare and transition from their high school and community life into successful college graduates.

Several presentations and workshops were conducted with young people to establish and bolster their sense of self in the context of their masculine and cultural identity. Several goals were emphasized: 1) how to institute and engage in self-care practices; 2) multiple discussions on healthy forms of masculinity, and 3) an emphasis on the importance of asking for help and 4) overcoming mental illness stigma. These are four areas that were prevalent during our interaction with students. We have been able to forge transformational interactions on this college campus. This is different from transactional interactions, which are based on one's job title. A transformational interaction is the ability to understand and interact with students on a deeper level (Ginwright 2018). In our MOE group meetings, we get a chance to understand their background, allow them the space to process their experiences, create an environment where we hold them accountable for their actions and hold them to high academic, social and leadership expectations.

7 MOE Results in Promoting a Growth Mindset

As mentors and facilitators of the MOE, we highlight and praise the efforts of the young men and focus on developing a growth mindset among members that embraces challenges and inspires maximum effort in their academic pursuits. We stress that intelligence is not fixed, which means that students can accomplish their academic and career goals, which is an important concept for them to internalize. The willingness to not be afraid to confront challenges, put forth maximum effort, possibly fail, learn from their experiences, and still be open-minded about the process, will prepare MOE members to accomplish their short and long-term goals. We emphasize to MOE members to follow through on their commitments, pursue a growth mindset, and that their brains change and grow as they face challenges and seek to accomplish their long-term goals. Overall, we attempted to create an environment in the MOE meetings that can positively influence the trajectory of college students.

Over the course of the program, the young men have had conversations that included their thoughts and feelings about the impact of not having a father or positive male mentor in their life, protective factors, discussed the stigma of mental illness and how we seek to promote resilience and healing by asking for help and being aware of the resources, supports and services that are available to them on the college campus. We have seen increased cohesion with peers where students offer mutual support and a supportive environment where students focus, highlight, and pinpoint their strengths rather than deficits.

8 Data Analysis

Much of the framework used with the male students in the Men of Excellence centered on the aforementioned themes. Students in the club were emailed a survey of closed and open-ended questions. The survey was sent to twenty-one active members, eighteen students responded providing a response rate of 86%. Both sets of responses are captured in this section. There was a 60/40 percent split in the group make up between upperclassmen and lowerclassmen at the time of the survey distribution. The data that is being displayed in this chapter is from year two of the program. We want to continue to collect data to improve the delivery of services in this program and continue to monitor and evaluate the effectiveness of this initiative.

Hurd et al. (2018, 1100–1112) discusses the value of supportive exchanges on college campuses that promotes healthy youth development and fosters the well-being and success of underrepresented racial/ethnic students attending predominantly White institutions of higher education. The authors discuss the importance of cultivating spaces where natural mentoring could develop and where faculty, students and staff have the opportunity to engage in meaningful collaboration. Table 9.1 explored if Men of Excellence (MOE) had a positive impact on students' ability to be successful at the College. Overwhelming, 72%

TABLE 9.1 Student views on persistence and retention

Question	Yes	%	No	%
Has your participation in MOE impacted your academic success?	13	72%	5	28%
Has MOE enhanced your perceptions of the value and importance of education and opportunities associated with it a college student?	16	89%	2	11%
Has MOE motivated you to stay at Springfield College?	9	50%	9	50%

SOURCE: AUTHOR GENERATED BASED UPON DATA COLLECTED FROM RESPONDENTS IN MEN OF EXCELLENCE.

of students affirmed participation in MOE has impacted their academic success and close to 90% of members agreed their awareness on the importance of an education and the opportunities granted as a result of a college degree increased. Interesting enough, only 50% of the students thought MOE had impact on them staying at the institution, which may speak to other variables that have significant influence or impact on retention at a small private college.

8.1 Selected Student Quotes/Responses

Has your participation in MOE impacted your academic success?
- "MOE has encouraged me to constantly strive for better grades and helped me focus more."
- "The group has helped with time management of my school-work."
- "Made me want to do better for myself."
- "I am held accountable by my brothers and pushed to do better academically. It is exciting to come together and say, "I just got an A in x class!" and have everyone be happy for you and congratulate you on your success."
- "I have been challenged to not settle for less and to achieve higher results in my academic work."

Has MOE enhanced your perceptions of the value and importance of education and opportunities associated with it a college student?
- "MOE has help build my work ethic more and being able to surround myself with self-motivated individuals has helped me to do better."

TABLE 9.2 Student views on self-care and developing healthy relationships

Question	Yes	%	No	%
Has your participation in MOE positively impacted your family interactions and communications?	12	67%	6	33%
Are you more conscious of engaging in self-care?	15	83%	3	17%
Do you engage in more self-reflection as a result of MOE?	16	89%	2	11%

SOURCE: AUTHOR GENERATED BASED UPON DATA COLLECTED FROM RESPONDENTS IN MEN OF EXCELLENCE.

- "For the first time ever, I see myself as a leader. I have gotten more responsible overall and act like an adult."
- "An organization that is fostering leadership and scholarship through cultural development, friendship, and community engagement. We push each other to be strong on the inside and out."

Has MOE motivated you to stay at college?

- "A place that is unique to any other place on campus because it is an atmosphere that allows me to truly be myself."
- "We HAVE to hold each other accountable for our goals and daily tasks. We NEED each other and cannot do everything alone. This is a place where we work to be accepted as not only males, but a variety of different males that come from different backgrounds and want to help and contribute to our society."
- "I like being able to have a group of guys on campus I can go to and trust to have my best interests at heart."
- "It made me feel accepted, it helps to let me know that I have a good group of brothers here to support and push me through my tough times."

Implementing self-care strategies is vital to the physical, emotional, and psychological health and well-being of African American males. The collective socialization and expectations of African American males to be strong, emotionally tough and disconnected, not to cry or express feelings, and be angry and aggressive takes a heavy toll and burden on young men to thrive and enter into healthy and sustaining relationships with others. Ginwright (2018) conveys the fact that oppression, inju-tice, and "social and environmental factors can promote or inhibit health" (Ginwright 2018, 9). Also important is a discussion of the impact of detrimental social and political practices and policies and "structural issues such as poverty, unemployment, underfunded schools, incarceration, lack of access to quality health care, and poor quality housing as the root causes of violence and causes of trauma" (Ginwright 2018, 9) that all intersect and hinder the growth and development of African American males and their well-being.

Table 9.2 reviews student responses on building healthy relationships. 67% of the respondents felt MOE positively impacted their familial relationships. That number jumped to 83% of students engaging in self-care and 89% utilizing self-reflection as a tool to promote a healthy well being. We stress the importance of self-reflection in their journey to help build emotional awareness. We pushed students to be deliberate frequently about what emotions they were having throughout the day or during an incident/or situation in order to gain a better understanding of their emotional triggers and strengths.

8.2 Selected Student Quotes/Responses

Has your participation in MOE positively impacted your family interactions and communications?

- "I'm more aware of my demeanor in public (making sure I don't look unapproachable and things like that), I take care of myself, I express my emotions more."
- "It means a safe place for men here on campus to be open about themselves and talk about ideas that are important to them. It also means that men can change the stigma associated with men of color and men in general."

Are you more conscious of engaging in self-care?

- "I take time to cleanse my mind and try doing things that make me happy."
- "I make sure that I am at a healthy state of mind and write things down on what I need to do and put effort toward my goals."
- "…treat my life just as important as anyone else's."
- "I was mindful of self-care before MOE, yet MOE made me appreciate it more. No longer was I alone on this journey of taking care of myself mentally as a man."
- "It is easy to feel alone as a man of color on campus. While MOE is not a club specifically for men of color, but it has a lot of us, men who look like me and experience the same things that I go through. The club allows me to feel comfortable and refreshed after every meeting."

TABLE 9.3 Student views on nurturing and self-actualization

Question	Yes	%	No	%
Has your participation in MOE made you more socially conscious?	14	78%	4	22%
Have you grown/developed in how you see yourself as a man?	16	89%	2	11%
Has MOE had a positive impact on your intimate relationship(s)?	14	78%	4	22%

SOURCE: AUTHOR GENERATED BASED UPON DATA COLLECTED FROM RESPONDENTS IN MEN OF EXCELLENCE.

Do you engage in more self-reflection as a result of MOE?
- "MOE to me means somewhere where we can come and speak our minds and get knowledge that normally would not be taught in the classroom. Also, it is somewhere that you can be a part of something great that gives back to the community for the good of it. Also something about the importance of 'when you know better you do better.'"
- "I take time to go to a quiet place to reflect on the past week or the upcoming week with my phone down just to really clear my head."

It is important to help African Americans successfully integrate into higher education settings. Owens, et al. (2010) states that African Americans may lack a sense of belonging and experience resistance, hostility, alienation, and culture shock in being in an environment that they are familiar with. It is essential to create safe spaces and a nurturing and supportive environment where students are welcomed, affirmed, validated, and valued. Table 9.3 explore responses around identity and nurturing. 78% of students thought MOE made them more socially conscious, which may correlate to the group having more campus events on race related topics. 89% had grown in how they saw themselves as a man; this could be a result of the safe and nurturing environment created during MOE meetings, which fostered for open and honest dialogue around a myriad of issues.

Finally, we were very pleased to see that 78% of the students felt MOE had a positive impact on their intimate relationship(s). Overall, the members of MOE valued the emphasis on healthy masculinity traits and the discussions about unpacking restrictive male gender roles. The discussions on this topic helped young men discuss their thoughts and vulnerabilities of being an African American male in today's society in a safe and affirming environment. In addition, young men were able to bolster their sense of identity, see the importance of being true to themselves, ask for help without being shamed, and get emotional support and resources from peers, adults, and organizations and offices on campus.

8.3 Selected Student Quotes/Responses

Has your participation in MOE made you more socially conscious?
- "What MOE means to me is an organization that is a brotherhood, a place where one can lean on their brother for advice, guidance, or simply someone to talk to. It is also an organization where we hold each other accountable on the journey of being men of excellence. During this journey everyone in the group is on their own path to greatness, we as brothers are simply there to make sure you are staying true to those goals and see to it that you are indeed a man of excellence."
- "The discussions that we have on certain social topics opened me up to different perspectives and knowledge on the subject. Some issues I never even thought about before I had to form my own stance on."
- "I am more aware of social issues happening around me because through conversations with the group and events we have hosted I have learned more, thus being able to educate others on these social issues and being an advocate to fight these issues."

Have you grown/developed in how you see yourself as a man?
- "I believe it means to give young men a space where they can improve to be better versions of themselves together through discussion on each other's perspectives of certain issues, holding each other accountable for our actions, and helping the community in ways that align with the organization's beliefs."
- "The men in group have kept me here and better yet the club itself has helped me better understand why I'm here and that is to make a difference."
- "It made me realize that for all of the actions I have taken up to this point that I need to take more responsibility for my life, in the sense that I need to make steps to ensure that my future is something I am proud to live in. I am not there yet."
- "What MOE means to me is an organization that is a brotherhood, a place where one can lean on their brother for advice, guidance, or simply someone to talk to. It is also an organization where we hold each other accountable

on the journey of being men of excellence. During this journey, everyone in the group is on their own path to greatness, we as brothers are simply there to make sure you are staying true to those goals and see to it that you are indeed a man of excellence."

Has MOE had a positive impact on your intimate relationship(s)?

- "I am more open about my emotions. I realized being walled off hurt my partner but myself even more."
- "I have because I know that toxic masculinity is something that is real and I know that I will not continue to be a part of that any longer."
- "MOE is a well-deserved environment for men to be themselves. Where educated men can come and express feelings that cannot be expressed to certain aspects in society."

The Men of Excellence organization has created a safe space on campus for African American men to understand the value and importance of education, implement self-care strategies, and allowed the young men to gain and provide support, accountability, networking, and fellowship with each other. There was also an emphasis on promoting positive masculinity traits and enhancing leadership skills. This group has helped young African American men to persist in their college education and affirmed in them that education can be a very powerful tool on their road to self-improvement and a successful career. We believe that institutions of higher learning should prioritize and have an institutional commitment to ensuring the development and success of African American male students and replicate this type of program in higher education settings nationally.

9 Recommendations/Conclusion

Institutions of higher learning must be re-engineered to better address the plight of African American male students, regardless of socio-economic status, are besieged with variables that undermine and impede their ability to be successful. Boys and men of color are exposed to traumatic experiences at significantly higher rates than are other demographic groups, which impacts graduating from 4-year institutions. Students are dealing with barriers that can negatively impact their success in institutions of higher learning. It is important for Colleges and Universities to help African American male student, heal from prior damaging K-12 experiences and socially toxic environments. College mentors can play an instrumental role in improving the educational outcomes of students of color in 4-year institutions of higher learning. Below are recommendations on how institutions can better serve and retain of American male students.

Recommendations are:

We wanted to share ideas of how to replicate this initiative in other institutions of higher learning. We propose the following five critical principles, six R's that institutions should focus on in the re-engineering of higher education for African American males.

Resources—Institutions of higher learning need to be in the forefront and allocate resources as an institutional priority to address issues of poor academic performance, a high truancy and drop-out rate, and punitive disciplinary practices in order to promote academic success for diverse college students. Institutions must model diversity and inclusion by hiring culturally competent administrators, faculty, and staff. In addition, it is essential to prioritize funding to promote and sustain these types of initiatives. Faculty and staff who mentor diverse students should be credited for this as a service to the college and a vital component to their performance evaluation. This work is also instrumental in helping African American students feel affirmed and have a sense of belonging on campus.

Relationships—Creating nurturing relationships with young men that are transformational based on respect, care, and compassion rather than just formal relationships that make it hard to understand, relate and make underrepresented students feel a sense of belonging on campus.

It is important for officials on college campuses to not only accept diverse students but also support students beyond just an academic support center that may provide additional tutoring, writing, and study skills and promotes their mental well being. Students may not be able to receive academic content when they are struggling with the fact that they are being targeted as young men of color and may not feel welcome and safe while at institutions of higher learning.

Reflection—More campus programming as well as curriculum content should provide greater opportunities to illustrate the experiences of diverse students. Helping the young men have awareness of their history, background, family of origin, community and the ability to be positive young men valuing their education and creating and sustaining healthy peer and romantic relationships. Institutions of higher learning need to have specialized training examining implicit biases, assumptions, prejudices and how these inform our practices, policies and interactions with African American students.

Representation—The importance of having mentors and role models that can relate to students, their culture, and build nurturing relationships. It is also essential to inspire and motivate students to excel academically and point them in the right direction with resources to help them prepare for their professional career. It is important to have administrators and faculty that are culturally competent. In addition, we must operationalize and show love, care, guidance, support, and compassion for students that may be first generation college students and experience culture shock, hardships, trauma, poverty, and a lack of resources as they attend institutes of higher learning.

Respite—provide a safe space and haven for students to discuss, process, vent and share their experiences of acclimating to the campus. It is a place of laughter, pointed debates and camaraderie with peers, faculty and staff. Colleges should partner with grassroot initiatives focused on providing black men with tools to heal and work on their mental wellness. For example, the Black Male Yoga Initiative; promote yoga as a stress management tool in addition to relying on faith and family for emotional support.

Resiliency—stressing to the students the importance of making the most out of their college education, establishing and augmenting their study habits, promoting self-directed learning, community service, and helping them by focusing on more than just their grades but making a contribution to their community and ultimately their profession. Resiliency also applies to institutions having long term commitment to ensure that African American male students are engaged in different manner with more holistic approaches to academic support and services and opportunities to heal, while addressing mental and social trauma many students have endured before stepping on a college campus.

Bibliography

Alang, Sirry, and Donna McAlpine, Ellen McCreedy, Rachel Hardeman. 2017. "Police Brutality and Black Health: Setting the Agenda for Public Health Scholars." *Am J Public Health*, 107 (5): 662–665. Published online 2017 May. DOI: 10.2105/AJPH.2017.303691, PMCID: PMC5388955.

Alexander, Michelle. 2011. *The New Jim Crow*. New York: New Press.

Anderson, Elijah. 1999. *Code of the Streets: Decency, Violence, and the Moral Life of the Inner City*. New York: W.W. Norton & Company Inc.

Aronson, Joshua, Carrie B. Fried, and Catherine Good. 2002. "Reducing the Effects of Stereotype Threat on African American College Students by Shaping Theories of Intelligence." *Journal of Experimental Social Psychology*, 38 (2): 113–125.

Barbadoro, Amelia. 2017. "The Socioemotional Impact of Disparate Student Discipline: An Examination of Racial Bias and Out-of-School Suspensions." CUNY Academic Works. https://academicworks.cuny.edu/gc_etds/2071.

Beneria, Lourdes, and Luis E. Santiago. 2001. "The Impact of Industrial Relocation on Displaced Workers: A Case Study of Cortland, New York." *Economic Development Quarterly, 15* (1), 78–89.

Bluestone, Barry, and Bennett Harrison. 1982. *The Deindustrialization of America*. New York: Basic Books.

Bridges, Brian. "African Americans and College Education by the Numbers." https://www.uncf.org/the-latest/african-americans-and-college-education-by-the-numbers.

Busselle, Rick, and Heather Crandall. 2002. "Television Viewing and Perceptions About Race Differences in Socioeconomic Success." *Journal of Broadcasting & Electronic Media*, 46 (2): 265–282. DOI: 10.1207/s15506878jobem4602_6.

Children's Defense Fund. 2018. "State of America's Children. 2017." https://www.childrensdefense.org/wp-content/uploads/2018/06/2017-soac.pdf.

Drier, Peter. 1996. "America's Urban Crisis: Symptoms, Causes and Solutions." In John Charles Boger and Judith Welch Wegner (Eds.), *Race, Poverty, and American Cities*, 79–139. Durham: University of North Carolina Press.

Engle, Jennifer, and Vincent Tinto. 2008. "Moving Beyond Access: College Success for Low-Income, First-Generation Students." Pell Institute for the Study of Opportunity in Higher Education.

Fainstein, Susan, and Mia Gray. 1996. "Economic Development Strategies for the Inner City." *The Review of the Black Political Economy* 24 (2, Winter): 29–38.

Fitzgerald, James, and William Patton. 1994. "Race, Job Training and Economic Development: Barriers to Racial Equality in Program Planning." *Review of Black Political Economy*, 23 (2): 93–112.

Ginwright, Shawn. 2016. *Hope and Healing in Urban Education: How Urban Activists and Teachers are Reclaiming Matters of the Heart*. New York: Routledge.

Goldsmith, William, and Edward Blakely. 1992. *Separate Societies*. Philadelphia: Temple University Press.

Graham, Phillip W., and Anna Yaros, Ashley Lowe, and Mark S. McDaniel. 2017. "Nurturing Environments for Boys and Men of Color with Trauma Exposure." *Clinical Child Family Psychology Review*, 20 (4): 105–116.

Holzer, Harry. 1998. "Barriers to Higher Employment Rates among African Americans." In Wilhelmina A. Leigh and Margaret C. Simms (Eds.), *The Black Worker in the 21st Century* (Vol. 1, pp. 91–146). Washington, DC: Joint Center for Political and Economic Studies.

Hurd, Noelle M., and Jamie Albright, Audrey Wittrup, Andrea Negrete, and Janelle Billingsley. 2018. "Appraisal Support from Natural Mentors, Self-Worth, and Psychological Distress: Examining the Experiences of Underrepresented Students Transitioning through College." *Journal of Youth and Adolescence*, 47 (5): 1100–1112.

Ihlanfeldt, Keith. 1997. Information on the Spatial Distribution of Job Opportunities within Metropolitan Areas. *Journal of Urban Economics*, 41 (2): 218–242.

Imbroscio, David. L. 1997. *Reconstructing City Politics*. Thousand Oaks: Sage Publications.

Jackson, Kenneth. 1985. *Crabgrass Frontier: The Suburbanization of the United States*. New York: Oxford University Press.

Kasarda, John. 1995. "Industrial Restructuring and the Changing Locations of Jobs." In Reynolds Farley (Ed.), *State of the Union* (Vol. 1). New York: Russell Sage Foundation.

Massey, Douglas, and Nancy Denton. 1992. *American Apartheid*. Cambridge: Harvard University Press.

Muyskens, John. 2018. *Fatal Force, 992 People Have Been Shot and Killed by Police in 2018*, https://www.washingtonpost.com/graphics/2018/national/police-shootings-2018/.

NAACP. "Criminal Justice Fact Sheet," http://www.naacp.org/criminal-justice-fact-sheet/ (last accessed May 2018).

Newman, Lynda Henry, Deborah M. Lyon, and Warren B Phillip. 1986. *Community Economic Development: An Approach for Urban-Based Economies*. Washington, DC: Institute of Urban Studies.

Noguera, Pedro. 2008. *The Trouble with Black Boys: And other Reflections on Race, Equity, and the Future of Public Education*. San Francisco: Jossey-Bass.

Onyeka-Crawford, Adaku, Kayla Patrick, K., and Neena Chaudhry. 2017. "Let Her Learn: Stopping School Pushout for Girls of Color." *National Women's Law Center*. https://nwlc.org/wp-content/uploads/2017/04/final_nwlc_Gates_GirlsofColor.pdf.

Owens, Delila, and Krim Lacey, Glinda Rawls, and JoAnne Holbert-Quince. 2010. "First-Generation African American Male College Students: Implications for Career Counselors." *The Career Development Quarterly*, 58: 291–300.

Rolen, Emily and Tossi, Mitra. 2018. "Career Outlook: Blacks in the Labor Force." U.S. Bureau of Labor Statistics. https://www.bls.gov/careeroutlook/2018/article/blacks-in-the-labor-force.htm.

Schramm, Richard. 1987. "Local, Regional, and National Strategies." In Severyn T. Bruyn and James Meehan (Eds.), *Beyond the Market and the State: New directions in Community Economic Development*, 152–170. Philadelphia: Temple University Press.

Thomas, June Manning, and Marsha Ritzdorf. 1997. *Urban Planning and the African American Community: In the Shadows*. Thousand Oaks: Sage Publications.

Topos Partnership and The Opportunity Agenda. 2011. *Media Representations and Impact on the Lives of Black Men and Boys*. https://www.racialequitytools.org/resource-files/Media-Impact-onLives-of-Black-Men-and-Boys-OppAgenda.pdf.

Tunstall, Jonli D. 2019. "Creating a College-Going Culture." In: Tyrone Howard, Patrick Camanigan, Earl J. Edwards, Maisah, Howard, Andrea C. Minkoff, Tonikiaa Orange, Jonli D. Tunstall, and Kenjus T. Watson, (Eds.), *All Students Must Thrive: Transforming Schools to Combat Toxic Stressors and Cultivate Critical Wellness*, 106–124. Rexford, NY: International Center for Leadership in Education.

United States Government Accountability Office. 2018. *K-12 Education – Discipline Disparities for Black Students, Boys, and Students with Disabilities.* https://www.gao.gov/products/gao-18-258.

Venezia, Andrea, Patrick Callan, Joni E. Finney, Michael W. Kirst, and Michael D. Usdan. 2005 (September). *The Governance Divide: A Report on a Four-State Study on Improving College Readiness and Success.* San Jose, CA: The Institute for Educational Leadership, the National Center for Public Policy and Higher Education, and the Stanford Institute for Higher Education Research.

Venezia, Andrea, and Michael W. Kirst, and Anthony L. Antonio. 2003 (March). *Betraying the College Dream: How Disconnected K–12 and Postsecondary Education Systems Undermine Student Aspirations.* Stanford, CA: National Center for Postsecondary Improvement.

Wade, Devone Tyrone, and Kasim S. Ortiz. 2017. "Punishing Trauma: How Schools Contribute to the Carceral Continuum through its Response to Traumatic Experiences." In Kenneth J. Fasching-Varner, Lori Latrice Martin, Ronald W. Mitchell, Karen P. Bennett-Haron, and Arash Daneshzadeh, (Eds.), *Understanding, Dismantling and Disrupting the Prison-to-School Pipeline*, 181–191. Lanham, MD: Lexington Books.

Wiewel, Wim, and Michael Tietz, Robert Giloth. 1993. "The Economic Development of Neighborhoods and Localities." In Robert D. Bingham and Robert Mier (Eds.), *Theories of Local Economic Development*, 80–99. Thousand Oaks: Sage.

Wilson, William Julius. 1996. *When Work Disappears.* New York: Random House Inc.

Index

abuse   81, 86, 87, 123, 135, 203, 205
accountability   97, 114, 204, 216
achievement gap: and higher education   201–202
  and Men of Excellence   207–208
  and safety of black males   202–205
  and solutions   207–208
  and structural realities of urban areas   205–207
  and theory to practice   208–209
adverse childhood experiences   202–203
affirmative action   165
antiblack   1, 51–53
arrears   61–63, 65–71
asset poverty   1
assimilation   4, 8
Atlanta School of Sociology   15, 18
authoritarianism   132

Barlow, Orlando   85
Baton Rouge, Louisiana   4, 82, 85, 88, 107
Bell, Sean   85
biological aging   123
Black British women   27
Black church: addressing economic inequalities in America   188–189
  and Black Liberation Theology   189–191
  the case for a living wage   191–194
  going forward   194–198
Black codes   58, 147, 156
Black community: and community policing   112–13
  and critical demography   104–105
  history of policing and   105–106
  law enforcement assessment of   108–109
  and public support of the police   106–107
  and War on Cops   107–108
Black fathers   48, 52, 59, 62, 67
Black feminism   29
Black Identity Extremists   108–109
Black Liberation Theology   17, 189–191, 196–198
Black Lives Matter   89, 93, 202
Black men: children with more than on partner   70

  discrimination against   56
  factory work   56
  and families   55–56
  imprisonment   36
  as migrants   41–42
  masculinity   67
  racialization of   70
  stereotyped and gendered   58–60
  unnatural deaths of   14
Black nationalist groups   14
Black Power   4, 14, 190
Black professors   10, 15
Black sociology   1, 6–10, 12–14
Black South Africans   27
Black women: academicians   173, 180
  blame   5
  domination of bodies   147
  double consciousness   168
  economic opportunities   55
  enslaved   59, 147
  habitus   166–167
  intersectionality   168–169
  labor force participation   202
  morality   57
  mortality during childbirth   42
  poverty   70
  public policies   54
  resisting benefits of marriage   147
  sexual violence against   2
  social mobility   17
  systematic racial oppression   147
  unnatural deaths of   14
  welfare queen stereotype   71
  welfare recipients   52
blood pressure   123–124
Brown, Michael   85, 103, 107
bullying   203
Busy Streets theory   113–115

capitalism   187, 193, 195
car window sociology   5
carceral migration   15–16
  Africana demography   27–30
  Africana demography's ancestries   26–27
  demography problem   36–37

carceral migration (cont.)
  migration 30–31
  reintegration 31–35
cardiovascular disease 123, 135–136, 138
Castille, Philando 103, 202
Charlottesville 5, 109
child poverty 1, 51–52, 70, 145, 194–195
child support: payments 16, 48, 62, 71
  orders 66–67
child support enforcement: anti-poverty or anti-black 51–53
  the black family 54–56
  Black men 58–60
  Moynihan Report 56–58
  nuclear family 53–54
  punish black fathers 16
  as social policy 48
  study of families 49–51
child tax credit 194
childbearing 49, 57, 59, 147, 157
Christianity 48, 105, 150, 190–191, 196–198
civil rights 4, 84
Civil Rights Movement 5, 13, 132, 146–148, 150, 153, 187, 196
Civil War 2, 106, 187
class mobility 169
cohabitation 53, 55, 147
collective efficacy 113
college attendance rates 205, 207
colonialism 148, 152
colorblind racism 154–156
colorblindness 168
community capital 39
community empowerment 114, 117
community partnerships 112
community policing 110, 112, 119
community service 208, 209, 218
Competencies 181
constructionist view 151–152
conventional demography 11, 15–16, 47, 53–54, 104
convict leasing 3
coping mechanisms 16, 124
courts 86, 121
Crawford, John 103, 106, 205
crime: absence of crime 111
  black neighborhoods 95
  and drug abuse 205

high-crime areas 82
  increases 5
  rates 56
  reducing crime 114–116
  teaching and educating children of color 95–96
  violent crime 81, 93, 110
  witnessing crime 203
criminal justice system 16, 18, 27, 37, 40–41, 81–82, 84–86, 92, 94–95, 122
criminologists 14, 35, 60
critical demography 1, 10–14, 25–27, 59, 103–105, 144, 158
Critical Race Theory 144, 150–151, 154, 158, 167–168, 181
cultural argument 146
cultural competencies 181
cultural deficit model 145
cultural racism 155
culture: black culture 57, 179
  culture shock 207, 218
  distinct culture 180
  history and 2
  culture of poverty 5, 8
  racist police culture 104
  Southern culture 124
  value of culture 28, 131–132
  versus structural arguments 145
  visual signs 174
culture shock 207, 218

Davis, Jordan 103, 106
demographic transition 53–54
dependency 71
depression 3, 123
deviance 36
Diallo, Amadou 84
disciplinary policies 95, 204, 217
discrimination: against black men 55
  forms of 94
  housing discrimination 5
  prejudice and 96
  racial discrimination 43, 54, 70
  responses to 121–124
  stereotypes and 133
  in social services 95
diversity 15, 147, 176, 217
divorce 51, 53

domestic violence 202
dominant group 2–4, 82, 87, 93–95
double consciousness 168, 174
Dred Scott 2
Du Bois, W.E.B. 5–8, 12, 14–15, 18, 55–56, 147, 168, 174
dysfunction 36, 52, 209

Earned Income Tax Credit 194
Eastern Sociological Society 6, 15
education: and class habitus 175
    and class mobility 169
    discrimination 122
    father's 62
    funds for 87
    higher education 17, 42, 201–202, 207, 210, 217
    human capital and 157
    lack of 55–56
    level of 67
    low attainment 49
    outcome 28
    privilege 173
    programs 90
    public education 206
    racial achievement gap 200
    settings 168
    standard of living 191
    systems 93, 97
    and zero tolerance 86
educational attainment 49, 63–66, 71, 94, 165, 174, 202–205
employment status 62–63, 66, 68–69
empowerment theory 113, 120
enforcement actions 61–63, 70, 205
essentialist view 151–152
ethnic groups 4–5, 50, 201, 207
ethnicity 8, 158, 169
Eurocentric universalism 148–149

fairness 96, 189
faith community 190–191
family: counterparts 67
    dysfunctional 52
    emotional support 218
    formations 57–59, 143
    and fear of crime 88–96
    and incarceration 35
    lessons from Du Bois and Frazier on the family 54–56
    life 29, 155
    living wage 192–193
    moral deficiencies 36
    as a national crisis 4
    nuclear 47, 53–54
    of origin 170, 174, 178, 180, 217
    poverty 52
    residential movements of 41
    roles 172
    as a social institution 18, 47
    social origins of 167
    sociology 17
    stigmatized community 202
    structure 16, 47–48, 143–150
    values 165
    welfarization of family law 52
    working-class 169
family law 52, 73
family structure 16, 47–50, 53–56, 60, 74, 143–150, 158–159
Farrakhan, Louis 114
fear of crime 16, 81, 83–88, 112–113
Federal Bureau of Investigation 107–110
Federal Housing Administration 3–4
federalism 195
female-headed households 47, 49, 55–56
fertility 11, 15–16, 47–50, 53–54, 59–69
Fourteenth Amendment 2, 4, 84
Frazier, E. Franklin 5–6, 8, 12–15, 18, 55, 87–88
freedom 2, 10, 96, 156, 187, 189, 191, 196–197

Garner, Eric 85, 106, 202
gender: ascribed status 174
    and critical demography 10
    double consciousness 168–169
    family and population change 54
    gender roles 30, 214
    habitus 177
    literature on incarceration 25
    privileges 147
    public policies 72
    sources of oppression 8, 173
    socialization 181
    stereotypes 58–60
globalization 206

Grant, Oscar   84–85
Gray, Freddie   85, 107, 110, 202
Gray, Kimani   85
Great Depression   3
Great Migration   3, 13

habitus   17, 166–169, 171, 173–182
hegemony   11, 29, 53, 64
higher education   13, 42, 168–170, 200–201, 207, 210, 214, 217
Home Owner's Loan Corporation   3–4
homeownership   153
housing   3, 5, 39, 81,84, 87, 94, 97, 121, 191, 205–206, 213
human capital   146, 157–158, 163
hybrid habitus   17, 174, 181–182
hypertension   124

identity construction   165
implicit bias   122, 205
incarceration   1, 5, 15, 25, 31–41, 58–59, 71, 86–87, 93, 95, 98, 150, 202–204, 206, 213
income: annual   52, 170
   child support as   51
   diversion   66
   and educational attainment   166
   household   62–69, 126
   inequality   1, 192–193
   middle   166
   racial gap   15, 166, 206
   religious attendance and   128
   tax   61
   universal   195
   upper   166
individualism   154
inheritance   193–194
injustice   82
inner-city   81–84, 205–206
Institutionalized Power Relations Theory   154
interdisciplinary   8, 49, 144
intersectionality   167–169
intracommunity   113–114

Jamestown, Virginia   1
Jim Crow   3, 58–59, 82, 132, 147, 150, 156
justice   4, 8, 96, 114, 159, 187, 189–91
   See also criminal justice system

King, Martin Luther   187
Ku Klux Klan   3
labor: of Black men   58
   cheap   94, 206
   emotional   39
   exploitable   87
   forced   2
   166
   extracting   148
   labor force   202, 206
   market   93, 97
   material conditions   152
   migrants   30, 33
   shortages   3

land takings   3
law enforcement   14, 31, 70, 88–90, 92, 103, 105–109, 111–112, 117, 202, 204
leadership   15, 189, 196, 208–209, 212, 216
living wage   17, 188, 191–192, 195, 198
low-income   17, 53, 86, 94, 143–145, 203
lynchings   59

mainstream sociology   15
marriage rates   53, 149
marriageable male hypothesis   145
Martin, Trayvon   85
masculinity   58, 200, 209, 214, 216
mass incarceration   15, 25, 203–204, 206
McDade, Kenrec   85
media   2, 10–11, 59, 82, 88–89, 109, 133, 155, 190, 202–203
medical care   121
Men of Excellence   208–216
mental health   17, 122, 124, 202
mentor   90–91, 96, 171, 207–210, 216–217
meritocracy   154, 168
microaggressions   121
middle-class   53, 166, 168, 174, 176, 179–181
migration   16, 26, 28, 30–31, 33–41
militarism   187
miscegenation   4, 58–59
mobility   17, 29, 42, 53, 123, 153
Money, Mississippi   84
Montgomery bus boycott   4
morality   29, 33, 52, 55, 57
mortality   15, 27, 42, 53, 123, 153

INDEX   227

Moynihan, Daniel Patrick   4–5, 15, 56–58,
    143, 145–146, 155
murder   58–59, 84–85, 88, 110

Nation of Islam   4, 14, 114, 116
neglect   86, 92, 148, 202–203
neighborhood: 10,000 Fearless Men and
    Women   114–116
  Black American   36
  black lower-income   36, 86
  decline of   206
  disadvantaged   85
  distressed   1, 5
  fear of crime and   85–98
  high crime urban   88
  incarcerated person's home   34
  inner-city   205
  migrants   38
  residential   29
  street activity   114
  unsafe   203
  urban   145, 206
  white   5
networking   216
New Deal   3
New Negro   3
non-marital births   53
noncustodial parent   51–52
nuclear family   47, 50, 53–55

Obama, Barack   5, 9, 187
ccupation   17, 61, 94, 107, 165–166, 169, 175,
    203
oppression   6–8, 13, 27, 54, 56, 58, 97, 105, 132,
    144, 147, 151, 169, 173, 213

Pan-African   28
parenthood   47, 50, 178
parole   35, 40
peer support   208
physical health   123
police: agencies   14
  attitudes about   16
  and the black community   103–116
  brutality   81–82, 108, 202
  discrimination   121
  deadly force   122
  fear of   81–98
  and safety of black men   202

  unemployed black people   5
policymakers   5, 72, 87, 145, 205
post-colonial   143–144, 148–150
post-colonial sociology   144, 148
post-racial   5, 81, 97, 146–148, 150, 153, 187, 201
poverty: anti-   51–53
  asset poverty   1
  black   56
  black families in   17, 143–159
    black women   70
  child   48–51, 70
  and crime   92
  culture of poverty   5, 8
  first generation college students and   218
  and incarceration   59
  poverty line   192–198
  racial inequality in   17
  school   204
prison: black fathers and   71
  Black Liberation Theology and   197
  criminological literature   35
  for-profit   87
  historical roots   84
  initial entry   32
  metaphorical   16
  place of origin and   34
  prison-industrial complex   86
  purpose of   94
  reentry   16
  return to   38
  school-to-prison pipeline   86, 204–205
  state   40
  system   31
  web of choices and   33
probation   40, 61, 66–67, 71
professors   10, 15, 17, 166, 170, 175, 181
psychological distress   207
public policy   1, 7–8, 13, 32, 51, 71–72, 144,
    205–206
public safety   112
public schools   94, 204, 209
punishment   59–60, 63, 67, 86, 97, 198

Quaker tradition   55
qualitative methods   38, 56, 70, 169
quantitative methods   38, 56, 72, 158

race-neutral   71, 143–146, 153, 156, 158
racial achievement gap   17, 200

racial attitudes   122, 131, 133
racial bias   81, 122
racial discrimination   4, 16, 54, 70, 121, 123–124, 149, 188
racial ideologies   151, 153–155, 157–158
racial profiling   81, 95
racial progress   56, 146, 149–150, 188
racial progress narrative   146, 149
racial realism   96
racial status quo   154, 156
racialized state   151, 153, 157–158
racism: Africana collective history   28, 82
   in America   50, 145
   black experience   29
   and capitalism   187
   colonialism   149
   colorblind   59
   continuing significance   96, 180, 192
   conventional demography   11, 54
   cure for   188
   demographers avoidance of the term   10
   demography and family scholars   52
   Du Bois and   55
   and education   207
   by faculty and staff   200
   family structure   16, 48, 144
   historical legacies   56, 152
   influence of   48
   individual well-being   203
   introductory textbooks   12
   permanence of   153–157
   and police violence   85
   social and economic constraints   47
   social programs   49
   system factors   34, 82, 146, 149
   structural   159
   theological response to   197
re-traumatization   205
Reconstruction   3, 147, 187
recruitment   15, 17, 170–171
reentry   16, 25, 30–33, 36–37, 40
reflection   107, 113, 213, 217
region   2, 16, 106, 121–134
reintegration   31–41
religion   8, 18
religious attendance   125–126, 128–130
remarriage   53
representation   3, 36, 82, 110, 217

residential segregation   156
resiliency   207, 218
respite   218
restrictive codes   3
Rice, Tamir   85, 103, 106–107, 110
right-wing extremists   109
rural   37–38, 55–56, 125, 127–131

school: and anti-black violence   1
   of Black Sociological Thought   27
   diploma   202
   first American School of Sociology   8, 15, 18
   Chicago School   8
   grade point average   201
   high school education   52, 62–64, 68, 96, 126, 166
   to prison pipeline   86
   and racial discrimination   121
   and War on Drugs   203
school discipline   204
school resource officers   204
school-to-prison pipeline   86, 204–205
Scott, Walter   4, 187
Second World War   4, 187
segregation   1, 30, 156
self-care   17, 192, 200, 209, 212–213, 216
sexism   11, 28–29, 34, 97
sexual aggression   133
sexuality   29, 58–59, 72, 133, 169
shaming   59, 72
sharecropping   3
single-parent households   47–52, 70, 72, 157, 178
slave patrols   105–106, 116
slavery   2, 28, 30, 55, 58–59, 84, 94, 105–106, 132, 146–147, 152, 154, 156, 204
social capital   113, 144, 149
social cohesion   113, 116
social construction of race   148, 150–152
social control: the black family   54–56
   and child support enforcement   51–53
   and conventional demography   49–51
   the Moynihan era   56–58
   neighborhood street activity   114
   and the nuclear family   53–54
   stereotypes of black men   58–60
social institutions   6, 13, 18, 47, 53–54, 82, 96

social interaction   115, 154
social movements   4, 85
social security   13
social services   81, 95, 97–98
socialization   132, 167, 173–174, 177, 181, 212
socioeconomic status   134, 165, 179–180
sociology   5–10, 12, 14–15, 17, 26–27, 60, 143, 146, 148, 150, 165, 167, 170, 173, 176, 179
South: 10,000 Fearless, civil rights movement   196
  experiences with discrimination   124–134
  and Great Migration   3, 13
  and Jim Crow   3
  policing   105
  portrayal of black population   81
  rural   55
  slave patrols   105–106, 116, 114
  U.S. Constitution   2
South America   37
southern culture   124, 131–132
Stansbury, Timothy   84
stereotypes   48, 52, 71–72, 132–133, 147, 179, 203, 205
Sterling, Alton   103, 202
stigma   33–36, 39, 60, 72, 95, 202, 209–210, 213
Stockton Economic Empowerment Demonstration   195
street patrols   115–116
stress   54, 124, 203, 218
structural argument   145
subordinate groups   151, 154
substance abuse   202
suburbanization   4

Temporary Assistance to Needy Families   63
terrorism   109
The 10,000 Fearless Men and Women in Atlanta   114–119
The Philadelphia Negro   12
The Scholar Denied   12
theory: black sociology   8
  Busy Streets theory   113–116
  and community safety   117

course   12
creation of   28
crime and policing   83
criminologists   14
  and critical demography   11, 104
  critical race theory   144, 150–151, 154, 158, 167, 181
  empowerment theory   113
  feminist theory   169
  grounded theory   170
  Men of Excellence   208–209
Thirteenth Amendment   2, 84
Till, Emmett   4, 59, 84
traditional family   53–54
trauma   8, 89, 200, 202–205, 209, 213, 216, 218
Truman, Harry   4
Trump, Donald J.   5, 187
trust   1, 13–14, 88, 90–92, 106, 112–113, 116, 212

unemployment   94–95, 149, 159, 195, 205, 213
Unite the Right   109
unmarried parents   50
urban   37–38, 55–56, 71, 83, 88, 145, 190, 205–207

values   7, 36, 61, 132, 165–166, 175, 180
violence   1, 2, 59, 85, 96, 103, 105, 108–110, 114, 117, 190, 202–205, 213
vulnerable   48, 50, 59, 71, 83, 85, 87, 205

wage gap   166
wage garnishments   61
Wall Street   5
War on Cops   103, 106–110
War on Drugs   203, 205
wealth   1, 3–4, 16, 27, 94–95, 153–154, 157, 188, 193–194
welfare   50–54, 59, 62–71, 111, 147, 153–154, 178
White virtual mobs   10
Whiteness   4, 9, 14–15, 58, 151, 153, 155–158
working-class   165–181

zero tolerance policies   86, 204–205
Zimmerman, George   85

www.ingramcontent.com/pod-product-compliance
Lightning Source LLC
Chambersburg PA
CBHW070921030426

42336CB00014BA/2483